Idaho

Real Estate Handbook

7th Edition

Chuck Byers

Professional Marketing Concepts, LLC, Nampa, Idaho

Idaho Real Estate Handbook, 7thEdition

Published by: Professional Marketing Concepts, LLC
                KDP Publishing

Idaho front cover page map is reprinted with permission by Travis Brown

ISBN:9798830014397

--

Table Of Contents

PREFACE

This book is intended to help students to prepare for a real estate career or the book can be used as a reference manual for the general public to acquire a basic knowledge about Idaho real estate.

It is highly recommended to have a general real estate book to accompany this book to further explain the basics of real estate and real estate terms. Such books are usually available at most Idaho real estate schools. General real estate text books may also be available at local book stores and public libraries.

Although the information contained in this book is intended to be current and up-to-date, newly legislated laws may be passed that supersede the publication date.

The information in this book follows the general sequence and flow of topics to learn about real estate in a logical sequence. Numerous laws with code identification are supplied for use as additional reference should the text be unclear or incomplete for reader comprehension.

At the end of each chapter, multiple choice questions are offered to test comprehension and knowledge to prepare the reader for the multiple choice question state exam. At the end of the book an answer key to chapter questions and index is available to assist the reader with pin pointing various subject areas.

ACKNOWLEDGMENTS

Thanks to the Idaho Real Estate Commission, real estate schools, real estate instructors and readers for their input and suggestions. Also, thanks to Pioneer Title Company for providing the sample closing statements. Special thanks goes to the Idaho Real Estate Commission Director, Melissa Furgerson and her staff for their assistance and suggestions.

The photos and figures used throughout the text are for illustrative purposes only and may not be reproduced in any manner without written permission from the copyright holder.

ABOUT THE AUTHOR

Chuck Byers has been actively engaged in the real estate industry since the mid 70's. During his career, Chuck has been an owner/broker of several real estate companies in Oregon and Idaho. He is a certified real estate instructor, past director of a real estate school, and subject matter expert (SME). Chuck has authored and published several text books, written real estate courses for Continuing Education approval, and has written articles addressing various real estate topics for publication.

Chuck holds a Bachelor of Science degree from the University of Oregon and has earned the Certified Residential Brokerage Manager (CRB), Graduate Realtors® Institute (GRI) and Internet Professional (e-PRO) designations from the National Association of REALTORS®.

Accomplishments include REALTOR® of the Year, Idaho Instructor Of The Year, and past Board Director of the Real Estate Educators Association.

Chapter 1

Getting Licensed In Idaho

Words Of Wisdom

"In laboring diligently and serving unselfishly,

I find the fulfillment of my purpose and destiny."

Charles Peter

Idaho Real Estate Commission

Idaho Real Estate Commission

Idaho Real Estate Commission

With the enactment of the Real Estate License Law in 1947, the Idaho Real Estate Commission became a self-governing agency of the State of Idaho.

IC 54-2005

The Division of Occupational and Professional Licenses provides consumer protection and safety through its regulation of licensees including those licensed by the Idaho Real Estate Commission.

The Idaho Real Estate Commission (IREC) is totally financed by mandatory fees paid by all active and inactive real estate licensees. Thus, no tax dollars are used to administrate and enforce real estate activities

IC 54-2007

Charged with protecting the public and the real estate industry, the Idaho Real Estate Commission is charged with administrating and enforcing the provisions of Title 54 of the Idaho code. The IREC also develops and oversees education and license exam programs to secure and maintain a real estate license.

Members
IC 54-2005
IC 54-2006

Commission Members

The commission members include 5 members; 4 active brokers from 4 districts (geographic areas) to represent the whole state of Idaho and 1 member of the public from the state at large with the interest in the rights of consumers of real estate services. All members are appointed by the Governor.

IC 59-509 (n)
IC 54-2007

As compensation, commission members receive an honorarium (not a salary) in the amount of $50 per day for actual time served (several days a month) for commission meetings.

IREC Meetings

When Does The Idaho Real Estate Commission Meet?

The IREC generally meets 6-8 times a year, primarily in Boise, and occasional meetings are held in other locations throughout the state. The meetings usually take a half to a full day depending on the agenda. The meetings are also open to the public including real estate licensees who can receive Continuing Education credit toward their license renewal.

Idaho Real Estate Education Council

Education Council

Education Council
The Idaho Real Estate Education Council serves as an advisory group to the Commission to recommend the education policy together with course content quality for all education courses to meet pre and post licensing requirements approved by the Commission.

The education council consists of 6 members including the education director, 1 commissioner, and 4 additional members appointed by the Commission from each of the 4 geographic areas of the state. Each council member is appointed for a 4 year term with compensation based on a per diam allowance for each day of approved service.

Activities Requiring a License

**Activities
Requiring A
License**

Activities Requiring A Real Estate License
A real estate broker or a salesperson, who, directly or indirectly, while acting for another, for *compensation* or a promise or an expectation thereof shall be required to have an active real estate license.

IC 54-2005 (35)
(36)

Real estate related activities requiring a license include:

- Offer to list, buy, sell, or negotiate for others;

- Negotiate the purchase, sale, option or exchange of real estate;

- Takes part in the procuring of prospects or closing of any transaction;

- Negotiate any real estate interest, option, or business opportunity for others.

Exceptions
IC 54-2003

Exceptions To Licensure
There are situations and instances that do not require a real estate license. Some examples include:

- A transfer of any interest in real property or business interest for a person's own account or use;

- Acquisition or disposal of real property or business opportunity interests within scope of his or her employment;

- Acting with a power of attorney for a single transaction in a parcel of real property or business opportunity;

- Any person selling based on default provisions of a deed of trust;

- Acting as an administrator, executor or personal representative of an estate;

- Acting as a property management, rental or leasing agent.

| IC 54-2003 (4) | Evading the exceptions to licensure shall be considered the unlicensed and unlawful practice of real estate. |

Types of Licenses and Requirements

Types Of Licenses
IC 54-2011

Types Of Licenses
There are 5 types of individual licenses granted in Idaho. A person may be licensed as a [1] salesperson, an [2] associate broker, [3] limited broker, [4] designated broker acting for a sole proprietorship or legal business entity and [5] a cooperative license.

Salesperson Or Associate Broker Affiliation
An active salesperson or associate broker must affiliate with a designated broker and cannot work without the supervision of a designated broker. The real estate salesperson or associate broker represents the designated broker.

Designated Broker
A designated broker is a licensed real estate broker who is designated by the brokerage company to supervise the activities of any licensees associated with the brokerage. The designated broker is also responsible for the supervision and operation of the brokerage company and unlicensed personnel.

IC 54-2038 (2)

Limited Broker
A limited broker is a individual broker qualified to do business in Idaho but who may not have associate brokers or salespersons licensed with that broker. Thus the term - limited broker.

IC 54-2011 (2)
IC 54-2017
Guideline 2 (5)

Cooperative License
A cooperative license is primarily designed to assist the commercial real estate arena. The nontransferable cooperative license may be issued to any out of state broker to work in cooperation with an actively licensed Idaho designated broker for the purpose of one Idaho commercial real estate transaction.

Minimum Requirements
IC 54-2012

Salesperson Minimum Requirements
Minimum requirements include each person seeking a real estate license:
1. Be an individual
2. Be 18 years of age or older
3. Have a high school education or equivalency
4. Not had a real estate or other occupational license revoked in Idaho or any other jurisdiction involving fraud, misrepresentation, or dishonest or dishonorable dealing within 5 years immediately prior to the date the application for license was submitted to the commission.
5. Not have been convicted of any felony. However, if after 5 years of the conviction, completed probation, confinement, or parole, the applicant may make a written request to the commission for an exemption review.
6. Complete all education requirements unless granted a waiver

7. Pass a commission approved real estate license exam
8. Be fingerprinted
9. Sign and file an irrevocable consent to service and provide the commission a full and current mailing address. All licensees shall notify the IREC of any change of address within 10 business days of the change.
10. Active licensees will provide the name and physical address of the designated broker with whom the licensee will be affiliated. An active licensee can only be licensed with 1 broker at a time.
11. Provide proof of meeting mandatory errors and omissions insurance requirements.

Broker Requirements
IC 54-2012 (2)

Broker Requirements

Some important requirements to become a designated broker, limited broker, or associate broker license include but are not limited to:

1. Provide evidence of being engaged on a full time basis for 2 of the last 5 years as a licensed real estate salesperson. Such evidence may require a certified report by the broker or brokers with whom the applicant has been associated. However, at the discretion of the commission, the experience requirement may be modified or reduced based on the applicants educational background or affiliated business experience.
2. Fingerprinting is required even if fingerprints are already on file since this is a new license and not an extension of an already existing license.
3. Designated broker must have a physical office location and business name.

Reciprocity
IC 54-2015 (1)

Reciprocity

Because Idaho does not have reciprocity agreements with any other state, individuals licensed in another state shall meet the minimum requirements set forth by Idaho. However, the applicant shall not be required to furnish proof of the educational requirements but will be required to provide a certified license history from the other licensing state.

Cooperative License
IC 54-2003 (13)
IC 54-2017

Cooperative Licenses

Idaho offers cooperative licensing to an individual broker who is currently and actively licensed as a real estate broker in another jurisdiction and wishes to work in cooperation with an Idaho real estate broker. A cooperative license is primarily designed to accommodate commercial transactions.

Some of the basic requirements include an application on a form approved by the commission must be submitted to include name, history, physical address of both brokerages, an irrevocable consent, proof of current errors and omissions insurance, and non refundable applicable license fee.

IC 54-2017 (9)

An out of state broker may cooperate with only 1 Idaho broker and an Idaho broker my cooperate with only 1 out of state broker per commercial transaction. However, an out of state broker may obtain a cooperative license for more than 1 commercial real estate transaction at a time.

IC 54-2017 (2)	A cooperative license is good for 12 months from the date of issuance or until the license of the out of state broker expires, or is inactivated, surrendered, suspended or revoked whichever occurs first, and may not be renewed. In the event a transaction is not completed within the 12 month period, a new cooperative license application may be submitted.
IC 54-2017 (4)	If an out of state broker changes a physical or mailing address, the Idaho Real Estate Commission shall be notified in writing within 10 business days of such change.
IC 54-2017 (5)	In addition, if either the out of state broker or Idaho broker wishes to terminate the cooperative relationship, written notice of the termination shall be provided to the commission within 10 business days of the termination

Real Estate Education

IC 54-2022 (1) (a)

Salesperson
Individuals seeking a salesperson license in Idaho shall successfully complete current commission-approved courses for a total of 90 classroom hours.

IC 54-2022 (1) (b)

Broker
Individuals seeking a broker or associate broker license, shall complete 4 additional specified courses for a minimum of 90 additional classroom hours.

IC 54-2016 (4) (b)

Designated Broker
If an individual is seeking to be a designated broker or branch office manager licensed separate and apart from the main office, the individual must take and pass the BCOO (Business Conduct and Office Operations) course prior to activating his/her license or managing the branch office.

IC 54-2022 (2)

Prelicense Course Timing And Attendance
All prelicense courses (salesperson or broker) must be successfully completed within 3 years prior to the date of license application. However, the 3 year requirement may be modified at the discretion of the commission.

IC 54-2022 (3)

All live course sessions (prelicense or continuing education) require 100% attendance as stated below from the Idaho Real Commission's written policy.

> *Regular attendance means 100% attendance at all sessions of a live (including courses taught by interactive video conference) prelicense or continuing education (CE) course. The Commission obligates instructors and course providers to monitor student attendance and strictly enforce this attendance policy. A certified instructor or course provider may have his/its certification withdrawn for failure to enforce the 100% attendance policy at all course offerings.*

Use of cell phones or other electronic devices (i.e., laptops, iPads, notebook computers, etc.) is not permitted during class time, unless required as part of the course. This includes texting, checking messages, note taking, incoming and outgoing calls, or any activities not related to the instruction of the course content.

A student who misses any portion (even a few minutes) of a course taken for CE elective credit may not receive credit for the course unless the provider allows the student to attend the corresponding class session(s) in a subsequent offering of the same course.

*A student who misses any portion (even a few minutes) of a prelicense course may, at the discretion of the instructor and provider, complete make-up work to satisfy the 100% attendance requirement. **Make-up work is allowed ONLY for prelicense courses.** Make-up work is defined as one or more of the following:*

1. Extra homework or other assignment given by the instructor; or
2. Attendance in the corresponding class session(s) in a subsequent offering of the same course; or
3. Supervised presentation of an audio or video recording of the class session(s) missed.

A student who does not complete the required make-up work within 90 days of the scheduled course completion date for a prelicense course may not receive credit for the course and will be issued an "incomplete."

IC 54-2036 (2) (d)	Approved classroom hours are based on 50 minutes of actual instruction. Approved course hours do not include exam time.
IC 54-2036 (2) (f)	Each prelicense course (salesperson or broker) must include a commission-approved final exam requiring a minimum passing score of 70%.

Waivers

Waivers
IC 54-2014 (3)
IC 54-2015 (2)

Waivers

An individual who is currently and actively licensed in another state or jurisdiction may, upon written notice to the Commission, obtain a certificate of waiver of the national portion of the exam required for Idaho licensure.

The form to request a waiver of the national exam is available on the Idaho Real Estate Commission website. The request must include a current (not more than 6 months old) original Certified License History showing the applicant holds a real estate license on active status in another state or jurisdiction.

If the applicants primary license is from a state with single licensure (everyone is a broker), the applicant might not qualify for an Idaho broker license. The applicant will receive an exam waiver for which the applicant is qualified under Idaho law.

Once granted, the Certificate of Waiver must be taken to the exam/test center, otherwise the applicant will be required to take both portions of the exam. No exceptions!

License Period

Initial Licence Period
IC 54-2018 (1)

The initial license period shall be for a period of 1 year plus the months up to and including the next birth date of the licensee, not to exceed a period of 2 years and shall expire on the last day of the month of the birth date of the licensee.

Or explained differently, from today go to the last day of your next birth month and add 1 year. As you can see, the initial license period will be shy of the 2 year license period but will subsequently renew in 2 year increments.

Each license shall be renewable for a period of 2 years by timely submitting a completed application. Applications must be received at the Commission office on or before 5 p.m., Mountain Standard Time, of the expiration date.

Continuing Education

Course Requirements

CE Course Requirements
IC 54-2004 (15)(16)

Each active licensee applying to renew their license or change from inactive to active status, shall complete two separate commission Core courses plus 12 hours of additional commission approved elective course credit prior to actual renewal.

Each commission Core course shall cover the 12 month period between July 1 and June 30 that covers that year's trends in real estate practice and changes in laws related to the real estate industry and related industries.

First Time License Renewal
IC 54-2023

To renew a salesperson license as an active licensee for the first time, whether active or inactive, a salesperson shall complete 2 separate commission Core courses, plus IREC required post license course(s) not exceeding 12 classroom hours of instruction.

Commission approved continuing education courses can be taken live with no exam but mandatory attendance is required based on the following commission policy the course provider must follow.

> However, enforcement of the 100% attendance policy is one of a provider's most important duties. The Commission expects all providers to consistently and strictly enforce the IREC attendance policy. It is a common "urban myth" that students are allowed to miss 10 minutes or some other period of time and still receive credit. This is NOT correct. Because live CE classes do not require a final exam, the only requirement to get the hours is to attend the _entire_ class.
> • Attendance Policy applies to LIVE classes only
> • 100% attendance is mandatory

The current IREC policies can always be located at irec.idaho.gov in the Education section under the "Policies" tab. Please check there often as there may be updates to this policy.

'Non Live' CE
IC 54-2036 (2) (e)
(f) (g)

Licensees *not* taking 'live' continuing education courses (online or distance learning courses) will be required to pass an approved course exam with a minimum score of 70%.

IC 54-2036 (2) (h)

If the student fails the retake exam for any continuing education course, the student must repeat the entire course and pass the final exam to receive credit.

IC 54-2023 (3) (4) (5)

Duplicate credit is not approved for having taken a continuing education course in the same license period. In addition, excess credits cannot be accumulated and carried over to the subsequent license renewal periods.

Also commission ordered continuing education for disciplinary action *cannot* be used as credit for license renewal.

The Idaho Real Estate Commission encourages licensees to attend a regularly scheduled meeting and receive a maximum of 4 hours for CE credit in any1 license period. Current meeting dates are available at the Idaho Real Estate Commission website.

It is very important for licensees to keep satisfactory proof of their having completed continuing education courses by keeping their course completion certificates in a safe place should the commission require such proof.

Rule 402

The commission has the final say to determine if courses accredited by another state or profession are within the scope of approved topics identified by Rule 402.

In order to make sure such courses will or will not be approved, the licensee should submit a Licensee Request for CE Credit at least 60 days prior to the end of the renewal period. In the event a course would be denied, the licensee will need to secure additional continuing education if the licensee does not have enough credit hours for renewal. So time is of the essence.

Prelicense and State Exams

Prelicense Exams
IC 54-2036 (2) (f)

Prelicense Course Exams
To satisfy the educational requirements to secure a Idaho real estate license, a commission-approved final exam must accompany each prelicense course (salesperson and broker) and requires a passing score of 70%.

IC 54-2036 (2) (h)

If the applicant fails the course exam, the course provider, at its option, may allow the applicant 1 opportunity to retake the exam within 1 month of the original course exam. If the student fails a retake exam for any prelicense course, the student must repeat the entire course and pass the final exam to receive credit.

State Exam
IC 54-2014

State Exam

Upon satisfying the educational requirements to secure a Idaho real estate license, the applicant will be required to take and pass the national and state 2 part exam.

Waiver

However, if an out of state licensee has obtained a written certificate to waive the national portion of the state exam (previously discussed), the licensee shall only be required to take and pass the Idaho portion of the state exam.

Pearson Vue
www.pearsonvue.com

Currently, Pearson VUE administers the state and national portions of the salesperson and broker exams. It is highly recommended the applicant carefully read the *Idaho Real Estate Candidate Handbook* published by Pearson VUE. A content outline is provided in the handbook for both the general and state portion of the exam showing subject areas and weight.

When ready, application to take the exam can be accomplished online through Pearson VUE at https://home.pearsonvue.com/id/realestate. As discussed earlier, if an applicant has an Certificate of Waiver for the general portion of the exam, they must take the waiver with them to the exam test site when they take the exam or the applicant will have to take both the general and Idaho portion of the exam.

The national portion consists of 80 questions plus 5 pretest questions that are not scored. The state portion consists of 40 questions for the salesperson exam and 50 questions for the broker exam. The national portion will contain 5 pretest questions that are not scored. The state portion adds 5-10 pretest questions that are not scored. All questions on both exams are multiple choice.

The passing rate for the salesperson exam is a minimum of 70% and the broker exam requires a minimum pass rate of 75%.

If the national or state portion of the exam is not passed, the applicant may retake the failed portion with a new registration and exam fee. There is no limit to the number of times the national or state portion of the exam may be taken but every retake does require new registration and exam fee.

Fingerprinting

Fingerprints
IC 54-2012 (1) (j)

Submitting Fingerprints

Before anyone can acquire a real estate license in Idaho, fingerprints must be submitted to the Idaho Real Estate Commission as a national criminal history check to determine qualification for licensure.

It is highly suggested that the fingerprint process be initiated when registering to take the state exam. Pearson VUE, who administrators of the exam, can also make a separate appointment for digital (LiveScan) fingerprinting after confirmation of your exam reservation is received at the Pearson VUE test center.

It should be noted that the background check is usually returned to the Idaho Real Estate Commission within 7-21 days for LiveScan fingerprints.

If a Pearson VUE test center is not available, you can contact the Idaho Real Estate Commission to obtain a special fingerprint card packet.

The packet includes a pre-addressed envelope and instructions on how to submit your fingerprints. You will take your fingerprint card to the nearest law enforcement agency for rolling and then submit to Morpho Trust for further processing.

Once your fingerprints have been submitted to the Idaho Real Estate Commission, you can track the fingerprint status via the IREC online services. All you have to do is register a user name at the IREC website -http://irec.idaho.gov/services.html

It should be noted you have only 6 months to submit your license application from the date your fingerprints are approved. No extensions will be given.

If and when you plan to upgrade from a salesperson to a broker license, new fingerprints will be required since you will be securing a new license.

Errors & Omissions Insurance

E&O Coverage
IC 54-2013 (1)
Rule 117

Who's Covered?
In Idaho, Errors & Omissions Insurance (E&O) coverage is mandatory for all active licensees. E&O is not required for inactive licensees and since they are not actively licensed they are not allowed to practice real estate.

Minimum Coverage
IC 54-2013 (7)
Rule 118 (02) (a)

Minimum Insurance Coverage
Because Idaho requires E&O insurance for all active licensees, the IREC shall make insurance coverage available for anyone and everyone under a Group Plan. The cost of the Group Plan shall not exceed $250 per year with a deductible amount no greater than $3,500 which includes cost of investigation and defense.

Rule 119

Although most licensees use the IREC Group Plan for their E&O coverage, they can also obtain E&O insurance independent of the Group Plan. An independent E&O insurance policy must have an A.M. Best rating of B+ or better and a financial size category of Class VI or better.

It should be noted that some real estate companies have their own company E&O insurance and require their agents to be added to their policy.

Whether using the Group Plan or an independent plan, the minimum liability coverage for each occurrence shall be not less than $100,000 and an annual aggregate of not less than $300,000 for individuals and $1,000,000 for independent firm policies not including costs of investigation and defense.

IC 54-2018 (2) (ii)

When you apply for an original or renewal license, certification that the applicant has met the mandatory errors and omissions insurance requirement for real estate licensees will be required.

Should you leave the industry, you may want to look into securing 'tail coverage' to protect you against claims made after you have left the industry for an event that occurred prior to cancellation of your policy. To be effective, 'tail coverage' must be purchased within 90 days after the effective date of cancelling you policy or non-renewal if insured through the Idaho Group Plan.

Failure To
Maintain
Rule 121

Failure To Maintain E&O Insurance

Failure of a licensee to obtain and maintain insurance required by section 117 shall result in inactivation of any active license issued pursuant to Idaho Real Estate License Law or denial of any application for issuance or renewal of an active license.

Notice of noncompliance will occur within 5 business days of the date the Commission is notified that a licensee does not have required coverage, the Commission shall notify the affected licensee of noncompliance.

Notice shall be sent by first class mail to the licensee's business or residence address, as reflected in the Commission's records, and a copy of the notice shall be sent to the licensee's broker, if any.

The notice shall provide that the licensee has 10 business days in which to comply with the law and these rules regulating Errors and Omissions insurance. Failure to comply at the end of 10 business days shall result in the license being automatically inactivated.

Rule 122

Falsification of insurance coverage shall be subject to disciplinary action, including but not limited to, suspension or revocation of your license.

License Application And Renewals

Whether applying for a salesperson or broker license, you fingerprints must clear *before* you submit your license application. You can check your fingerprint status online by registering at the IREC website.

License
Application
IREC website

Both the salesperson and broker license applications and instructions are available from the IREC website - https://irec.idaho.gov/index.html. It's critical that you read over the application carefully to make sure you have all the necessary supporting information prior to submission.

Some required support information may take time to acquire or produce such as securing a copy of your high school diploma or equivalency, or securing an original certified license history if licensed in another state and coming to Idaho.

If you are already licensed in another state, you will need an original certified license history from that state which can sometimes take 3 to 6 weeks to receive. So it is important you order the license history early to minimize delays.

IC 54-2018 (10)

An application that is incomplete or lacking the required fees shall be returned to the applicant and no license shall be issued until a completed application and all required fees are received at and actually approved by the Commission.

IREC Application
Form

Once you submit your application for approval, allow 10 days for processing. When you application is approved, your license will be placed inactive until you affiliate with a broker.

Make sure you have Errors & Omissions insurance in place before you activate your license.

In conclusion, a checklist for license application needs to include:
- License fee payable to the IREC
- Copy of high school diploma or equivalency
- Document showing legal presence
- Certification of E&O insurance (if going active)
- Fingerprints approved by the IREC
- Verification of passing license exams

License Renewal
IREC website

License Renewal

To renew your license and check your education records, all licensees must register at the IREC website and log in to create a user name and password in order to process license renewal.

IC 54-2018 (2)

License renewal applications must be received no later than 5 p.m. (Mountain standard or daylight) of the expiration date at the Commission office in Boise.

Certification that the licensee has met the Continuing Education requirements for renewal is also required if renewing on an active basis.

The licensee must also certify they met the mandatory E&O insurance requirements if renewing on an active basis. If the licensee is renewing as an inactive licensee, E&O insurance is not required. An inactive licensee cannot practice real estate.

IC 54-2018 (9)

Personal Information

Whether active or inactive, a licensee must notify the IREC in writing, of any change of a personal name, change of personal residence or personal phone number, within 10 days of the change.

If a personal name has been changed, the licensee shall submit legal proof of the change and if the licensee is on active status, the licensee is to have the broker submit the notice of change to the commission.

Approximate Cost To Get Licensed

Approximate Costs To Get Licensed

The initial costs to secure a Idaho real estate license might approximate:

$ 600 Salesperson pre-license courses *
$ 1,200 Broker pre-license courses*
$ 80 State exam (not including retakes)
$ 65 Fingerprinting (digital through PearsonVue)
$ 155 E&O Insurance (basic plan; excludes add ons)

Rule 100

$ 160 Idaho real estate license (salesperson or broker)

* Course costs and additional items will vary between different real estate schools and individual needs. Also, once licensed, there will be more expenses including but not limited to – Multiple Listing Service (MLS) membership, memberships in trade organizations, such as the National Association of REALTORS®, and other expenses related to the practice of real estate.

Understanding The Basic Concepts Of Real Estate

Before one can practice real estate with confidence and understanding of the real estate industry, one needs to review and learn about various categories revolving within the real estate industry'.

Important categories that need to be understood, include but are not limited to:

- Federal, state, and local regulations
- Real estate laws, rules, and guidelines
- Contract law
- Agency representation
- Finance options
- Risk management
- Property valuation
- Limitations on rights of ownership
- Forms of ownership
- Water rights
- Property descriptions
- Title Insurance and closing transactions
- Environmental issues
- Property taxes

Once you learn the concepts of the categories mentioned above and pass the state exam, you will be ready to prepare for and practice real estate. The preparation and actual practice of real estate will be discussed in detail later in this text book.

General Exam Content Outline for Salespersons and Brokers

Effective: June 01, 2020

The general portion of the real estate exam is made up of eighty (80) scored items, which are distributed as noted in the following content outline. The general examination also contains five (5) pretest items that are not counted toward the score. These items are used to gather statistics on performance and to help assess appropriateness for use on future examinations. Because pretest items look exactly like items that are scored, candidates should answer all the items on the examination.

I. REAL PROPERTY CHARACTERISTICS, LEGAL DESCRIPTIONS, AND PROPERTY USE (SALES 9; BROKER 9)

A. Real property vs. personal property
1. Fixtures, trade fixtures, emblements
2. Attachment, severance, and bill of sale

B. Characteristics of real property
1. Economic characteristics
2. Physical characteristics

C. Legal descriptions
1. Methods used to describe real property
2. Survey

D. Public and private land use controls – encumbrances
1. Public controls – governmental powers
   a. Police power, eminent domain, taxation, escheat
   b. Zoning ordinances
2. Private controls, restrictions, and encroachments
   a. Covenants, conditions, and restrictions (CC&Rs), HOAs
   b. Easements
   c. Licenses and encroachments

II. FORMS OF OWNERSHIP, TRANSFER, AND RECORDING OF TITLE (SALES 8; BROKER 8)

A. Ownership, estates, rights, and interests
1. Forms of ownership
2. Freehold estate
   a. Fee simple absolute
   b. Fee simple defeasible, determinable, and condition subsequent
   c. Life estate
   d. Bundle of rights
3. Leasehold estates and types of leases
   a. Estate for years and from period to period (periodic estate)
   b. Estate at will and estate at sufferance
   c. Gross, net, and percentage leases
4. Liens and lien priority
5. Surface and sub-surface rights

B. Deed, title, transfer of title, and recording of title
1. Elements of a valid deed
2. Types of deeds

3. Title transfer
   a. Voluntary alienation
   b. Involuntary alienation
4. Recording the title
   a. Constructive and actual notice
   b. Title abstract and chain of title
   c. Marketable title and cloud on title
   d. Attorney title opinion, quiet title lawsuit, and title insurance

III. PROPERTY VALUE AND APPRAISAL (SALES 11; BROKER 10)

A. Concept of value
1. Market value vs. market price
2. Characteristics of value
3. Principles of value

B. Appraisal process
1. Purpose and steps to an appraisal
2. Federal oversight of the appraisal process

C. Methods of estimating value and Broker Price Opinions (BPO)
1. Sales comparison approach (market data)
2. Cost approach
   a. Improvements and depreciation
   b. Physical deterioration, functional, and economic obsolescence
   c. Reproduction or replacement costs
3. Income approach
4. Gross rent and gross income multipliers
5. Comparative Market Analysis (CMA)
6. Broker Price Opinion (BPO)
7. Assessed value and tax implications

IV. REAL ESTATE CONTRACTS AND AGENCY (SALES 16; BROKER 17)

A. Types of contracts
1. Express vs. implied
2. Unilateral vs. bilateral

B. Required elements of a valid contract

C. Contract performance
1. Executed vs. executory
2. Valid vs. void

3. Voidable vs. unenforceable

4. Breach of contract, rescission, and termination

5. Liquidated, punitive, or compensatory damages

6. Statute of Frauds

7. Time is of the essence

D. Sales contract

1. Offer and counteroffer

2. Earnest money and liquidated damages

3. Equitable title

4. Contingencies

5. Disputes and breach of contract

6. Option contract and installment sales contract

E. Types of agency and licensee-client relationships

F. Creation and termination of agency

G. Licensee obligations to parties of a transaction

V. REAL ESTATE PRACTICE (SALES 14; BROKER 13)

A. Responsibilities of broker

1. Practicing within scope of expertise

2. Unauthorized practice of law

B. Brokerage agreements between the broker and principal (seller, buyer, landlord, or tenant)

1. Seller representation – Types of listing agreements

   a. Exclusive right-to-sell and exclusive agency listing

   b. Non-exclusive or open listing

   c. Net listing (conflict of interest)

   d. Multiple listing service (MLS)

2. Buyer representation

3. Property management agreement

   a. Accounting for funds

   b. Property maintenance

   c. Leasing property

   d. Collecting rents and security deposits

4. Termination of agreements

5. Services, fees, and compensation

C. Fair Housing

1. Equal opportunity in housing

2. Protected classes

3. Fair housing laws

4. Illegal practices, enforcement, and penalties

5. Prohibited advertising

6. Housing and Urban Development (HUD)

7. Americans with Disabilities Act (ADA)

D. Risk management

1. Supervision

2. Compliance with federal regulations; including Privacy and Do Not Contact

3. Vicarious liability

4. Antitrust laws

5. Fraud and misrepresentation

6. Types of insurance

   a. Errors and Omissions

   b. General Liability

VI. PROPERTY DISCLOSURES AND ENVIRONMENTAL ISSUES (SALES 8; BROKER 8)

A. Property conditions and environmental issues

1. Hazardous substances

   a. Lead-based paint

   b. Asbestos, radon, and mold

   c. Groundwater contamination and underground storage tanks

   d. Waste disposal sites and brownfields

   e. Flood plains, flood zones, and flood insurance

2. Clean Air and Water Acts

3. Environmental Protection Agency (EPA)

   a. Comprehensive Environmental Response, Compensation, and Liability Act (CERCLA)

   b. Superfund Amendment and Reauthorization Act (SARA)

   c. Environmental site assessments (including Phase I and II studies) and impact statements

   d. Wetlands protection

B. Disclosure obligations and liability

VII. FINANCING AND SETTLEMENT (SALES 7; BROKER 7)

A. Financing concepts and components

1. Methods of financing

   a. Mortgage financing – conventional and non-conventional loans

   b. Seller financing – land contract/contract for deed

2. Lien theory vs. title theory and deed of trust

3. Sources of financing (primary and secondary mortgage markets, and seller financing)

4. Types of loans and loan programs

5. Mortgage clauses

B. Lender Requirements

1. FHA requirements

2. VA requirements

3. Buyer qualification and Loan to Value (LTV)

4. Hazard and flood insurance

5. Private mortgage insurance (PMI) and mortgage insurance premium (MIP)

C. Federal Financing Regulations and Regulatory Bodies

1. Truth-in-Lending and Regulation Z

2. TILA-RESPA Integrated Disclosures (TRID)

   a. Consumer Financial Protection Bureau (CFPB)

   b. Loan Estimate (LE)

   c. Closing Disclosure (CD)

3. Real Estate Settlement Procedures Act (RESPA)

   a. Referrals

   b. Rebates

4. Equal Credit Opportunity Act (ECOA)

5. Mortgage fraud and predatory lending

D. Settlement and closing the transaction

VIII. REAL ESTATE MATH CALCULATIONS
(SALES 7; BROKER 8)

A. Property area calculations

1. Square footage

2. Acreage total

B. Property valuation

1. Comparative Market Analysis (CMA)

2. Net Operating Income (NOI)

3. Capitalization rate

4. Gross rent multiplier- **Broker Only**

5. Gross income multiplier- **Broker Only**

6. Equity in property

7. Establishing a listing price

8. Assessed value and property taxes

C. Commission/compensation

D. Loan financing costs

1. Interest

2. Loan to Value (LTV)

3. Fees

4. Amortization, discount points, and prepayment penalties

E. Settlement and closing costs

1. Purchase price and down payment

2. Monthly mortgage calculations- principal, interest, taxes, and insurance (PITI)

3. Net to the seller

4. Cost to the buyer

5. Prorated items

6. Debits and credits

7. Transfer tax and recording fee

F. Investment

1. Return on investment

2. Appreciation

3. Depreciation

4. Tax implications on investment

G. Property management calculations

1. Property management and budget calculations

2. Tenancy and rental calculations

Idaho State Exam Content Outline
for Salesperson and Broker Examinations

Effective: July 15, 2017

The state-specific examination is made up of forty (40) scored items for salesperson candidates and fifty (50) scored items for broker candidates.

The salesperson and broker examinations also contain five to ten (5-10) pretest items. The pretest items are not identified and will not affect a candidate's score in any way.

The following examination content outline is applicable to both real estate salespersons and real estate brokers.

I. **DUTIES AND POWERS OF THE REAL ESTATE COMMISSION (SALESPERSON 5%, BROKERS 4%)**
   A. General Powers
   B. Investigations, audits, hearings, appeals
   C. Sanctions
      1. Fines
      2. License suspension and revocation

II. **LICENSING REQUIREMENTS (SALESPERSON 10%, BROKER 4%)**
   A. Activities requiring a license
   B. Eligibility for licensing
   C. License renewal
   D. Change in license/status
   E. Education

III. **LICENSE LAW AND RULES OF THE IDAHO REAL ESTATE COMMISSION (SALESPERSON 40%, BROKER 30%)**
   A. Advertising/Use of business name
   B. Broker-salesperson relationship
   C. Sales Commissions and fees
   D. Document handling and record keeping
   E. Handling of monies/Consideration (Items of value)
   F. Trust accounts
   G. Offers, counteroffers, acceptance
   H. Office operations and business practices
   I. Prohibited conduct

IV. **BROKERAGE REPRESENTATION (AGENCY LAW) (SALESPERSON 25%, BROKER 20%)**
   A. Agency contracts
   B. Types
   C. Obligations to parties
   D. Termination of agency
   E. Limits of confidentiality
   F. Disclosing agency relationships

V. **CALCULATIONS AND CLOSING COSTS (SALESPERSON 5%, BROKER 10%)**

VI. **IDAHO PRINCIPLES AND PRACTICES (SALESPERSON 15%, BROKER 12%)**
   A. Financing
   B. Trust deeds, notes, mortgages, contract for deed
   C. Foreclosure
   D. Ownership/Possession and Community Property
   E. Real estate valuation
      1. Property taxes/assessed value
      2. Homeowner's exemption
   F. Recording
   G. Mobile homes/manufactured housing
   H. Water rights
   I. Land use controls; zoning, subdivision

VII. **BROKERAGE MANAGEMENT (BROKER ONLY 20%)**
   A. Broker Supervision
   B. Requirements to maintain a Brokerage License
   C. Brokerage Operations

Purpose of Idaho Real Estate Commission
Purpose of Education Council
Licensure exceptions
Broker requirements
Continuing Education for renewal

Activities requiring a real estate license
Types of real estate licenses
Minimum salesperson requirements
Course and State exam requirements
Fingerprinting process

Questions - Chapter 1

1. The primary purpose of the Idaho Real Estate Commission is to:

   A. Protect the public and industry
   B. Defend the public and industry
   C. Protect private property rights
   D. Defend complaints against licensees

2. Initial application for a real estate license is administrated by:

   A. Idaho Employment Department
   B. Idaho Department of Occupational Licensing
   C. Idaho Real Estate Commission
   D. Idaho Secretary of State

3. Where does the money come from to operate the Idaho Real Estate Commission?

   A. State of Idaho general fund
   B. All active licensees
   C. All licensees
   D. All brokerage companies

4. The Idaho Real Estate Commission consists of how many member commissioners?

   A. 3
   B. 4
   C. 5
   D. 6

5. The Idaho Real Estate Commission generally meets:
   A. Once a month
   B. Four times a year
   C. Twice a year
   D. Six to eight times a year

6. Course make-up work is allowed only for:

   A. Any certified IREC approved course
   B. Continuing Education (CE) courses
   C. Any pre-license courses
   D. All pre-license and CE courses

7. Prelicense courses must be successfully completed prior to license application within:

   A. 1 year
   B. 3 years
   C. 5 years
   D. 10 years

8. Change of personal information be submitted to the IREC no later than:

   A. 1 week
   B. 10 days
   C. 1 month
   D. 30 days

9. How many IREC Core classes are required for license renewal

   A. One
   B. Two
   C. Three
   D. Four

10. An independent E&O insurance policy must have an A.M. Best rating of at least:

    A. A
    B. B+
    C. B
    D. C+

11. License renewal must be received no later than _____ of the expiration date at the Commission office in Boise.

    A. Midnight
    B. 5 p.m Pacific time
    C. 5 p.m. Mountain time
    D. Post marked by 5 p.m.

12. What is the minimum pass rate score for a broker taking the Idaho state exam?

    A. 65%
    B. 70%
    C. 75%
    D. 80%

13. Who is required to have a real estate license to practice real estate?

    A. Anyone assisting another to sell their property
    B. Anyone, with expectation of compensation, while acting for another, offers to list property for sale
    C. Anyone, with expectation of compensation, offers to sell personal property
    D. Anyone, for compensation, leases a commercial building

14. An example of an exception to being required to have a real estate license is:

    A. Purchasing real property for another for compensation
    B. Listing real property for another for compensation
    C. Negotiates for another an option for real property for compensation
    D. Offering property management or leasing for another for compensation.

15. What's the minimum age to secure a real estate license in Idaho?
    A. 16
    B. 18
    C. 20
    D. 21

16. Minimum elective hours of Continuing Education required to renew a real estate license are:

    A. 16 hours plus 1 Core
    B. 16 hours including 2 Core
    C. 12 hours plus 1 Core
    D. 12 hours plus 2 Core

17. When does a real estate license expire?

    A. The last day of licensees birth month
    B. The first day of licensees birth month
    C. 2 years from the date of licensing
    D. 2 years from date of completing CE

18. A student, whose birthday is June 5, passed their state exam on April 8, and applied for and received their license on April 18, 2016. When does their license expire?

    A. April 18, 2017
    B. June 5, 2017
    C. June 30, 2017
    D. April 18, 2018

19. When do initial fingerprints expire prior to receiving a real estate license?

    A. Fingerprints are fingerprints, they don't expire
    B. Fingerprint results are valid for 6 months
    C. Fingerprints are valid for 1 year
    D. Fingerprints aren't required if the license applicant already has them

20. What type of insurance is required for an inactive real estate licensee?

    A. Errors & Omissions Insurance
    B. Automobile liability insurance
    C. Personal liability insurance
    D. None

21. To be effective, tail coverage for E&O insurance must be purchased within how many days from cancellation?

    A. Tail coverage is automatically included with E&O insurance.
    B. 60 days from cancellation
    C. 90 days from cancellation
    D. 120 days from cancellation

22. What document needs to accompany an application for a real estate license?

    A. Verification of taking a license exam
    B. Fingerprints taken a year ago
    C. Proof of automobile insurance
    D. High school diploma or equivalency

23. A cooperative license applies to:

    A. Building contractors
    B. Residential transactions
    C. Commercial properties
    D. Developers

Legal Descriptions

Transferring Real Property

Before real property can be transferred from one party to another, an adequate legal description must be identified on all deeds and mortgages. Legal descriptions create an exact way to describe property as opposed to street address or parcel number which do not identify exact property dimensions.

3 Different Types Of Legal Descriptions

There are three different types of legal descriptions that can be used to meet Idaho requirements. They are:

- Government Rectangular Survey
- Metes and bounds
- Recorded plat (aka lot and block or subdivision)

One of the above systems will be used to properly and completely identify the exact location of the property that is to be transferred. Street address or tax parcel number alone will not meet acceptable standards to transfer property. A legal description must be able to adequately describe the exact size, shape and location of the property.

The basis for all surveys (except for the original 13 colonies) of the United States is based on a 'standardized' survey system under an ordinance of the Continental Congress passed in 1785 and officially adopted by the government in 1805 and is known as the Government Rectangular Survey system.

Initial Point Location

Rectangular Survey System - Initial Point

The rectangular survey system requires a 'initial' point from which *all* surveys originate. In Idaho, the 'initial' point is located on top of a lava butte one mile east of the Swan Falls Road out of Kuna, just east of the Kuna Caves. The initial point was established in 1867 and is identified with a U. S. Geological Survey stainless steel marker.

Where the east/west base line (latitude - N43°22' 31") intersects with the north/south longitude line (longitude 116 ° 24' 15"), it serves as the initial point which is the basis for *all* legal descriptions in Idaho.

Boise Meridian

This starting point is referenced as the Boise Meridian also known as B.M. Remember, the government rectangular survey system utilizes the concept of township and range. Township 65 North (T65N) is the most northern township and Township 16 South (T16S) is the most southern township.

Each township is 6 miles by 6 miles and contains 36 sections which, as you remember from basic real estate, are 1 mile by 1 mile and contain 640 acres. Each acre is 43,560 square feet. Correction lines, known as a government check, will occur every 24 miles on the guide meridian to accommodate for the curvature of the earth.

Along the borders of a state and around large bodies of water, there will be undersized and oversized sections which are known as fractional sections.

The western border is Range 6 West (R6W) and the eastern border is Range 46 East (R46E). Given these coordinates, one could say that Idaho is 486 miles long and 312 miles wide at its widest and longest points.

Metes-And-Bounds

Metes-And-Bounds

Properties that cannot be described by the government rectangular system will be irregular in shape and described with longitude and latitude bearings identified in feet including tenths or hundreds of a foot. It is important to note that inches are *not* used at anytime to identify the length or width of property.

Identification of these irregular lots must be prepared by a licensed surveyor and a legal description prepared from the survey. The initial point of beginning (POB) will be a corner of a section or township that connects the metes-and-bounds to the government rectangular survey. The actual point of beginning will be a point of the metes-and-bounds description. In order to have a 'closed' legal description, the actual point of beginning will begin and end at the same point.

To assure accurateness, some surveyors will triangulate the legal description from two different initial points. If they both come up with the same results, the description has minimized errors. However, it is not unusual to have two different surveyors come up with close but not exact numbers when surveying the same parcel of ground if they use different beginning points.

Recorded Plat
IC 50-1301 (17)

Recorded Plat

Recorded plats are used for developments that consist of multiple lots. Idaho Code describes a subdivision as a tract of land divided into 5 or more lots, parcels, or sites for the purpose of sale or building development, whether immediate or future. The definition shall not include a bone fide division or partition of agricultural land for agricultural purposes

A bone fide division or partition of agricultural land for agricultural purposes will be a division of land into lots, all of which are 5 acres or larger and maintained as agricultural lands.

It is important to know that cities or counties may adopt their own definition of subdivision in lieu of the state code and may be more restrictive.

After a subdivision has been formally approved and recorded in the county in which the property is located, the legal description will reference lot and block of a specified subdivision; example might read - lot 4 block 7, Sunnyside Slope, Ada County, Idaho.

Unplatted Lots
IC 50-1316

It should be noted that any person who disposes of or offers for sale any lots in a city or county before a plat is duly acknowledged and recorded shall forfeit and pay $100 for each lot sold or disposed of or offered for sale.

Within the plat, there will be reference to the government rectangular description, metes and bounds description, and finally the lot and block identification. Because the plat contains all the necessary items to create a valid legal description, reference by lot and block uncomplicates the process and offers easier identification.

Measuring Elevations

Measuring Elevations

A datum is a point, line or surface in which vertical height or depth is measured and most large cities have a datum point from which benchmark monuments are established beyond the original datum point.

The benchmarks are used by most surveyors due to the permanence of the monuments and are usually topped with an aluminum or brass cap. The cap will usually identify a monument number and the company who did the survey. From that information, additional information, including but not limited to, will give the date, elevation, monument coordinates (GIS) section, township, and range plus additional information showing the exact location accompanied with a sketch or map plus the stamp of the registered land surveyor.

It's not uncommon to find these monuments located in the middle of streets or somewhere where close by where the surface won't be disturbed. There are many uses for benchmark elevations including mining, agriculture, storm drainage, flood plains, roadway construction, landscaping, and on and on.

Air Lots
IC 55-1504

Air Lots (also known as elevation surveys)

Like other legal descriptions, a licensed surveyor will prepare the plat to identify 'air lots' in which condominiums are identified. Each unit is identified by elevation but later referred to as a particular unit within an approved and recorded plat.

The requirements of the Condominium Property Act shall apply to condominiums only if (a) there shall be recorded in the county in which such condominiums are located or to be located a declaration, as provided in the act, together with a plat or plats, and (b) if said documents or either of them, contain an expression of intent to create a project which is subject to the provisions of the act.

Condominium Elevations
IC 55-1504 (ii)

The Condominium Property Act identifies elevations with diagrammatic floor plans in sufficient detail to identify each unit, its relative location and approximate dimensions, showing elevations where multi-level or multi-story structures are diagramed.

Most cities have a local official datum(s) for surveyors to use for an initial point of elevation. As a note, most airports (even the little ones) have a elevation point located somewhere near or on a runway for elevation verification.

Although not used directly for legal descriptions, topography or contour maps are very useful to identify elevations. Topo maps are helpful with large development plans for planned view sites, roadways, common areas, and other important factors to determine feasability.

Flood Plain

Flood Plain
Although a legal description identifies the exact location of a property, a legal description does not identify the strata or physical characteristics of the property. So it's important that one observes whether there is water located on or near the property that could impact or restrict the building or use of the property.

Flood Plain Definition

A flood plain is 'land located close to or adjacent to a stream or river that is naturally subject to flooding and is known as a flood zone'. However, such a definition can be deceiving. A property could be located five miles or more from a river or stream and yet be subject to flooding from the overflow of river banks or even water canals.

FEMA

FEMA, Federal Emergency Management Agency, administers the program and flood elevations are determined by the U. S. Army Corp of Engineers who is in charge of maintaining the U. S. waterways. Special Flood Hazard Areas are identified and often called the '100-year floodplain'. Flood zone maps are published for every municipality and county exclusively by the U. S. Army Corps of Engineers.

Federal Banking Regulations

Federal banking regulations require certain flood zone properties to carry flood insurance as a condition of extending a loan to a borrower.

Therefore, it is very important that a real estate licensee be familiar with the Special Flood Hazard Area in which the flood zones are shown in detail on the National Flood Insurance Program map. It's also important to make sure the most current maps are identified as flood plains mapping can change periodically.

If a structure is located in a flood plain but is above the flood plain elevation, a 'foundation survey' may be required to prove that the structure is not subject to flood insurance.

Survey Monuments
IC 54-1227

Survey Monuments
A land survey, performed by a licensed professional land surveyor, is to set permanent and reliable, magnetically detectable monuments. The minimum size shall be at least ½" in diameter and 2 feet long. Such monuments must be permanently marked with the license number of the surveyor placing the monument.

IC 54-1234

If any person willfully defaces injure, or removes any signal, monument or other object set as a permanent boundary survey marker, benchmark or point set in control surveys by agencies of the United States government or the state of Idaho, he shall forfeit a sum not to exceed $1,500 for each offense, and shall be liable for damages sustained by the affected parties.

Recording Surveys
IC 55-1904

Recording Of Surveys

After a survey has been completed, a record of survey shall be filed within 90 days after completing a survey that:

1. Discloses a material discrepancy with previous surveys of record;

2. Establishes boundary lines and/or corners not previously existing or of record;

3. Results in the setting of monuments at corners of record which were not previously monumented;

4. Produces evidence or information which varies from, or is not contained in, surveys of record relating to the public land survey, lost public land corners or obliterated land survey corners.

Easements

Easements

Legal descriptions identify the specific dimensions and location of a property but may or may not address use by others that are allowed within the boundaries of the property such as easements; whether recorded or unrecorded.

**Easements Right
To Use**
IC 55-603

Because easements provide the right to use the land of another for a particular purpose, it is very important for all parties to know and understand that an easement can create serious limitations. Its also important to remember that a transfer of real property passes all easements attached thereto, and creates in favor thereof an easement to use the other real property of the person whose estate is transferred, in the same manner and to the same extent as such property was obviously and permanently used at the time the transfer was agreed upon or completed.

**Easements Pass
With Transfer**

Any easements, contained within a legal description, need to be reviewed very, very carefully. Some examples of limitations are: ingress, egress, set back requirements, solar easements, utilities, etc.

A transfer of real property passes and creates in favor of an easement to use other real property of the person whose estate is transferred. Such property was obviously and permanently used for the benefit and by the person at the time when the transfer was agreed upon or completed.

Easements should also identify any limitations, restrictions and obligations. Are easements for roadways where they are supposed to be? Who maintains the easements for ingress and egress? Are the roadways for anyone to use or are they restricted to specific users? Are the roadways public or private? Are there encroachments into any roadway easements by adjoining properties?

**Double Check
Property
Descriptions**

Double Check Legal Descriptions

The transfer of real property from one party to another is evidenced by a proper and correct legal description. It is very important that real estate licensees double check legal descriptions and any additional issues surrounding the closing to verify exactly what is being transferred.

In today's society, it's easier than ever to come close to actual survey points with electronic devices such as smart phones, gps, and laser measuring equipment. But for the transfer of real property, the property lines must be exact. That's where licensed professional surveyors can provide the necessary documentation.

Disclose Adverse Material Facts
IC 54-2086 (1) (d)
(E)
IC 54-2087 (4) (a)

Once a property has been identified, everyone involved should make sure any additional issues such as water (flood plain) or access by others (easements) be observed and acknowledged. Remember, real estate agents are required to disclose any adverse material facts actually known or which reasonably should have been known by the licensee.

Roadway Easement

Roadway Easements

Extreme care should be taken to verify the roadway easements and the actual use of a roadway. In addition, is the full easement being used? For example, if a roadway easement is for 50', is a full 50' being utilized or could there be an encroachment by the party giving the easement due to non use? The best way to verify the exact location of the easement is with a survey from a licensed surveyor.

View Easements

View And/Or Solar Easements

Another example could involve elevation easements. Hillside view lots may need protection to preserve the views with 'view easements' to restrict other improvements or foliage from blocking views from the subject property. These types of restrictions may not be directly addressed in the legal description but may be contained in the covenants, conditions and restrictions (CC&R's). If so, what are the specifics?

If property lines are important to either the buyer or the seller, perhaps a new survey would be in order to assure all parties exactly where the property lines are located. It's not unusual to have fences erected outside or inside the property lines. Accurate legal descriptions are especially important when dealing with commercial properties. Zero lot lines can often overlap causing delays and even transaction cancellations.

Common Area Easements

Common Area Easements

Platted residential and condominium divisions may contain easements that are not easily visible. For instance, a walkway to a recreational facility or maybe a body of water may be platted but not yet developed. Or, what about common area easements that are placed between occupied lots or buildings for public access or maintenance?

Double check the recorded plat for any easements that are platted but not developed or used.

Figure 1 – Boise Meridian and Initial Point

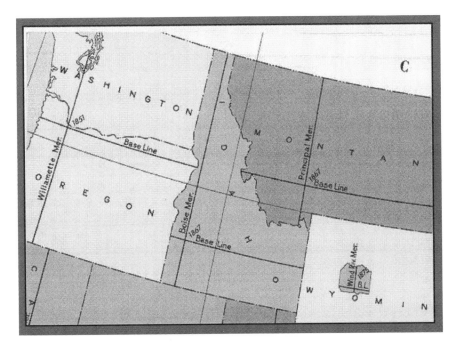

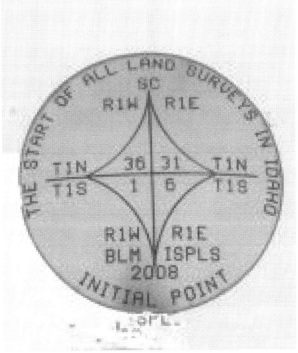

Figure 2 - Plat map and lots

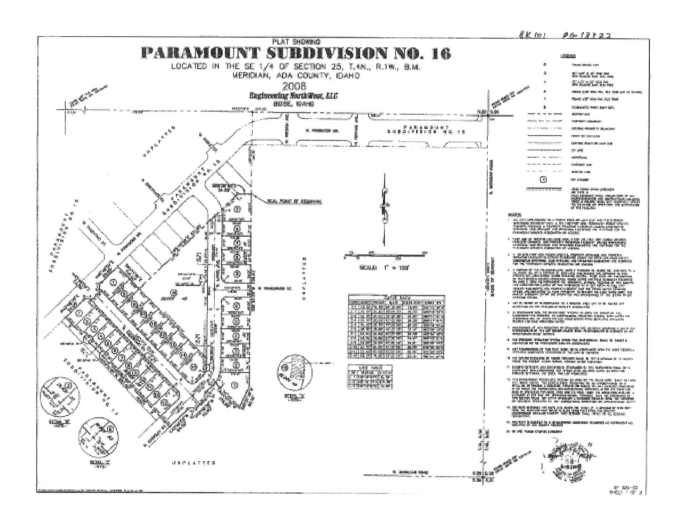

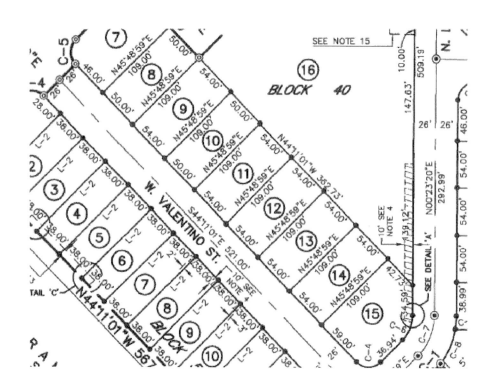

BEFORE ANSWERING QUESTIONS – can you define or explain:

Government Rectangular Survey	Initial point
Boise Meridian	Metes And Bounds
Recorded plat	Idaho definition of subdivision
Air lots	Foundation survey
Recording of Surveys	Survey monuments
Purpose of easements	View easements
Townships	Point of beginning
Flood plain	Flood insurance

Questions - Chapter 2

1. How many different types of surveys are recognized in Idaho.

   A. One
   B. Two
   C. Three
   D. Four

2. What type of description will not meet acceptable standards to transfer property.

   A. Tax parcel number
   B. Government Rectangular Survey
   C. Metes and Bounds
   D. Recorded plat

3. The 'initial point' (Boise Meridian) is closest to what community?

   A. Meridian
   B. Boise
   C. Nampa
   D. Kuna

4. What township borders Canada?

   A. Township 16 North
   B. Township 56 North
   C. Township 65 North
   D. Township 85 North

5. If the western border is Range 6 west and the eastern border is Range 46 east, how wide is Idaho?

   A. 276 miles
   B. 282 miles
   C. 312 miles
   D. 360 miles

6. Idaho describes a subdivision as a tract of land divided into at least how many lots for the purpose of sale or development?

   A. 3
   B. 5
   C. 7
   D. 9

7. A legal description using 'lot and block' is using what method to describe the parcel?

   A. Tax parcel number
   B. Government Rectangular Survey
   C. Metes and Bounds
   D. Recorded plat

8. What period of time does a completed
record of survey need to be filed?

    A. 90 days
    B. 120 days
    C. 180 days
    D. 365 days

9. The minimum size of survey pins shall be not
    less than:

    A. ½ inch diameter – 2 feet long
    B. ¼ inch diameter – 1 foot long
    C. ½ inch diameter – 1 foot long
    D. ⅞ inch diameter – 2 feet long

10. A datum point and subsequent benchmarks are
    used to measure:

    A. Road easements
    B. Air lots
    C. Solar easements
    D. Personal property

Chapter 3

Rights And Interests In Real Estate

Words Of Wisdom

"I have been impressed with the urgency of doing. Knowing is not enough; we must apply. Being willing is not enough; we must do."

Leonardo da Vinci

Real Estate And Real Property

Real Estate And Real Property

As one can imagine, the terms 'real estate' and 'real property' are general terms that describe a vast and complex subject. Real estate includes land plus added permanent additions such as structures. Real property covers a greater area to include the rights, interests, and benefits (also known as the 'bundle of rights') associated with the ownership of land and real estate.

Just think of real property as being everything from the center of the earth to the heavens above, attached or unattached (air rights) to the land together with the interests, benefits and rights to own, occupy, or use.

Deed Or Bill Of Sale

For a better understanding, 'real property' needs to be broken down into different increments with separate explanations. The instrument used to transfer ownership in real property is a *deed*. Personal property, on the other hand, is transferred with a *bill of sale*.

Chattel

One area known as personal property or 'chattel' is generally movable or annexed onto real property. Examples include annual growing crops, fixtures used in a trade or business, and other types of personal property that are transferable and separate from real property. For instance, in Idaho, a water right is an example of a unique form of personal property.

Water Rights

Range Wars

In the 1800's our country was challenged with 'range wars' as a result of expansion of our population moving west. Conflicts flared up for a number of reasons. There were conflicts between large cattle ranchers and homesteaders plus many disagreements between ranchers over water rights.

Water Wars

Today, 'range wars' are being replaced with 'water wars'. As a result of climatic changes, many parts of our country, especially the west, have and are experiencing long drawn out droughts. These droughts are creating challenges for allocation of available water resources and how available water will be distributed.

With water resources dwindling and demand growing, the use and distribution of water is becoming a key topic of discussion in designing our economic future. Water rights will be the final say in determining when and how water will be distributed, especially in areas of extreme drought.

Riparian Rights

In states that recognize 'riparian rights', an owner of land has the right to make use of the ground water flowing on, through or along the borders of the owned land. A riparian right is not limited by priority date and cannot be lost by non-use.

IC 42-104

Idaho does *not* recognize riparian rights under the laws of Idaho. In Idaho, a water right must be for some useful or beneficial purpose and can only be established by appropriation and once established, *can* be lost if not used.

Prior Appropriation

Prior Appropriation
IC 42-103

Unlike the eastern United States where water rights are tied to the land through riparian rights, most of the western United States follows the doctrine of 'prior appropriation', which is based on 'first in time, first in right' principle.

Idaho is 1 of 17 states to employ prior appropriation to the exclusion of the riparian doctrine. Rights acquired by appropriation are the right to the use of the unappropriated waters of rivers, streams, lakes, springs, and of subterranean waters of other sources within the state shall be acquired only by appropriation under the application, permit and license procedure as provided by the law.

However, it should be noted that each state operates independently of each other. Thus, the administration of the rights will differ from state to state.

IC 42-101

All the waters of Idaho are declared to be the property of the state when flowing in their natural channels including the waters of all natural springs and lakes within the boundaries of the state.

Priority Date

Priority Date
42-106

As mentioned above, 'first in time, first in right' will create a priority date. It determines who gets water when there is a shortage. If there isn't enough water to satisfy all of the water rights, then the oldest or senior water rights are satisfied first and so on in order until there is no water left. It is the new or junior water rights that do not get water when there isn't enough to satisfy all the water rights.

However, there may be water rights that do not require 'appropriation'. For example, some persons have the right to receive water as share holders in a ditch company. The ditch company has the appropriation and the users are the share holders of the ditch company.

IC 42-101

Additional examples would be persons who receive water from a city, irrigation district, or a water utility company where the user has the right to receive water but does not have an appropriation. The right is usually accompanied with a fee and the water delivery can be withheld if the charges or fees are not paid.

IDWR
www.idwr.idaho.gov

Idaho Department Of Water Resources
The Idaho Department Of Water Resources (IDWR) is the regulatory agency that administers water rights and has a duty to supervise the appropriation and allotment for beneficial purposes.

Distribution of water from public or natural water sources in accordance with water right priority dates, shall be administered by the Director of the Idaho Department of Water Resources (IDWR)

Water And Irrigation Districts
IC 43-101

Irrigation districts are generally created for new irrigation development or acquiring existing irrigation projects. Whenever 50, or a majority of the owners of lands that can be irrigated from the same or different sources and by the same or different systems works to provide irrigation, Idaho Code authorizes the formation of Irrigation Districts.

Water delivery within an irrigation district is performed by irrigation district staff and referred to as 'ditch riders' or 'watermasters'.

Lesser known districts include Ground Water Management Districts, Aquifer Recharge Districts, Water and Sewer Districts, Canal Companies, and Lateral Ditch Water Users Associations. We will not go into discussion about these districts but you can contact the IDWR for further information. If water isn't available from water or irrigation districts, one may have to resort to drilling a well.

Use Of Public Waters
IC 42-107

Use Of Public Waters
Anyone intending to use public waters of any natural streams, springs, lakes, seepage waters, or ground water shall make application for a permit from the Idaho Department of Water Resources before commencing to construct, enlarge, or extend any ditch, canal, well, or other distributing systems.

If the diversion works or irrigation system is represented by a corporation or irrigation district, consent must be obtained from the corporation or irrigation district before approval can be made by the Director of the Idaho Department of Water Resources.

Well Permit
IC 42-230
IC 42-235
IC 42-238 (2)

Well Drilling Permit Required
It is unlawful for anyone to drill a well deeper than 18' in vertical depth below land surface and cannot be drilled in Idaho without a licensed well driller and operator of drilling equipment.

The Department of Water Resources has the statutory duty and responsibility for regulating the drilling of wells and licensing of drillers and operators in the State of Idaho. Without urban water and sewer districts, most rural homes and ranches have wells drilled for their own domestic use.

Domestic Water Usage

Domestic Water
IC 42-111

The use of water for homes and any other purpose in connection with home type use is limited to irrigation up to ½ *acre* of land. The total use of water is not to exceed 13,000 gallons per day.

A real estate licensee needs to be very careful when listing homes on small ranchette type properties that are irrigated from a domestic well, especially if more than ½ acre is being irrigated. If in doubt, contact the local water district to verify usage. If the water district does not have any record of the homeowner, it's possible there is a violation. The IDWR also uses Infrared sensors from satellites to identify those parcels in which violations are occurring.

It is certainly possible that the smaller parcels are irrigated with multiple water rights for domestic uses. However, multiple water rights cannot overlap in a manner to satisfy a single combined water use or purpose. The purpose of the limitation is to prohibit the diversion and use of water to supply a use that does not meet the domestic use definition.

License To Use

**Water Right
License To Use**
IC 42-219

If a water right is to be used for irrigation or municipal purposes and not for domestic use, an application, permit/license procedure must be followed.

Once the application has been properly submitted and approved by the IDWR, a notice of application will be published. If the application meets the requirements a permit will be issued including a deadline in which the appropriation must be completed including a 'Proof of beneficial use' form.

After filing the proof form, a field examination will be conducted by a certified field examiner to ensure that water is being used as described in the permit. If so, the IDWR will issue a license that describes the appropriation has been completed.

Use It Or Lose It

Use It Or Lose It
IC 42-222 (2)

If after the holder of a water right has ceased to put the water to a beneficial use for any *5 year period of non use*, the water right will be lost and forfeited. Such lost right shall revert to the state and be again subject to appropriation.

**Non Use
Forfeiture
IC 42-222 (12)**

No portion of any water right shall be lost or forfeited for nonuse if, after the 5 year period of nonuse, use of the water is resumed prior to a claim of right by a third party.

The water right holder shall have the right to an administrative hearing if requested in writing 15 days from the date of service to petition for reinstatement.

IDAPA 37.03.09

In addition, a well *cannot* be abandoned unless a report is submitted to the director of the IDWR describing the abandonment by a licensed well driller in compliance with administrative rules.

**Recharging
Ground Water
IC 42-4201**

Recharging Ground Water

Unforseen circumstances such as drought, lack of snow pack, and other situations that could jeopardize ground water basins could leave water users high and dry.

Idaho's farmers have done an excellent job with water conservation and irrigation practices.

However, some of the conservation practices could in fact reduce the amount of natural recharge into the ground water.

In order to minimize excessive draw down of aquifer storage, the IDWR has the authority to appropriate recharge from the Snake River. The purpose is to replace the waters displaced from the aquifer.

Water has been and will continue to be a very important aspect of property ownership. It is very important that real estate licensees and the public are both aware of water law and the use of water in Idaho. In the old days, we had 'range wars'. Today, many parts of the country are experiencing 'water wars'.

**Geothermal
Energy
IC 42-4002**

Geothermal Energy

In Idaho, a geothermal resource is defined as ground water having a temperature of 212 degrees Fahrenheit or more in the bottom of a well.

Being neither a mineral nor water resource, geothermal resources are considered *sui generis* because of the close relationship to each other.

In order to secure geothermal energy, one has to make application for a geothermal resource well permit from the Idaho Department of Water Resources.

**Selling Water
Rights**
IC 42-2604

Sale Of Water Rights

All contracts and deeds for the sale of water rights shall be in the form approved by the Department of Water Resources. The contracts or deeds shall be numbered plainly and consecutively. It shall be the duty of the owner of such irrigation works to file for record in the proper county recorder's office.

The IDWR will determine the number of water rights, units or shares of water which may be sold and the number of acres which may be irrigated. The purchasers will receive a certificate in appropriate form certifying or showing the amount of water rights which may be sold. The certificate will then be recorded in the county recorder's office in each county in which the lands are located.

Manufactured Home Residency Act

**Idaho Code
Ch 20**
IC 55-2001 thru
55-2019

Purpose

Because of the nature of a manufactured/mobile home and the fact it could be moved or relocated, the Manufactured Home Residency Act was created in 1980. The purpose of the act is to address issues not covered under the basic rights of the typical landlord-tenant laws between park owners and park residents.

Rental Agreement
IC 55-2001 thru
IC 55-2019

Rental Agreement

The landlord offering a lot for rent shall provide the prospective resident a *written* rental agreement.

Any changes or adjustments to rent, services, utilities or rules require a 90 day written notice to residents. Furthermore, the landlord may not amend the rental agreement more than once in a 6 month period.

However, a rental agreement may include an escalation clause for increases or decreases in the community's ad valorem taxes, utilities or other services charged in the monthly rent and only requires a 30 day written notice to the resident after the effective date of the change.

IC 55-2009A

Past Due Rent Protection To Landlord

If the resident becomes 60 days late in rent, the landlord can notify and advise the lien holder of the liability for space rent owing. The lien holder shall be responsible for utilities from the date of notice. However, the landlord shall be entitled to a maximum of 60 days of rent due prior to notice to the lien holder.

Any and all costs then become the responsibility of the legal owner or lienholder. The manufactured/mobile home cannot be removed from the space without written landlord approval.

IC 55-2010	**Rental Agreement Termination**

Repeated violations of written rules or non payment of rent or other charges require the resident to receive written notice of such violations. If the resident doesn't comply within three days, the resident may be given a 20-day notice to vacate.

If the resident no longer intends to renew a rental agreement, written notice is to be provided to the landlord 30 days prior to renewal date.

If the landlord terminates the agreement by not renewing, the landlord shall give written notice to the resident not less than 180 days prior to the expiration date of the rental agreement.

If notification is not given by either party, the rental agreement renewals are automatic.

IC 55-2015	**Retaliatory Conduct By Landlord**

The landlord shall not terminate a tenancy, refuse to renew, increase rent, or decrease services normally supplied, or threaten repossession of a manufactured/mobile home because the resident has complained about:
- health and safety issues
- maintenance or condition of the park
- rent charged
- rules and regulations

Floating Homes Residency Act

Title 55
Chapter 27
IC 55-2704

What Is A Moorage Marina?

A floating home moorage marina is a waterfront facility for the moorage of 1 or more floating homes and the land and water premises on which it is located.

Some issues need to be addressed due to limited availability of moorage sites and the cost of relocating floating homes.

IC 55-2706

Rental Agreement

Any landlord offering a moorage site for rent shall provide a written agreement to be executed by both parties.

The term of a rental agreement shall be for 12 months unless the landlord and tenant agree to a lesser or longer period. The agreement shall identify the specific moorage site and remain site specific unless agreed upon by landlord and tenant.

IC 55-2708

Rental rates shall be reasonable with a minimum of 90 day written notice to increase or decrease such rates prior to expiration of any existing rental agreement. All things being equal, rental increases shall be uniform throughout the floating home marina.

If a master meter for utilities is provided, the cost of the utilities must be separately stated in each billing period. The landlord must also post the current rates charged by the utility in at least 1 conspicuous place in the marina.

If 25% or more of the tenants within a marina disagree with what may be termed 'reasonable', the dispute will be resolved by arbitration.

IC 55-2709

Rental Renewal
The landlord shall not terminate or refuse to renew a rental agreement without first giving a written notice to the tenant to remove the floating home from the marina within a period of not less than 90 days specified in the notice.

IC 55-2710

Eviction
Grounds for eviction in which a tenancy may be terminated are:

- Conduct constituting a nuisance
- Repeated violations of reasonable rules and regulations
- Non payment of rent
- Other material breach
- Condemnation of the marina

Homestead

Homestead Protection

Homestead Protection
Homestead rights don't exist under common law but 27 states have enacted homestead protection including Idaho.

Protect Against Unsecured Creditors
IC 55-1003

The home or property is protected by law from *unsecured creditors* during the occupants lifetime. The owner can only have one homestead at a time.

$175,000 Maximum Protection
In Idaho, the homestead protection (exemption) includes the net value of the dwelling, manufactured home, lands, and improvements not to exceed $175,000 in net value. Net value is defined as market value less all liens and encumbrances.

Automatic Exemption
IC 55-1004

Homestead exemption is automatic in Idaho providing:

- The property must be occupied as the principal residence;

Minimum 6 Month Occupancy

- Property must be occupied continuously for at least 6 months;

- If the property is land and is not occupied, a declaration of homestead must be filed.

If the owner already resides on a parcel of property that has a claim of homestead but wants to move to another piece of property which they also own, what must they do?

Declarations   The owner must file a declaration of abandonment on the property they reside and also file a declaration of homestead for the new location. The declaration(s) must be filed in the county or counties where the property(s) are located.

The declaration of homestead must contain:
1. A statement that the person making it is residing on the premises or intends to reside thereon and claims the premises as a homestead;
2. A legal description of the premises;
3. An estimate of the premises actual cash value.

The declaration of abandonment must contain:
1. A statement that the premises occupied as a residence or claimed as a homestead no longer constitutes the owner's homestead;
2. A legal description of the premises;
3. A statement of the date of abandonment.

Leasehold Estates

The creation of occupancy with a landlord/tenant relationship becomes a contract between landlord and tenant.

Statute Of Frauds   The lease or rental agreement can be oral or in writing if the agreement is for less
IC 9-503   than one year. However, the Statute of Frauds does state that an agreement to rent or lease for longer than one year is invalid unless the agreement is in writing.

As a precaution to having an invalid contract, it would be advisable to have a rental/lease agreement in writing regardless of the time frame.

www.ag.idaho.gov   Although Idaho does not currently regulate property management operations, the Idaho Office of the Attorney General offers an excellent booklet titled *Landlord and Tenant Guidelines* and can be downloaded from the AG's website.

Rental Property Maintenance
Specific   During the tenant's occupancy, the landlord must maintain the premises and
Performance   protect the tenant's health and safety. The landlord must comply with city and
IC 6-320   county ordinances together with state laws regarding housing conditions.

Examples that could contribute to violations might include:

- Missing doors or windows
- Defective plumbing
- Exposed wiring
- Non-functioning heating
- Insect infestation
- Leaks
- Environmental issues endangering health

Notice To Landlord
IC 6-320 (6) (d)

Tenant Remedies

The tenant must provide the landlord a written list of the violations in person, certified mail, or with an employee at the landlord's usual place of business.

The landlord has 3 days to fix the violations. Failure to fix the problems allows the tenant to sue for compliance. The landlord will receive a summons and complaint at least 5 days before trial.

Landlord Remedies

If the tenant damages the property through carelessness or negligence, the tenant may be required to pay the landlord for damages and may even be evicted.

Like the tenant remedies, the landlord must give written notice of the violation(s) and be delivered in person or left with a competent person at the tenant's residence or place of business If the tenant is unavailable, the landlord must post a copy of the notice in a conspicuous place on the property or leave a copy with any person living at the property and mail a copy to the tenant at the property address.

The tenant now has 3 days to fix the problem. Failure of the tenant to fix the problem gives the landlord the right to evict the tenant and recover costs for repair of the damage.

If the landlord has reasonable grounds to believe any person is or has been engaged in the unlawful delivery, production, or use of a controlled substance, the landlord can initiate immediate eviction proceedings.

Termination
IC 55-208

Termination Or Evictions

Proper 3 day or not less than 1 month notice to terminate must be given in writing depending on the circumstances surrounding the termination.

IC 6-303

The 3 day notice is only available if the tenant or subtenant:

- Continues possession after the expiration tenancy agreement
- Failed to pay rent
- Violated the terms of the rental or lease agreement
- Engaged in an unlawful activity

Unlawful Detainer
IC 6-303

Unlawful Detainer Action

If, upon proper notice to the tenant, the tenant fails to comply with the terms of the notice, the landlord must file an unlawful detainer action to force the tenant to leave the property.

If tenant or subtenant continues possession after default of payment of rent, pursuant to the lease or agreement and 3 days notice, in writing has been served to the tenant or subtenant, the landlord can initiate action to regain the property.

Such notice shall notify the tenant that if a court enters judgment against him, he will have 72 hours, if residential or 7 days if commercial with a tract of land 5 acres or more to remove his belongings from the premises.

Change In Rent
IC 55-307

Rent Increases - Month-To-Month Tenancy
If the landlord plans to increase the month-to-month rent, the landlord must provide a written notice at least 15 days before the increase becomes effective.

Termination
IC 55-208

Termination - Month To Month Tenancy
A tenancy at will may be terminated by the landlords' giving written notice to the tenant, in the manner prescribed by the code of civil procedure, to remove from the premises withing a period of not less than 1 month to be specified in the notice.

The tenant can terminate a tenancy at will by giving notice in writing to the landlord and the tenant will be vacating the premises, on a date as specified in the notice, but not less than 1 month from the date of the notice.

Security Deposits
IC 6-321

Security Deposits
Deposits with the landlord other than payment for rent shall be deemed security deposits. With the exception of 'normal wear and tear', security deposit refunds shall be made within 21 days if no time is fixed by agreement. Such refund shall be made within 30 days after the surrender of the premises by the tenant.

IC 6-321 (4)

Third party property managers shall put security deposits into a federally insured financial institution that is separate from the third party's operating account.

Any amount refunded less than the deposited security deposit shall be accompanied with a detailed statement itemizing repair and cleaning amounts that are retained by the landlord.

Before And After Photos

As a precaution based on 'opinion' of condition when terminating, it's a good idea to take photos of the rental unit when the unit was first rented and when it was vacated. The photos will assist in determining the condition when the unit was first occupied (and show any pre-existing issues).

Easements

Easement - Right To Use

Simply put, an easement is the nonpossessory *right* to use the land of another for a limited purpose. The basic types of easements revolve around granting access of others to or over privately owned property for a specific purpose.

Easement Examples

Some easement examples include driveways, roadway easements, utility easements, pipelines, ditch easement, water delivery systems by irrigation districts, solar, conservation easement, and yes, even view easements.

IC 55-603

Right to use easements can be divided into 4 different categories which once established, are attached to and pass with the transfer of real property.

Easement Categories

4 Easement Categories

1. Easement by necessity - is a right granted by law where there is no access to a person's land. Idaho does not have any specific laws requiring access from a public road to landlocked property. However, there may be many circumstances that could invoke an easement by necessity so legal counsel should always be considered.

IC 5-203

2. Easement by prescription - is acquired by using land of another without permission for a prescribed period of time which in Idaho is 20 years before the commencement of the action.

3. Easement in gross - is a right of a person or corporation to use land owned by another for a specific purpose. The best examples are utility easements such as power, gas, and telephone companies. Another example could be for a neighbor to use the property (such as hunting) and terminates when the person holding the easement dies and is not transferable.

4. Easement appurtenant - is a right that runs with the land from the servient estate to the dominate estate. An example is a driveway from the front lot to a back lot. Although the back lot benefits from the easement, it must be noted the front lot is burdened.

It's very important that real estate licensees explore and ask questions especially where it appears the servient estate is possibly being used by another party.

License To Use

License To Use

Granting access to a property for a particular purpose for a specific period of time, will incorporate a 'license to use' and might be known as a restrictive easement.

Ending Date

An example might be a timber company needing road access to the property where the timber is located, would need to cross over other private property to get to the timber. Thus, the timber company would be granted a 'license' to use under specific conditions and would incorporate a ending date of the license. Upon expiration of the license, the use would no longer be valid.

Another example might be where a farmer is granted a 'license' to use in order to move equipment from one field to another by cutting through a separate piece of property. The license might only grant the license with specific time frames when the use can be executed. The 'license' would probably not allow other uses or access by any other party except the farmer and the license would automatically expire when the use is no longer utilized.

The main thing to remember is that a 'license' is a temporary use and not permanent.

Questions - Chapter 3

1. An example of 'chattel' is?

   A. A stand of trees
   B. A newly constructed home
   C. A building lot
   D. Annual growing crops

2. Personal property is transferred with what type of instrument?

   A. Certificate of Sale
   B. Bill of Sale
   C. Deed
   D. Title

3. Who 'own's the water in Idaho?

   A. Federal government
   B. State of Idaho
   C. Irrigation districts
   D. Individual property owner

4. Domestic water usage for land irrigation is limited to?

   A. Unlimited
   B. 5 acres
   C. 1 acre
   D. ½ acre

5. Daily use of domestic water is not to exceed how many gallons per day?

   A. 1,000
   B. 5,000
   C. 10,000
   D. 13,000

6. A holder of a water right can lose a water right if not put to beneficial use for what period of time?

   A. 1 year
   B. 3 years
   C. 5 years
   D. 7 years

7. Who is required to notify the Idaho Department of Water Resources to abandon a water well?

   A. Property owner
   B. Central Health District
   C. Licensed well driller
   D. Building permit department

8. Who has the authority to appropriate ground water recharge?

    A. Idaho Department of Water Resources
    B. State of Idaho
    C. The member's irrigation district
    D. The property owner

9. Unless declared as real property, manufactured home ownership will be transferred with:

    A. Certificate of Title
    B. Bill of Sale
    C. Deed
    D. Certificate of Sale

10. If there isn't enough water to satisfy all the water rights, who get the water?

    A. All water shared equally
    B. Junior water rights holder
    C. Senior water rights holder
    D. Water is shut off if there isn't any

11. Who can legally drill a water well?

    A. Water witcher
    B. Property owner
    C. Licensed well driller
    D. A registered well driller

12. What's required before a well can be drilled?

    A. A soil test
    B. A drilling permit
    C. A building and drilling permit
    D. A drilling permit and soil test

13. If a person filed for and received a water right to use water from a navigable river, the water right is a unique form of?

    A. Farm property
    B. Real property
    C. Private property
    D. Personal property

14. Homestead protection protects the home or property from:

    A. Bankruptcy
    B. Secured lenders
    C. Automobile repossession
    D. Unsecured creditors

15. The maximum net value of the dwelling for homestead protection is:

    A. $ 50,000
    B. $ 75,000
    C. $175,000
    D. $125,000

16. To qualify for homestead protection in Idaho, the property must be occupied for a continuous period of:

    A. Only needs to be owned, not occupied
    B. Occupied 100% of the time
    C. At least 6 months out of the year
    D. Not less than 1 year

17. An owner moves from one permanent residence to another. What must the owner do to receive homestead protection.

    A. Nothing is necessary; homestead protection is automatic
    B. File for a new declaration of homestead
    C. File for abandonment
    D. File for abandonment and file a declaration for homestead for the new location.

18. A verbal lease for more than one year is:

    A. Valid
    B. Illegal
    C. Worthless
    D. Invalid

19. What kind of notice must the tenant provide the landlord to get a water heater replaced?

    A. Written notice
    B. Certified mail
    C. Leave a voice mail
    D. Email

20. Given proper notice, how long does a landlord have to resolve a violation?

    A. 1 day
    B. 3 days
    C. 5 days
    D. 7 days

21. If a landlord plans to increase the rent on a month-to-month rental, how much notice must be given?

    A. At least 7 days notice
    B. At least 15 days notice
    C. At least 30 days notice
    D. Not less than 1 month

22. How much advance notice to terminate a month to month tenancy is required?

    A. At least 7 days notice
    B. At least 15 days notice
    C. At least 30 days notice
    D. Not less than one month

23. After a tenant surrenders premises, security deposit refunds must be made within:

    A. 10 days
    B. 21 days
    C. 30 days
    D. 60 days

24. Lot rent for a manufactured home is required to be:

    A. In writing
    B. At least verbal
    C. Recorded in county records
    D. Filed with county assessor

25 How much notice to tenant is required to increase utilities in a mobile home park?

    A. 30 days
    B. 60 days
    C. 90 days
    D. 120 days

26. How much advance notice must a landlord of a mobile home park give to the tenant to not renew a lot lease prior to expiration?

    A. Not less than 180 days
    B. Not less than 90 days notice
    C. Not less than 60 days notice
    D. Not less than 30 days notice

27. A right granted by law where there is no access to a person's land.

    A. Easement appurtenant
    B. Easement in gross
    C. Easement by necessity
    D. Easement by prescription

28 A right that runs with the land from the servient estate to the dominant estate.

    A. Easement appurtenant
    B. Easement in gross
    C. Easement by necessity
    D. Easement by prescription

29. Using land of another without permission for prescribed period of time.

    A. Easement appurtenant
    B. Easement in gross
    C. Easement by necessity
    D. Easement by prescription

30. Right of a person or corporation to use land owned by another for a specific purpose.

    A. Easement appurtenant
    B. Easement in gross
    C. Easement by necessity
    D. Easement by prescription

31. A license to access property for a specific period of time:

    A. Can be used by anyone
    B. Must be recorded
    C. Is a permanent easement
    D. Is a temporary use

32. Once a positive field examination for a
    water right has been conducted within the
    proof time period, a municipality will be
    issued a:

    A. Permit
    B. Beneficial use certificate
    C. License
    D. Certificate

Chapter 4

Forms Of Ownership

<table>
<tr><td>Words Of Wisdom</td></tr>
<tr><td>"A pessimist sees the difficulty in every opportunity;

an optimist sees the opportunity in every difficulty ."

Winston Churchill</td></tr>
</table>

Fee Simple Estate

A fee simple estate is the highest estate possible and gives the holder all rights to the property. Unless expressed otherwise, Idaho law presumes fee simple interest will be conveyed.

But it isn't unusual to own property that is subject to various limitations or qualifications with the transfer of a fee simple estate. Adding limitations or qualifications to a fee simple estate will create a defeasible fee estate.

Defeasible Estate

A defeasible estate is subject to the occurrence or nonoccurrence of something happening. Words such as 'while', 'provided that', 'so long as', and 'during the period' are examples that can be incorporated by the grantor for the transfer.

3 Limitations

Limitations created by the grantor for a qualified fee estate fall into three categories - determinable, condition subsequent, and condition precedent.

An example of condition determinable - Mr. Harris donates a parcel of land to a school district *so long as* it is used for elementary education. But, if some other use is made, then the land reverts back to the grantor (Mr. Harris).

An example of condition subsequent - In the example above, Mr. Harris would have the right to re-enter and take the property back when it no longer is used for education.

An example of condition precedent - Transfer of ownership would not occur until a condition is performed. Using the same example above, the transfer wouldn't occur until the school is built and is actually in operation.

An estate that cannot be for a definite period of time, but rather for the duration of one's life, is known as a life estate.

Life Estate

Life Estate
A life estate conveys an estate for the duration of someone's life that can be tied to the life of the life tenant or to a third party. Upon death, the life estate will convey to the named remainderman. Even though a remainderman has been named, the mere possibility (based on expectation) is not transferable.

Statutory or legal estates are created by state law and include dower, curtesy, and community property. Like most states, Idaho has abolished dower and curtesy and advocates community property. Idaho, together with 8 other states, (Arizona, California, Louisiana, Nevada, New Mexico, Texas, Washington and Wisconsin) statutorily incorporate community property.

Choosing a form of ownership and deciding on how ownership shall be held should be carefully evaluated before advising or making any decisions. If there are any questions whatsoever, competent legal and tax advisors should be consulted.

Sole Ownership

Sole Ownership

Sole ownership is also known as severalty or to 'sever from all others' and is the simplest form of ownership since it only involves one owner or entity.

As a reminder, it should be noted that different types of business ownerships involve single entities. Some examples include:

- Partnerships
- Corporations
- Limited Liability Companies
- Real Estate Investment Trusts
- Land Trusts
- Joint Ventures

Limited Liability Company
IC 30-6-201

Limited Liability Company

A popular type of business ownership is a limited liability company. It's not unusual to find commercial real estate to be owned by a limited liability company. Idaho has a complete chapter in the Idaho Code known as the Idaho Uniform Limited Liability Company Act.

Some highlights surrounding a limited liability company in Idaho is that the company must reserve a name which the Secretary of State shall reserve for 4 months.

The formation of a limited liability company can consist of one or more persons by signing and delivering to the Secretary of State a Certificate of Organization for filing.

Annual Report
IC 30-6-209

An annual report of a limited liability company shall be delivered to the Secretary of State each year before the end of the month the company was initially organized.

Failure To Report
IC 30-6-705

It is very important that the LLC not forget to file the annual report. Failure to deliver its annual report to the Secretary of State can be grounds for an administrative dissolution.

However, reinstatement is possible if application is made to the Secretary of State for reinstatement within 10 years after the effective date of the dissolution.

Two Or More Owners

Tenants In Common
IC 55-104

Default For 2 Or More Owners - Tenants In Common

When 2 or more persons, other than executors or trustees, own real estate in Idaho, the default will be tenants in common unless specified differently. The ownership interests will be equal unless stated otherwise. Tenants in common can hold unequal interest in ownership but the deed must state the percentage of ownership.

Because there are so many different types of ownership, they can result in making different ownership allocations and possible tax consequences. It is always advisable to consult legal and tax counsel if an owner is unsure of what type of ownership best suits their needs.

Living Trust

Living Trust

With estate planning, there is a growing trend toward creating living trusts including placing real estate ownership into a living trust.

The trust can be revocable or irrevocable. If revocable, the person creating the trust will become trustee of the trust and retains the right to use the property and reserves the power to revoke or change the terms of the trust. The trust document will name someone to take over after death known as a successor trustee and avoid probate. Upon death, the trust qualifies for homestead allowance.

Joint Tenancy

Joint Tenancy

Joint tenancy is a form of joint ownership which includes the right of survivorship. The surviving owner automatically owns the property when the other owner dies. No probate is necessary to transfer the property.

IC 15-6-401

Community property in Idaho allows for the right of survivorship but applies only to a husband and wife. Joint tenancy ownership on the other hand, allows two or more people who are not married with equal ownership, the right of survivorship.

An example of where joint tenancy would work well for the owners might be where a mother and son, or a father and son, own a piece of property together.

Tenancy By The Entirety

Tenancy By The Entirety

Because of potential conflicts with Idaho community property statutes, tenancy by the entirety <u>cannot</u> be used. However, it can be used on property that either spouse owns separately. The conveyance needs to state the intention to be with the 'right of survivorship and not as community property' or another forms of co-ownership.

Community Property

Common Law Marriage

Common law marriage was outlawed on January 1, 1996 but shall not invalidate any marriage created by consenting parties prior to January 1, 1996.

Consent alone will not constitute marriage. However, with the law now requiring the issuance of a marriage license, common law marriage prior to January 1, 1996 will not be invalidated.

IC 32-202

To be legally married, both male and female must be 18 years of age or older. If either the male or the female is under the age of 18, the consent of the father, mother, or guardian is given, or that such underaged person has been previously but is not at the time married; and that the parties applying for the rites of marriage, and making such contract, have a legal right to do so.

In Idaho, marriage arises out of a civil contract between a *man and woman*. Consent or mutual assumption alone will not constitute marriage. It must be followed by the issuance of a license and a solemnization as authorized by law.

Sole & Separate
IC - 32-903

Property Owned Prior To Marriage

All property of either husband or wife owned prior to marriage or received afterward as gift, bequest, or acquired with proceeds of his or her separate property shall remain his or her sole property.

**Income Is
Community
Property**
IC 32-906

Income Is Community Property

All other property acquired after marriage is community property and any income including rents and profits of all property, separate or community, is community property. The exception would be if both spouses, by written agreement, specifically state it will be treated as separate property of one of the spouses. However, any property maintained as 'sole and separate' must be just that; no co-mingling of funds for maintenance.

**One To Buy;
Two To Sell**
IC 32-912

Binding Community Property

Either the husband or wife shall have the right to manage and control community property and either may bind the community property by contract. Neither the husband nor wife may sell, convey or encumber the community real estate unless the other joins in. However, either the husband or wife may give to the other by expressed power of attorney, the right to sell, convey or encumber community property.

**Right Of
Survivorship**
IC 15-6-401

Right Of Survivorship In Real Property

Effective July 1, 2008, Idaho authorized real property held by a married couple as 'community property with rights of survivorship'. The new law allows married couples an income tax basis step-up for the entire community real property and a simple title transfer through the 'joint tenancy' designation.

This allows transfer of the real estate to the surviving joint tenant by recordation of a death certificate in the county where the real estate is held, thereby avoiding a probate of such real estate. However, one should consult legal or accounting counsel to make sure there isn't conflict with estate and tax planning.

Manufactured Homes

Manufactured Homes

Manufactured Homes

According to the Idaho Housing and Finance Association in 2018, approximately 64,000, or 8.75% of Idaho's 735,762 housing units, are manufactured/mobile homes. The classification of manufactured/mobile homes is somewhat unique. They can be classified as personal property, real property, or a combination of both. Adding to the confusion, the licensing of salespeople is also a little unique.

Retailer Licensing
IC 44-2102 (3)

The manufactured home retailer must be licensed and can sell new or used units that are determined to be personal property on the tax roles.

If a used unit has been determined to be real property, it may only be offered for sale, listed, bought for resale either directly or indirectly by a licensed real estate broker or real estate salesman.

A licensed real estate broker or real estate salesman representing a licensed real estate broker, may participate in new manufactured homes sales that include real estate if a real estate broker or salesman has a valid, written agreement with a licensed retailer to represent the interest of the retailer in this type of transaction.

Transfer MH To
Real Property
IC 63-304

Transfer Manufactured/Mobile Home To Real Property

If a manufactured/mobile home is sold as personal property, a certificate of title will be used to transfer ownership. To properly transfer the manufactured home from personal property to real property, the running gear must be removed and the land must be owned by the owner of a manufactured/mobile home.

When the manufactured/mobile home is properly affixed to a permanent foundation the owner shall make an application on an approved form to the county assessor for the intent to treat the manufactured home as real property.

The form will be submitted to the county assessor for approval. Once approved, the transfer will be recorded, in the county the manufactured/mobile home is situated and will be reclassified as 'real' property.

Reversal from
Real Property To
Personal Property
IC 63-305

If one wants to revert from 'real' property back to 'personal property' Idaho code allows for a reversal of declaration with certain requirements. This would allow the owner to remove the manufactured home from the real property. This would allow the owner to sell the manufactured home as personal property and retain the remaining property as real property.

However, a manufactured home cannot be removed without proper and legal notification to the county assessor. At least 30 day notice is required for the intended removal. The homeowner shall make application for certificate of title within 5 days of removal.

STATEMENT OF INTENT TO DECLARE
MANUFACTURED HOME REAL PROPERTY

Owner Name(s):			
Mailing Address:			
Property Address:			
Legal Description:			
Real Property Parcel #:		Manufactured Home Parcel #:	
Land Ownership:	☐ Deed ☐ Contract of Sale	☐ Recorded ☐ Unrecorded	
Manufactured Home Description:	Make:	Model:	Year:
Serial Number:	Size:	Lien Holder, if any:	

The undersigned, being duly sworn, states that the above information is true and correct, and does hereby exercise a STATEMENT OF INTENT, declaring the above manufactured home to constitute real property according to Section 63-307B, Idaho Code. The undersigned further represents that the running gear of the home has been removed and that the manufactured home will be permanently affixed to a foundation on land which is owned or being purchased by the owner or purchaser of the manufactured home.

Signature:	Date:	Signature:	Date:

STATE OF IDAHO)
) ss.
COUNTY OF ADA)

On this _____ day of _____, 20____, before me, the undersigned notary public in and for said State, personally appeared _____ or identified to me to be the person(s) whose name(s) is/are subscribed to the within instrument, and acknowledged to me that ___he___ executed the same.

IN WITNESS WHEREOF, I have hereunto set my hand and affixed my official seal the day and year in this Statement first above written.

(SEAL)

_____
Notary Public in and for the STATE of IDAHO

Residing at_____, Idaho

Commission Expires _____

Signatures - Pursuant to Section 63-307B, Idaho Code

BUILDING & ZONING DEPARTMENT OR OTHER AUTHORIZED OFFICIAL:

    A. Removal of running gear.
    B. Permanently affixed to a foundation.
       (See Idaho Code § 44-2205)

_____
Authorized Signature   Date

COUNTY ASSESSOR

_____
Authorized Signature   Date

    Ownership of land and manufactured home.
    Payment of sales tax on new manufactured home verified.

_____
Authorized Signature   Date

CONSENT OF LIENHOLDER: _____
                        Name / Company

_____
Authorized Signature   Date

REVERSAL OF DECLARATION OF A
MANUFACTURED HOME AS REAL PROPERTY

(See instructions on the back of the form.)

1. Owner Name(s)	
2. Mailing Address	
3. Property Address	
4. New Parcel Number for Manufactured Home	
5. Manufactured Home Description: Make_____ Mode _____ Year_____ Size_____ Serial Number _____ Lien Holder (if any)_____ Mailing Address _____	

6. This document rescinds the Statement of Intent To Declare this manufactured home as real property, which was recorded on_____ **Date**
with _____ .
      Instrument Number

☐   Destroyed   I hereby certify that the above described manufactured home has been destroyed. Date of removal _____

The undersigned, being duly sworn, states that the above information is true and correct, and does hereby exercise a "Reversal," declaring the "Statement of Intent to Declare" the above referenced manufactured home as real property to be null and void according to Idaho Code Section 63-305.

Signature	Date	Signature	Date

STATE OF IDAHO   )
) S.S.
COUNTY OF   )

_____

On this ____ day of _____, in the year of 20___, before me, _____,
personally appeared_____, proved to me on the basis of
satisfactory evidence to be the person(s) whose name(s) is (are) subscribed to this instrument and acknowledged that he (she)(they)
executed the same.

S
E
A
L

                 _____
                 Notary Public

                 My Commission Expires on _____

Signatures - Pursuant to Idaho Code Section 63-305

8. COUNTY TREASURER'S SIGNATURE   9. COUNTY ASSESSOR'S SIGNATURE

_____ _____   _____ _____
Authorized Signature   Date   Authorized Signature   Date

PA00043-1
11-1-15

BEFORE ANSWERING QUESTIONS – Can you define or explain:

Fee simple estate

Examples of sole and separate property

Failure to report LLC annual report

Tenants in common

Transfer MH to real property

Limited Liability Company annual report

Tenancy by the entirety

Community property

Questions - Chapter 4

1. A partnership, 'ABC Partners', constitutes what type of ownership?

   A. Tenants in common
   B. Sole ownership
   C. Tenancy by the entirety
   D. Community property

2. The formation of a limited liability company is filed with:

   A. Secretary of State
   B. Attorney General
   C. State Tax Commission
   D. Department of Insurance

3. Failure of an LLC to file an annual report can result in:

   A. Mandatory audit from IRS
   B. State imposed fine
   C. Administrative dissolution
   D. Loss of business license

4. All property of either husband or wife acquired prior to marriage shall remain:

   A. Community property
   B. In trust
   C. Tenants in common
   D. Sole and separate

5. Unless stated otherwise, any income or profits from all property after marriage, separate or community, will be treated as:

   A. Sole and separate
   B. Community property
   C. Both sole and community property
   D. Limited liability partnership

6. When is the annual report by a limited liability company to be filed?

   A. Before the last day of the current year
   B. No later than Jan 1 of following year
   C. No later than April 15 of the following year
   D. Before the end of the month the company was organized

7. 'Community property with rights of survivorship' will:

   A. Avoid probate
   B. Automatically require probate
   C. Delay probate
   D. Require separated probate action

8. If an LLC is dissolved, an application for reinstatement may be possible if filed within what period of being dissolved?

   A. Cannot be reinstated
   B. 1 year
   C. 5 years
   D. 10 years

9. Unless declared as real property, manufactured home ownership will be transferred with:

   A. Certificate of Title
   B. Bill of Sale
   C. Deed
   D. Certificate of Sale

10. Prior to permanently removing a manufactured home off of real property, intent to remove must be given to:

    A. Idaho State Tax Commission
    B. County Commissioners
    C. County Assessor
    D. City or county building department

Chapter 5

Land Use Controls and Environmental Issues

Words Of Wisdom
"I've missed more than 9000 shots in my career. I've lost almost 300 games. 26 times I've been trusted to take the game winning shot and missed. I've failed over and over again in my life and that is why I succeed."
Michael Jordan

Ownership Misconceptions

Perhaps a big misconception about real estate ownership is that ownership gives unlimited use and right to private property. After all, the owner of a property should be able to do as they wish. Unfortunately, this may not be true.

One by one, some of the sticks from the bundle of rights can be removed for various reasons based on limitations imposed by the powers of the government, by the seller with deed restrictions, or Homeowner Associations with Covenants, Conditions, and Restrictions

Land Use Controls

Purpose Of Police Power

Police Power
Police power is the authority of the government to adopt and enforce laws governing the use of real estate based on the need to promote public safety, health, and general welfare.

In regard to real estate, police power allows for the adoption and enforcement of various regulations, including but not limited to: zoning, building codes and environmental regulations and eminent domain.

State Land Use Planning Act (Ch 65) IC 67-6502

State Land Use Planning Act
In keeping with the 'police power' concept, the Idaho land use planning purpose includes:

- Allow planned development for low cost housing
- Ensure public facilities and services at a reasonable cost
- Protect local and state economy
- Ensure that environmental features are protected
- Encourage agriculture, forestry, and food production
- Encourage urban development within cities
- Avoid undue overcrowding of population

- Ensure development on land fits physical characteristics
- Protect against natural hazards, water hazards, and disasters
- Protect fish, wildlife, and recreation resources
- Avoid undue water and air pollution
- Allow school districts to participate in planning

Based on the State Land Use Planning Act, counties and cities throughout Idaho have adopted local and regional comprehensive plans for local control.

P&Z Commission
(Ch 65) IC 67-6504

Planning And/Or Zoning Commissions

A planning commission or a zoning commission or a planning and zoning commission acting in both capacities, may act with the full authority of the governing board (city council members or county commissioners) excluding the authority to adopt ordinances or approve land subdivision.

The powers of the board of county commissioners shall apply to the unincorporated area of the county.

Membership shall consist of not less than 3 nor more than 12 voting members appointed by the mayor or chairman of the county board.. Each member must have resided in the county for at least 2 years prior to appointment and remain a resident of the county during his service on the commission.

All meetings and records shall be open to the public. At least 1 regular meeting shall be held each month for not less than 9 months in a year.

Supreme Court Observation

The Idaho Supreme Court made a very interesting observation between planning and zoning in the case, *Giltner Dairy, LLC v Jerome County* in 2008. The Court said:

Givens Pursley Land Use Handbook - Pg 38

Planning is long range; zoning is immediate. Planning is general; zoning is specific. Planning involves political processes; zoning is a legislative function and an exercise of the police power. Planning is generally dynamic while zoning is more or less static. Planning often involves frequent changes; zoning designations should not. Planning has a speculative impact upon property values, while zoning may actually constitute a valuable property right.

The court continued, *".....while zoning designations should generally follow and be consistent with the long range designations established in the Comprehensive Plan, there is no requirement that zoning immediately conform to the Plan. The Plan is a statement of long-range pubic intent; zoning is an exercise of police power which, in the long run, should be consistent with that intent. Planning is a determination of public policy, and zoning, to be legitimate exercise of the police power, should be in the furtherance of that policy."*

(Ch 65) IC 67-6509

Any changes or amendments to the comprehensive plan requires at least 1 public hearing with a public notice at least 15 days prior to the hearing.

Zoning	## Zoning While a comprehensive plan set the framework for future development, zoning is the 'legal' tool a municipality uses to regulate land use. Items such as height and size of buildings, size of lots, setbacks, parking, landscaping and density can be regulated to meet the needs and goals of the community.
Zoning Districts	Zoning ordinances will identify uses and density into different areas or zones for specific land use. There isn't any uniformity for the classifications but for convenience, zoning districts are often identified with abbreviations such as I or M for industrial or manufacturing, C for commercial, A for agricultural, R for residential and so on.
Classifications	Then each zoning classification may have subheadings such as R1, R2 or R3 for residential density requirements. The same may be said for commercial such as C1, C2, C3 for types of use. There can also be some special classifications such as PUD for Planned Unit Development or RPD for Residential Planned Development.
Enforcement	Within the each zoning classification are allowed uses. If the allowed uses are violated, the business or home can be shut down or 'red tagged' until the violation has been resolved.
Grand Fathered Use	## Zoning Changes Not all zoning classifications fit all situations. Mechanisms need to be available to address those special situations that might allow zoning changes. Issues such as nonconforming uses might be 'grand fathered' so the existing owner can continue the use, even though it does not conform to the new zoning.
Zoning amendment	Another example may involve an amendment to the existing zoning to be rezoned. Any zoning change requests must be sent to surrounding property owners and a public hearing must be held so the property owners and the public can both voice their opinions.
Zoning variance	A third example could address a variance allowing the owner to deviate from the current zoning requirements for a piece of property. Perhaps the owner needs a setback change to accommodate a particular structure design.
Annexation	## Annexation There are all kinds of reasons to annex land into cities including but not limited to more police or fire protection, access to water and sewer, accommodation of growth, and other public services.
3 Categories To Annex IC 50-222	There are 3 categories in which annexation by cities can occur. Category A - requires all private landowners to consent to annexation. If all private landowners have consented, the area may extend beyond the city if it is contiguous to the city and the comprehensive plan includes the area to be annexed.

Category B - addresses subject lands containing *less* than 100 separate private ownerships and platted lots of record where not all such landowners have consented to annexation or, subject lands containing *more* than 100 acres and where more than 50% of the landowners have consented to annexation prior to the annexation process.

Category C - involves annexations where the subject lands contain more than 100 separate private ownerships and where more than 50% of the area of the subject lands have not consented to annexation prior to the annexation process.

There are specific procedures to comply with each category. The implementation of any annexation proposal wherein the city council determines that annexation is appropriate, it shall be concluded with the passage of an ordinance of annexation.

After it has been decided to annex, all the property owners within the land to be considered and within 300 feet of the external boundaries of the land being considered and any additional area that may be impacted shall be notified by mail of a hearing for annexation. Notice shall also be posted on the premises not less than 1 week prior to the hearing.

Council Approval
IC 50-222 (5) (c)

At the hearing, the panel will accept both verbal and written testimony before voting. The city council shall review the results and if the owners of the majority of the land area have consented, the city council may enact an ordinance to annex.

Section 1401
15 U.S.C.

Interstate Land Sales Full Disclosure Act

As a method to protect consumers from fraud and abuse in the sale or lease of land, Congress enacted the Interstate Land Sales Full Disclosure Act patterned after the Securities Law of 1933.

The Act requires land developers to register subdivisions of 100 or more non-exempt lots with HUD and provide each purchaser with a full disclosure document about the subdivision known as a Property Report.

Before a buyer signs a purchase and sale agreement the buyer should:
- Know the rights of a buyer
- Know something about the developer
- Know the facts about the development
- Be able to resist high pressure sales campaigns

The developer must file with HUD:
- Copy of corporate charter and financial statement
- Info on local ordinances and health regulations
- Info about the land and title opinion
- Info on facilities such as schools, hospitals, transportation
- Availability of utilities, water, sewage
- Roads, maps, plats, suppliers of water and sewer

Information that will be contained in the property report:
- Distances to nearby communities over paved or unpaved roads
- Existence of any existing mortgages or liens on the property
- Contracts to be placed in escrow and applied to purchase
- Availability and location of recreational facilities
- Availability of water, sewer, septic tanks, and wells

- Present and proposed utility services and charges
- Number of homes currently occupied
- Soil and foundation conditions and any problems with septics
- Type of title and when the buyer will receive it

Examples of dishonest sales practices (high pressure)
1. Concealing or misrepresenting facts about value
2. Failure to honor refund promises or agreements
3. Misrepresentation of facts about the subdivision
4. Failure to develop the subdivision as planned
5. Failure to deliver deeds and/or title insurance policies
6. Abusive treatment or high-pressure sales tactics
7. Failure to make good on sales inducements
8. 'Bait and Switch' tactics
9. Failure to grant rights under Interstate Land Disclosure Act

The information discussed is especially important to Idahoans, since Idaho is surrounded by 6 states and 1 foreign country. Add many out of state investors and developers, and the Interstate Land Sales Full Disclosure Act even becomes more important for all parties.

Subdivision
IC 50-1301 (17)

Subdivision

Idaho statute defines a subdivision to be a parcel of land divided into 5 or more lots for the purpose of sale or building development. However, Idaho Code excludes partitions of agricultural land for agricultural purposes.

Idaho Code also provides that cities and counties may adopt their own definition of subdivision in lieu of the state definition. It may not be unusual for local governments to define subdivision to be the division of land into 2 or more lots, building sites, or other divisions for the purpose of sale or building development.

Certification Of Plat
IC 50-1309

The owner of the land shall make a certificate with the correct legal description together with a dedication of all public streets and rights-of-way on the plat. The professional land surveyor making the survey shall certify the correctness with his seal, signature and date on the plat.

Recording Plat

Once the plat is approved, it will be recorded in a book or file designated as 'Record of Plats'.

Penalty For Selling Unplatted Lots
IC 50-1316

Any person who shall dispose of or offer any lots for sale in any city or county, before the plat has been acknowledged and recorded, shall forfeit and pay $100 for each lot and part of a lot sold or disposed of or offered for sale.

Idaho Building Code Act
IC 39-4105

Building Codes

The Idaho Building Code Act has adopted the International Building Code and the International Fire Code as the basis for all construction. The purpose of the building codes is to ensure the health, safety and construction standards are adhered to with uniformity.

Building Permit Application

It is unlawful for any person to allow any construction, improvement, extension or alteration of any building, residence or structure without first applying for a permit in accordance with the local government ordinance or ordinances.

Bear in mind, not all alterations or construction requires a building permit but one should check first before starting any construction project. Also, it should be noted that what may require a permit in one jurisdiction may not require a permit in another; or the construction requirements in one jurisdiction may be different in another jurisdiction.

The building permit process initiates inspections to make sure the construction meets the requirements of whatever building code(s) may be involved (construction, electrical, plumbing, gas, etc).

Certificate of Occupancy

After the construction is completed, a 'final' inspection will be ordered and if everything passes, the building permit will be signed off and an 'Certificate of Occupancy' will be issued which allows occupancy and habitation.

Easements

Easements

An easement is the right of one party to use the land of another for a special purpose consistent with the general use of the land. The use can extend from the earth below the surface to the heavens above. Thus, easements can include subsurface rights as well as air rights.

Access easements to allow ingress and egress, such as roadways, will be discussed in another chapter.

However, solar and conservation easements will be included in this chapter. Idaho is aware of the need to protect the ability to take advantage of alternate forms of energy. The purpose of a solar easement is to allow the exposure of solar energy to a device capable of storing such energy. Forms of solar easements are not new. A doctrine based on English law known as 'Ancient Lights' was adopted in 1832 to preserve use of light.

Solar Easements
IC 55-615

Solar Easements

A solar easement shall be in writing and subject to the same recording requirements as any other easement.

A solar easement shall include but not be limited to:
- Vertical and horizontal angles, expressed in degrees, at which solar easement extends over the real property subject to the solar easement;

- Any terms or conditions or both under which the solar easement is granted or will be terminated;

- Any provisions for compensation of the owner of the property benefitting from the solar easement in the event of interference with the enjoyment of the solar easement or compensation of the owner of the property subject to the solar easement for maintaining the solar easement.

Solar Lot Line

The angle in which a shadow could encroach onto another property is often referenced by the shadow that is cast on December 21 (winter solstice) between 10 am and 2 pm. The key is to keep the shadow from encroaching upon the the solar capturing property. Thus, if the neighbor's shadow encroaches beyond the lot line setbacks, the neighbor would be in violation of the solar easement.

Many new subdivisions incorporate solar easements in their CCR's (conditions, covenants, and restrictions). Solar easements will attach to the property and pass to another owner when title is transferred.

Homeowner's Association Restrictions
IC 55-115 (4)

No homeowner's association may add, amend, or enforce any covenant, condition or restriction in such a way that prohibits the installation of solar panels or solar collectors on the rooftop or any property or structure within the jurisdiction of the homeowner's association.

View Easements

View Easements

For example, hillside view lots may need protection to preserve the views with 'view easements' that basically restricts other improvements or foliage from blocking views from the subject property. These types of restrictions may or may not be directly addressed in the legal description on the deed or in the CCR's if applicable.

However, view easements contained in the deed as a deed restriction must be addressed on *all* deeds of the servient and dominant estates that are affected by the view easements.

The restrictions usually contain limitations based on stated elevations which could be verified with a elevation survey by a licensed surveyor.

Conservation Easement
IC 55-2101

Conservation Easement

A conservation easement is a tool that can be used between landowners and a government agency to protect natural resources including water resources and habitat, scenic views, open space, and farm land. Conservation easements can limit the right to develop, now and in the future.

Conservation easements can also be used to preserve historical, architectural and cultural aspects of real property.

In addition, there are tax benefits to the landowner. The land can be bought and sold but the easement 'runs with the land' and applies to all future owners. Twelve non profit land trusts hold approximately 59,000 acres in conservation easements in Idaho.

Water Issues

FEMA

Flood Plain Management

Many of Idaho's cities and communities are located along rivers and waterways. The Federal Emergency Management Agency (FEMA) is the agency responsible for the overall administration of the National Flood Insurance Program.

It's important that buyers and sellers alike be made aware of possible rivers, waterways, and water hazards including proximity to large irrigation canals, ditches and reservoirs.

http://maps.idwr. Idaho.gov/	If a property is located near or adjacent to these water hazards, it would be wise to get a copy of a Flood Insurance Rate Map. The map more precisely defines a floodplain located in a Special Flood Hazard Area and is used by lenders to determine if a property will need flood insurance. The vertical datum currently adopted by the federal government as a basis for measuring heights is the North American Vertical Datum of 1988 to establish the Base Flood Elevation. Properties located in such areas can be subject to restrictive construction requirements as well as additional construction and insurance costs.
Idaho State Disaster Preparedness Act (Ch 10) IC 46-1011	The Idaho State Disaster Preparedness Act allows local governments to adopt local floodplain zoning ordinances within their jurisdiction. A floodplain map will identify areas that would require protection and/or floodproofing based on an acceptable vertical datum from which all elevations are determined.
Flood Damage Prevention Ordinance	As a result, the Idaho legislature has authorized local governments to adopt a floodplain map and floodplain management ordinance that identifies floodplains and provides minimum development requirements known as the Idaho Flood Damage Prevention Ordinance
Violations	In addition, there are very strict requirements regulating any diversion of a waterway or alteration of the land. Penalties can be a fine of not more than $1,000 or imprisoned for not more than 180 days or both. Each day of the violation shall be considered a separate offense!
30 Day Wait	If a homeowner owns their home free and clear or does not have a federally related loan, the homeowner is not required to have flood insurance but the insurance is still available to the homeowner. Typically there is a 30 day wait period from the date of purchase till the policy takes effect.
Navigable Waters	**Navigable Waters** What happens when a property has a stream running through it? Can anyone use the stream for fishing or recreational use? It depends,.
Definition IC 36-1601	In Idaho, the definition of a navigable stream is any stream in its natural state during normal high water flow, will float cut timber having a 6" diameter or greater. The public is allowed access between the flow of ordinary high water lines for business or recreational purposes. Access is limited with the normal navigability of the stream. Portaging over private land and around irrigation dams or other obstructions is expressly permitted by statute but the boater must reenter the stream immediately below the obstruction or the nearest safe point to reenter.
Trespass IC 18-7008	Idaho Code regarding trespass is extensive but as a recap, trespassing on property that is posted against trespassers with signs or painted fence posts, or where the owner gives oral or written personal communication to leave the property, failure to leave will be a misdemeanor.

Private Ponds

Private Ponds
IC 42-212

Private Ponds

Although ponds and lakes not exceeding 5 acres in surface area are allowed on private property without interference from the Department of Water Resources, ponds or lakes that contain fish creates a different situation.

F & G Approval
IC 36-706

The use of any fish approved by the Department of Fish and Game for noncommercial purposes requires an application for a private pond permit. The application includes the water source, description of the fish pond, and identification of the fish species contained in the pond.

Eminent Domain

Eminent Domain
IC 67-8002
IC 7-701

Eminent Domain

There will be issues when private property needs to be taken by the government to make way for development for public needs including, but not limited to, roadways and highways, public parking, power lines, urban renewal, etc. The taking of private property is known as eminent domain and the process is condemnation.

If a state or local governmental entity plans to make a regulatory taking of private property, a written request for an analysis of the taking can be made by an owner of real property.

Compensation
IC 7-712

The property owner will receive compensation based on an appraisal of fair market value as of the date of the summons. No improvements put the property subsequent to the date of the summons shall be included in the assessment of compensation or damages

Dying Without A Will

Escheat

IC 33-902 (d)

Escheat

Escheat is the reversion of a person's property to the state when a person in Idaho dies without a will and has no heirs. All moneys and effects will accrue and be transferred to the public school permanent endowment fund based on the constitution of the state of Idaho.

However this rarely happens because the laws are designed to get one's property to anyone who was even remotely related to the decedent. Examples would be a spouse, children, siblings, parents, grandparents, aunts or uncles, or aunts, neices or nephews, cousins of any degree, or the children, parents, or siblings of a spouse who dies before the decedent died.

Environmental Issues

Asbestos

Asbestos

Asbestos was considered a miracle building material in the late 19th century because of its many uses including sound insulation and its resistance to heat. As a flame-retardant and insulating factors, it was extensively used in construction. In housing, asbestos was used in ceiling insulation, fireproof drywall and drywall joint compound, flooring, roofing, and pipe insulation.

Asbestos was used outside the construction industry and was a major component for brake linings and clutches in the automotive industry.

Unfortunately the ingestion and inhalation of asbestos fibers can create serious lung disease known as asbestosis. Scarred lung tissue cannot expand and contract normally and cannot perform gas exchange. With no known cure, the disease can ultimately result in death.

Because of the serious health hazards, asbestos was outlawed in the housing industry by the EPA starting in 1977 with its use in textured paint and patching compounds used on wall and ceiling joints.

Lead Based Paint

Lead Based Paint

Congress found that pre-1980 housing contained more than 3,000,000 tons of lead in the form of lead based paint. The majority of homes build before 1950 contained substantial amounts of lead based paint.

As many as 3,800,000 homes endangered the health and development of children with chipping or peeling paint. These homes afflict as many as 3,000,000 children under the age of 6, who are the most vulnerable.

As a result, the EPA outlawed lead based paint in housing in 1978. Later the Lead-Based Paint Reduction Act of 1992 was created to set some rules and guidelines to inform the purchaser or lessee about housing constructed prior to 1978 for lead based paint or plumbing with lead or lead solder.

However, in 2008 the laws were strengthened with the EPA's Renovation, Repair, and Painting (RRP) Rule and HUD's Lead Safe Housing Rule which became effective on April 22, 2010.

RRP
40 CFR 745.223
(Federal Regulation Code)

Renovation, Repair, And Painting Rule

The purpose of the RRP is to give owners, tenants, and individuals performing renovations, better protection from lead hazards. The new ruling only applies to persons who perform renovations for compensation in target housing and child care facilities.

The term renovation includes but is not limited to:
- Removing, modifying or repairing painted surfaces or painted components. Examples include modifying painted doors, surface restoration, window repair, and surface preparation that includes sanding and scraping that may generate paint dust.
- Removing building components such as walls, ceilings, plumbing or windows
- Weatherization projects such as cutting holes in painted surfaces to install blown in insulation or to gain access to attics, or painting thresholds to install weather-stripping.

The RRP doesn't apply to just painters. It applies to any contractor including electricians, plumbers, HVAC contractors and anyone who disturbs the painted surface areas.

If the interior surface exceeds 6 square feet or 20 square feet exterior surface is disturbed, all renovation must comply with the rule. HUD's rule still remains at 2 square feet of interior surface and 20 square feet exterior or 10% of the surface area of a small building component.

A pamphlet, *Renovate Right: Important Lead Hazard Information for Families, Child Care Providers, and Schools* must be used exclusively for any renovations.

Individuals and firms performing renovations must be properly trained and certified. Re-certification is required every 5 years. All records of each renovation must be kept for not less than 3 years. Penalties for non compliance can be as much as $37,500 per violation, per day!

Radon

Radon

Radon is an odorless, tasteless and invisible radioactive gas created from natural deposits of uranium and radium in the soil. Radon testing was screened on 1,018 homes in Idaho. Around ⅓ of the homes had high levels of radon.

The EPA has a threshold of 4 pCi/L (pico curries per liter). Anything over the threshold is considered dangerous. According to the Idaho Department of Health and Welfare, the average indoor radon level for Idaho is 6.4 pCi/L. In August 2005, it was reported that around 6,668 homes have reported testing results with 37% of the homes testing high for radon.

There are pockets in Idaho that have very high levels of radon present. Local building codes may require installation of radon-resistant construction by installing a pipe to remove radon gas from below a concrete floor or crawl space.

Urea Formaldehyde

Urea Formaldehyde

Urea formaldehyde can be found in all kinds of products including adhesives, finishes, MDF, molded objects, foam, and insulation.

In the 1970's many homes were insulated with urea-formaldehyde foam insulation as an energy conservation measure before it was discovered that the emissions could be a dangerous health hazard.

In Idaho, many mountain cabins with high pitched roofs contain this product. Although the emissions decline over time, there can still be exposure. Early health symptoms include eye, nose, and throat irritations as well as coughing and breathing difficulties. Usually these irritants disappear once the pollutant has been removed or 'airs' out.

Carbon Monoxide

Carbon Monoxide

Known as the 'silent killer', carbon monoxide is a colorless, odorless, tasteless, toxic gas created by incomplete combustion of fuel such as wood, gasoline, kerosene, propane or natural gas.

Contributing causes of carbon monoxide include:
- unvented space heaters
- leaks in furnaces and chimneys
- back drafts from gas water heaters, or furnaces

• gas ovens and ranges
• auto exhausts

Although not a federal law for residential housing, it is recommended that a CO detector be installed if the house has fuel-burning appliances. Another precaution is to crack windows when using unvented appliances and don't use gas stoves or ovens to heat your home.

Electronic Magnetic Fields (EMF's)

Electromagnetic Fields   (EMF's)

Idaho Power has monitored the issue of health effects of electromagnetic fields since the early 1970. The research has identified that EMF's exist everywhere in our modern society as invisible forces created by any electric charge. However, the forces decrease rapidly in magnitude as one moves farther away from the source.

Although some states have established EMF exposure limits, there are no federal or Idaho-established limits. However, Idaho Power has addressed several good questions.

• Q - Do underground power lines limit EMF's?
A - Not necessarily. The maximum magnetic field will generally be higher for underground lines, but much depends on the method of construction.

• Q - Should I have an EMF strength reading done in my home?
A - Idaho Power will measure EMF strength upon request and will discuss the results with the customer.

• Q - Should I limit my exposure to electrical appliances?
A - The research does not suggest that people need to change the way they use electrical appliances, or limit the amount of time they use certain appliances.

Mold

Mold

Many states have legislated laws surrounding toxic mold and disclosure requirements. California enacted the Toxic Mold Protection Act in 2001 to establish permissible exposure limits along with assessment standards and remediation. Other states followed California in developing regulations including New York, Massachusetts and Texas.

Additional states have adopted or created disclosure requirements for evidence of mold or excessive moisture issues.

IC 55-2808

Although Idaho does not have specific disclosure laws addressing mold, the Property Condition Disclosure Act does require disclosure with any problems with basement water, plumbing, drainage or other water issues; all of which could contribute to breeding grounds for toxic mold.

Adverse Material Facts
IC 54-2086 (1) (d)
IC 54-2087 (4) (a)

If known, toxic mold (stachybotrys) could constitute an adverse material fact and would need to be disclosed.

Clandestine Drug Laboratory Cleanup
IDAPA 16.02.04

Methamphetamine

Meth is highly toxic and creates extremely dangerous conditions for humans and property alike. In 2006, Idaho Administrative Code adopted very specific requirements labeled 'Clandestine Drug Laboratory Cleanup'. Part of the process requires that the contaminated home will remain vacant until such time a 'clearance sampling' renders the home safe.

The property will also be listed on a Clandestine Drug Laboratory Site Property List available to the public until it is delisted. The Idaho Department of Health and Welfare offers a lot of information including a property list, cleaning up a former meth lab, cleanup contractors, qualified industrial hygienists, and laws/rules.

Forcible Entry And Unlawful Detainer
IC 6-303 (5)

Idaho code does allow a landlord the use of 'rapid eviction' if any person is, has been, or engaged in the unlawful delivery, production or use of a controlled substance on the premises of the leased property.

Underground Storage Tanks

Underground storage tanks or USTs are regulated by the U. S. Environmental Protection Agency and are required to comply with specific conditions. Not regulated as underground storage tanks are:

- Farm or residential tanks of 1,100 gallons or less storing motor fuel for non-commercial purposes
- Tanks used solely for storing fuel oil for home heating
- Tanks with a storage capacity of 110 gallons or less

Underground Storage Tank Act
IC 39-8801 thru 39-8812

The Idaho Underground Storage Tank Act addresses protection of the environment from leaking underground tanks (LUST). Leaking underground storage tanks can create huge problems with contamination of the ground water.

On-site inspections shall be conducted at least once every 3 years to determine compliance. If the Idaho Department of Environmental Quality (DEQ) conducts the inspection, it shall not charge a fee for the inspection.

Rules regulating underground storage tanks in Idaho include:

- Federal standards regulating underground storage tanks
- Measures to protect ground water from contamination
- Training requirements
- Inspections
- Delivery prohibition
- Maintenance of an underground storage tank database

Real estate practitioners should obtain a copy of a booklet titled, *Real Estate Professionals and Underground Storage Tanks*, if working with any customers or clients who have underground storage tanks on their property.

The 12 page booklet is available at no charge from the Idaho Department of Environmental Quality and can be downloaded online. It's a good resource on how to handle various issues, including the removal of home heating oil tanks.

Hazardous Waste Management
IC 39-4402 (b)

Waste Disposal Sites

The purpose of Idaho's hazardous waste management laws are to protect the public health and safety, and the environment that might be threatened when hazardous wastes are not managed in an environmentally sound manner.

Based on the federal Resource, Conservation and Recovery Act of 1976, no person shall treat or store hazardous waste, nor shall any person discharge, incinerate, release, spill, place or dispose of any hazardous waste in a manner that would endanger the environment.

Idaho DEQ

The Idaho's Department of Environment Quality is the state agency that is delegated responsibility by the EPA to implement waste management in Idaho. The DEQ's Hazardous Waste Program issues permits, oversees inspections of facilities that generate hazardous waste, provides technical assistance and takes corrective action. The program also oversees remediation of radioactive and hazardous wastes at the Idaho National Laboratory (INL) site.

The State Response Program oversees the development and operation of municipal and non-municipal solid waste disposal sites in Idaho. It is important that landfills in Idaho be carefully managed and regulated since more than 95% of households water comes from ground water.

Questions - Chapter 5

1. The property of a person who died, had no heirs, and reverts to the state is known as:

   A. Eminent domain
   B. Escheat
   C. Police power
   D. Accession

2. A solar lot line is often referenced on what date?

   A. June 21
   B. September 15
   C. December 21
   D. January 16

3. Scenic views and open space can be protected with:

   A. Conservation easement
   B. Easement by prescription
   C. Solar easements
   D. Access easement

4. A zoning regulation is an example of:

   A. Eminent domain
   B. Police power
   C. Economic changes
   D. Federal regulations

5. Any changes to the comprehensive plan require how many public hearings?

   A. 1
   B. 2
   C. 3
   D. 4

6. To modify the comprehensive plan, how much notice must be given prior the hearing

   A. 7 days
   B. 15 days
   C. 21 days
   D. 30 day

7. Zoning ordinances are used to identify?

   A. Population
   B. Traffic patterns
   C. Density
   D. Age groups

8. If an owner needed a setback change to accommodate a structure design, the owner would request:

   A. Grandfathered use
   B. Comprehensive plan change
   C. Zoning amendment
   D. Zoning variance

9. Who certifies the correctness of a plat for a planned subdivision?

   A. City or county planning commission
   B. County recorder
   C. Professional land surveyor
   D. The developer of the subdivision

10 What's the penalty for offering subdivision lots for sale from a preliminary plat but has not yet been approved and recorded?

   A. Shut down all future subdivision sales
   B. $100 for each lot
   C. $500 for any lot
   D. Cannot close the sale until the subdivision is approved

11. How many categories are available to cities to annex land into cities?

   A. 1
   B. 2
   C. 3
   D. 4

12. What building code has been adopted for all construction?

   A. Uniform Building Code
   B. State of Idaho Construction Code
   C. National Building Code
   D. International Building Code

13. Contractors doing major surface repairs to homes built prior to 1978 must be:

   A. Certified
   B. Licensed
   C. Registered
   D. Approved

14. Idaho statute defines a subdivision to contain how many lots?

   A. 2 or more
   B. 5 or more
   C. 7 or more
   D. 10 or more

15. Use of navigable waters passing through private property can only be used by:

   A. Anyone
   B. The property owner(s)
   C. Commercial enterprises
   D. Kayaks

16. Private ponds containing fish must apply for a private pond permit from:

   A. Department of Water Resources
   B. Department of Environmental Quality
   C. City or county Building Department
   D. Department of Fish and Game

17. Who is responsible to implement the waste management program in Idaho.

   A. Environmental Protection Agency
   B. Department of Water Resources
   C. Department of Environmental Quality
   D. Department of Hazardous Materials

18. Lead based paint was outlawed to be used in housing built prior to:

   A. 1950
   B. 1978
   C. 1985
   D. 1990

19. A requirement for persons performing renovations to target housing is:

    A. Building permit
    B. DEQ approval
    C. EPA approval
    D. Compensation

20. What are the limits for electromagnetic fields in Idaho?

    A. None
    B. 4 pico curries per liter
    C. 0 to 3 kHz
    D. 10 kHz

21. A methamphetamine contaminated home must:

    A. Be 'red tagged'
    B. Be torn down
    C. Be vacated
    D. Be cleaned up

22. Underground storage tanks are not regulated if the tanks have a storage capacity less than:

    A. 55 gallons
    B. 110 gallons
    C. 500 gallons
    D. 1,000 gallons

23. Approximately what percentage of Idaho homes have high levels of radon?

    A. 25%
    B. 33%
    C. 50%
    D. 60%

24. Planning and/or zoning members are:

    A. Elected
    B. Appointed
    C. Hired
    D. Promoted

Chapter 6

Transferring & Recording Title

Words of Wisdom

"Minds are like parachutes - they only function when open."

Thomas Dewar

Transferring Title

Trigger Events

Different events can trigger the transfer of title or ownership of real estate. Examples of such events include:

- Death of an owner
- Ownership by accession
- Title by occupancy
- Voluntary and involuntary transfer

Conveyance
IC 55-601

Conveyance

A conveyance of an estate in real property may be made by an instrument in writing, subscribed by the party disposing of the property. The name of the grantee (party receiving) together with a complete mailing address must also appear on the instrument (document).

There are many documents that convey an interest or ownership in real estate including deeds, mortgages, release of mortgages, and power of attorney that has been acknowledged. Also included in conveyances are transcripts of judgments or decrees which affect the title or possession of real property including water rights.

The transfer of ownership of real property from one party to another is with a deed. With the execution of a deed, the owner transfers, conveys, and releases any interests in their ownership to another. The deed serves as evidence of ownership.

Transfers of ownership must be in writing and signed to meet the *statute of frauds* including a deed.

5 Required Elements

Although Idaho does not have a statutory deed format, one should know and understand 5 elements that make up a valid deed.

1. A deed must identify the grantor (the party giving up ownership) and a grantee (the party acquiring ownership). Because the deed is 'granting' ownership, the grantor must be of legal age and of sound mind.

2. A deed must state consideration to identify something of value is being transferred. Such statement may state, *For one thousand ($1,000) and other good and valuable consideration*, or perhaps a condensed version, *For valuable consideration* could meet the legal requirement.

3.	The deed must contain a granting clause with words of conveyance. The format of the wording will identify the type of deed and to what extent ownership is being conveyed.
Examples of words of conveyance:

> *"Conveys, grants and warrants"*
> Provides the most protection to the buyer and warrants against encumbrances by prior owners.

> *"Grant, bargain, and sell"*
> Only implies ownership transfers the implied ownership without warranty.

> *"Convey, release, remiss, and forever quit claim"* Least protection of all deeds to the grantee. There are no covenants or warranties of any kind. The grantor is merely 'quitting' any claim to the property.

4.	A deed must contain a legal description that cannot possibly be misunderstood. Acceptable legal descriptions can be by government survey system, metes and bounds, or recorded plat. If an easement or air right is part of the transfer, the deed should state that fact along with the legal description.

5.	The signature of the grantor. In order for the deed to be recorded, the signature must be acknowledged and witnessed by someone authorized by a notary public, authorized public officer or someone approved by state law.

Once the deed is signed, it must be personally delivered to the grantee for acceptance to validate the public records and establish priority.

Evidence Of Death
IC 15-1-107 (a)

Death Of An Owner

A certified or authenticated copy of a death certificate by an official or agency is prima facie proof of the fact, place, date, and time of death of the decedent.

The issue of a person means all of his lineal descendants of all generations, with the relationship of a parent and child of each generation, being determined by the definitions of a child and parent contained in the Idaho code.

Intestate
Distribution
IC 15-2-102

Distribution Without A Will (intestate)

Upon death of a married person living in Idaho who does not have a will, the intestate share of the surviving spouse's distribution will be as follows:

Separate Property
- If there is no surviving issue or parent of the decedent, the entire intestate estate;
- If there is no surviving issue but the decedent is survived by a parent or parents, ½ of the intestate estate;
- If there are surviving issue of the deceased spouse, ½ of the intestate estate.

Community Property
- The ½ of community property which belongs to the decedent passes to the surviving spouse.

If there is no surviving spouse, Idaho Code defines the distribution process from kinship to maternal relatives (IC 15-2-103).

Legal Age

Distribution With A Will   (testate)
The Idaho State Bar on Estate Planning, states a person of legal capacity must be 18 years of age or older to make a will. A will can be prepared anytime during the property owner's lifetime but cannot take effect until the owner's death.

Witnessed Will

The person making the will is known as the testator. The will must be signed and witnessed by at least two persons. A verbal will (noncupative) may be made under special circumstances in immediate anticipation of the maker's death. Idaho Probate Code does not have any provision for the use or enforceability of this type of will.

Ownership By Accession
One example of accession can include shoreline property in which natural forces can increase the shoreline with soil washing up and depositing onto the shoreline. Or, if the water line is permanently reduced, the land can 'grow' in size.

Because Idaho owns all the water, it also regulates and controls the use or disposition of lands in the beds of navigable lakes, rivers and streams, to the natural or ordinary high water mark.

High Water Mark
IC 58-104 (9)

The natural or ordinary high water mark is defined to be the line which the water impresses on the soil by covering it for sufficient periods to deprive the soil of its vegetation and destroy its value for agricultural purposes.

Another example of accession is with the addition of an improvement that becomes a permanent fixture upon the land. A home, building, sidewalks, and even fences are examples of 'adding to the land'.

Transfer By Occupancy

Transfer By Occupancy
With the adoption of the Homestead Act of 1862, a tract of unoccupied public land, 160 acres in area, could be permanently acquired after 5 years of continuous occupancy and payment of a fee. Expansion of this concept led to 'squatters rights' which works off the doctrine of possession and the statute of limitations.

Adverse Possession

In Idaho, a property must be held and adversely possessed for 20 years. A person claiming adverse possession must present clear and convincing evidence that the property has been protected by a substantial enclosure and has been usually cultivated or improved. In addition all the taxes, state, county or municipal which have been levied upon the land according to law must be paid by the party or persons, their predecessors and grantors.

20 Year Holding
IC 5-207

Included in the adverse possession claim, can be an easement by prescription except for the payment of taxes. An easement by prescription must also be held and possessed or controlled for 20 years and when it consists of a tract divided into lots, the possession of 1 lot is not deemed a possession of any other lot on the same tract.

Before purchasing a property, it's a good idea to look closely for any evidence of some use that may have been created by some outside source. If something looks out of place, ask questions.

Abandonment

Abandonment

Can claims of use or ownership be lost due to non use or abandonment? The answer is not only yes, but there may be specific requirements to complete the process.

Water Rights
IC 42-222 (2)

For example, a *water right* can be lost in Idaho by abandonment or forfeiture. If the water right is not used for 5 consecutive years, the right will be forfeited unless a formal application is applied for to extend the water right. If a well is abandoned, the well must be certified by a licensed well driller of such abandonment.

Rights-Of-Way
IC 40-203

Highways and public *rights-of-way* can be abandoned but only with a proper public hearing. No highway or public right-of-way shall be abandoned or vacated that leaves any real property without access to an established highway or public right-of-way.

Until abandonment is authorized by the commissioners, public use of the highway or public right-of-way may not be restricted or impeded by encroachment or installation of any obstruction restricting public use. Because highway right-of-way abandonment is somewhat complex and cross references many laws, legal counsel should be sought to understand the whole process.

Automatic Protection
IC 55-1004

Homestead Protection

The homestead protection (protection against unsecured creditors) is automatic. If the homeowner retains their homestead and moves to another home, that will become their new homestead, and the owner must file for change in homestead.

An owner who selects a homestead from unimproved or improved land that is not yet occupied as a homestead must execute a declaration of homestead and file the same for record in the office of the recorder of the county in which the land is located. However, if the owner also owns another parcel of property on which the owner presently resides or in which the owner claims a homestead, the owner must also execute a declaration of abandonment of homestead on that other property and file the same for record with the recorder of the county in which the land is located.

Involuntary Transfer

Unfortunately, involuntary transfer of rights or ownership occurs when one or more parties either do not want to make the transfer or the parties to the issue cannot come to agreement.

Eminent Domain

Eminent Domain

The Idaho State Constitution states in part, 'private property may be taken for public use, but not until a just compensation, to be ascertained in the manner prescribed by law, shall be paid therefor'.

Section 14, Article 1	Thus, under the federal and state constitutions, private property may not be taken for public purposes without payment of just compensation. The Idaho attorney general establishes and reviews the process to assure the actions of 'a taking' do not result in an unconstitutional taking of private property.

Forfeiture

Forfeiture

Violations of the uniform controlled substances act resulting in a person found guilty of, or enter a plea of guilty, shall forfeit any of the person's property used or intended to be used to facilitate the violation.

Title 37, Ch 28 IC 37-2802	Property subject to criminal forfeiture includes: real property, including things growing on, affixed to, or found on the land. Additional property subject to criminal forfeiture includes tangible and intangible personal property, including rights, privileges, interests, claims and securities.

Bankruptcy

Bankruptcy

Bankruptcy can be either voluntary or involuntary. Typically bankruptcy results from debts exceeding assets with little or no ability to recover. Although bankruptcies are initiated for various reasons, 3 out of 5 personal bankruptcies are due to medical debt.

Voluntary Bankruptcy	A voluntary bankruptcy begins with the filing of a petition in the Bankruptcy Court. Part of the federal court system, Bankruptcy Courts are established in every state. The debtor is required to file schedules of assets and liabilities, current income and expenditures. Only chapters 7 and 11 can qualify for involuntary bankruptcy. Chapters 7, 11, 12, and 13 can qualify for voluntary bankruptcy
Chapter 7	Chapter 7 - results in total liquidation or 'wipe out'. All assets and non-exempt properties are turned over to a trustee who converts them into cash to pay the debtor's creditors.
Chapter 11	Chapter 11 - is used primarily for business bankruptcies and restructuring. This chapter gives businesses the opportunity to reorganize themselves. It is far more complex and expensive than Chapter 7.
Chapter 12	Chapter 12 - is designed for the family farmer and is less complicated and expensive than chapter 11.
Chapter 13	Chapter 13 - is a smaller version of Chapter 11. The debtor still retains the property and may be allowed one to keep additional property that would otherwise not be exempt. Chapter 13 is designed to give a fresh start but you have to submit to the bankruptcy court how you intend to pay off your debts over a 3-5 year period of time for as little as 10 cents on the dollar. You may not incur any significant new credit obligations without consulting the trustee.

Title Insurance

Abstract Of Title

Abstract Of Title

An abstract of title contains a condensed history of the title to a piece of land in addition to a summary of conveyances. In Idaho abstract searches will go back to 1890 and the original patents. Abstractors are required to be bonded for $10,000. It's very important that there aren't any breaks in the 'chain' of historical ownership. A break in the chain could lead to someone claiming an interest in the property and create legal issues.

Abstracts are rarely used in Idaho today because if a problem exists in an abstract, the only recourse is the financial well being of the person or company producing the abstract. But with title insurance, the financial risk is virtually eliminated.

Title Insurance
Title 41, Chapter 27

Title Insurance

Title insurance is the certification or guarantee of title or ownership, or insurance of owners of property against loss by encumbrance, defective titles, invalidity, or adverse claim to title.

IC 41-2705

In Idaho, the title insurance industry is regulated by the Idaho Department of Insurance. The Department of Insurance also requires rates for premiums for title insurance and escrow fees and title insurance agents to be filed with them.

Illegal Rebates
IDAPA 18.01.56
011

In addition, title insurance companies are regulated against offering illegal inducements or rebates. This includes quoting or reducing any charge for title insurance for less than the currently filed rate with the Department of Insurance.

The duplicated records title insurance companies secure from the county recorder are put into 'tract' books and filed by date. A patent title plant will have records going back to the first Idaho recordings beginning in 1890.

Title insurance helps bridge the issue by performing a title search to examine all public records pertaining to the property including a "chain of title" which reviews the history of ownership starting with the current owner and going back to the original owner.

In addition, the search will reveal any title-related problems with the property and report all publicly recorded liens and encumbrances against the property.

To be within the unbroken chain of title, the instrument must be discoverable or traceable through linking conveyances from the present owner through successive owners to a common grantor.

If the chain is broken, a "gap" exists in the chain, creating a "cloud" on the title. If the "cloud" cannot be resolved, it may be necessary to establish ownership by a court action called a 'suit to quiet title'.

When a title search is complete, the information is gathered on a commitment document for title insurance. This document shows any defects to the property that would be listed as exceptions to the policy plus any requirements that need to be resolved before the policy can be issued.

Marketable Title	A title that is free from objectionable defects and encumbrances will be deemed as being 'marketable'. Marketable title enables the owner to sell or freely transfer his property to others.

Title Commitment	## Title Commitment

Once a title insurance company is satisfied with their title search, they can offer a title commitment which is a promise to issue an insurance policy on a piece of property. A Title Commitment is equivalent to a binder for other types of insurance and identifies:

1. Who is being insured
2. The amount of the insurance
3. What is being insured
4. What is required to insure the title
5. What is not insured

Policies	## Title Insurance Policies

There are two basic types of title insurance; Owners Policy and a Lenders Policy.

Owner's Standard Policy	*Owner's or Standard Owners Policy (owner)*

The Standard Owner's title insurance is usually based on the *real estate purchase price*. It is purchased for a one-time fee at closing and lasts as long as the owner has an interest in the property. The Standard Owner's policy fully protects the buyer should a problem arise with the title and it was not discovered during the title search. However, the policy only covers events prior to closing.

Owner's Extended Policy	*An Extended Owner's Policy* should be seriously considered if there has been recent construction or new construction. The policy may not always be available or could be available with additional requirements or expense.

It protects the owner for future acts or claims that may have occurred prior to closing but would not be of public record until after closing. A good example of such claim could be a Mechanic's Lien. The claim took place prior to closing but was filed after closing.

Lender's Extended Policy	*Lender's or Extended Lenders Policy (mortgagee policy)*

Most lenders require a lenders policy when they issue a loan. The lenders policy is usually based on the *dollar amount of the loan*. It protects the lender's interest in the property should a problem arise with the title. The coverage decreases with the reduction in outstanding loan amount and will eventually disappear when the loan is paid off.

In addition to the basic policies, endorsements may be required which will add additional costs to the base title insurance costs. Endorsements could include zoning, easements, encroachments, condominium compliance, planned unit development, and environmental issues.

Endorsements	Endorsements protect against those issues that may not be of public record but could easily have a legal effect upon the property.

UCC

Uniform Commercial Code

The Uniform Commercial Code deals primarily with commercial transactions, including business opportunities, that involves the transfer of personal property in real estate.

UCC Filing
IC 28-9 Part 5

The Secretary of State's UCC (Uniform Commercial Code) Division is the agency which receives and files liens, thereby making the liens public record, as well as providing a date and time of the filing. The UCC division also maintains a database of lien filings for future documentation, as necessary.

Various liens that can be filed with the Secretary of State's office include:

Basic lien
Commodity lien
Farm lien
IRS lien
Labor lien
Medical lien
Seed lien
Utility lien

Recording

Statute Of Frauds

Recording Concept

The concept of recording is based on English common law together with the Statute of Frauds which state certain documents *must* be in writing to be valid.

The difference between common law title and a Torrens title is that a Certificate of Title is absolute. An example of a Certificate of Title is an automobile.

On the other hand, common law transfer of title is based on the premise that the recording system does not determine who owns the title or interest in land. That determination is made through litigation in the courts. As a safety measure, most transfers of real property include title insurance, which was discussed earlier.

Recording Priority

With a government sponsored public recording service, public records would be open and free of charge to anyone confirms 'he who is first in time is preferred in right' which leads to the 'chain of title'.

Idaho Recording Law
IC 55-801

All states, including Idaho, have passed recording acts to provide for the recording of every document in which an estate, interest, or right in land is created, encumbered, or transferred.

The primary purpose of recording is to give notice to others that an interest is claimed on real property to:

1. Provide constructive notice to the public of a real estate transaction;

2. Provide a perpetual history of the title to a particular parcel of land.

IC 55-809

An instrument is deemed to be recorded, when, being duly acknowledged, or proved and certified, it is deposited in the county recorder's office for record.

Place Of Recording
IC 55-808

Place Of Recording

Any instruments that affect real property must be recorded in the county recorder's office of the county where the affected real property is located. Recordable documents that do not specifically deal with real property are normally recordable in the county where the business is being conducted or a part to the document resides.

English Required
IC 73-121

Idaho also requires that 'any document required to be filed or recorded . . . . shall be in the English language or shall be accompanied by a <u>certified</u> translation in English'.

If the property is closed at a title company in the morning, it usually can be recorded the same day or the next business day.

Upon presentation to the county recorder, the recorder's office shall immediately write or stamp an instrument number. The numbers so stamped shall be consecutive in the order of filing in only one series of numbers. The priority of number shall be prima facie evidence of priority of filing in the order the instruments actually came to the recorder. If more than one instrument is received from the same source, the recorder may follow such directions as the sender may give in relation to the numbering.

Reception Book
IC 31-2413

A reception book will be maintained by the county recorder for recorded instruments. The format consists of 8 parallel columns to enter the required information as follows:

1st column - instrument number
2nd column - day, hour, and minute of filing
3rd column - grantor or person executing instrument
4th column - grantee or person to whom executed
5th column - character of the instrument
6th column - book and page where recorded
7th column - brief description of the property
8th column - name of person to whom delivered

By the way, other resources for investigating records are the title insurance companies. They all have a 'duplicate' set of all recorded records for their use in title searching.

In fact, it may even be easier to search the title company records since they use a different format to retain records that are very quick and efficient with cross reference information to trace a specific property back to original recordings.

Transfer Taxes
Idaho has none

Transfer Taxes

Idaho is one of 13 states that *does not* have any transfer fees or taxes.

37 states that have transfer taxes that range from a low of .01% in Colorado to a high of 1.5% in New Hampshire. Many others may incorporate graduated scales.

Of those states that surround Idaho, only Nevada and Washington have transfer taxes. Nevada transfer tax ranges from .13% to .25% and Washington has a flat 1.28% transfer tax on all transfers of real estate. However, it should be noted that neither Nevada nor Washington have state income tax.

Oregon (except Washington County), Montana, Wyoming, and Utah do not have transfer fees.

Instruments For Recording
IC 31-2402

Instruments That May Be Recorded In Idaho

Some examples of real estate related documents that can be recorded include:

Deeds
Mortgages
Deeds of trust
Power of Attorney
Leases
Judgments affecting title
    Partition action
    Water rights
    Quiet title action
    Condemnation action
U. S. Patents
Affidavits
    Facts showing marital status
    Possession through tax deed
    Plats and legal descriptions
Notices of mechanic's liens
Financing statements (UCC)
Platting
Condominium instruments
Conservation easements
Manufactured homes statement of intent
Sale of water rights

All these documents, and many more not listed above, may assist the public to determine the quality of ownership with historical information regarding any real estate.

Constructive Notice
IC 55-811

Constructive Notice

In Idaho, recording is not part of the actual conveyance process. When the grantor delivers a properly executed deed to the grantee, and the grantee accepts the delivery, the conveyance of title to the real property is effective.

The act of recording establishes constructive notice and priority among competing interests in the same parcel of real property. An unrecorded instrument is valid as between the parties to the instrument. The Idaho Supreme Court made the following observation about the primary purpose of the recording laws:

The primary purpose of the recording statutes is to give notice to others that an interest is claimed in real property, and thus give protection against bona fide third parties who may be dealing in the same property.

Matheson v. Harris, 98 Idaho 758, 572, P.2nd 861, at 864 (1977)

**Recording
Requirements
IC 55-707
IC 32-912**

Requirements To Record

The acknowledgment of an instrument must not be taken, unless the officer taking it knows, or has satisfactory evidence from a credible source, that the person making such acknowledgment is the individual who is described in, and who executed, the instrument. Upon verification, the document will be properly notarized allowing the document to be recorded.

It should be noted that neither the husband nor wife may sell, convey or encumber the community real estate unless the other joins in executing the sale agreement, deed or other instrument of conveyance.

It is possible that a husband or wife could own property as 'sole and separate' during marriage. However, a title company will probably require a 'quit claim' deed to make sure the property being conveyed is in fact 'sole and separate'.

Not all documents require acknowledgment. Some examples of documents that do not require proper acknowledgment are:

- Patents & other instruments recorded by the United States
- Authenticated judgments
- Notice of Lis Pendens
- Mechanic's liens

**Endorsement
IC 31-2410**

Endorsement And Index System

Once a properly executed instrument is deposited in the recorder's office with the proper officer to record, the recorder will endorse the document with the time it was received including the year, month, day, hour, and minute of its reception. The document will then be placed in the proper index.

**Book And Page
IC 31-2411**

Also included will be the book and page or instrument number in which it is recorded and then it is delivered upon request to the party leaving the same for record.

**27 Indexes
IC 31-2404**

Constructive notice does not occur until the document is indexed. In Idaho, there are 27 different indexes that the county recorder must keep. They include:

1. Grantors (deeds)
2. Grantees (deeds)
3. Mortgagors
4. Mortgagees
5. Release of mortgagees
6. Release of mortgagors
7. Power of Attorney
8. Lessor
9. Lessee
10. Marriage Certificates - men

11. Marriage Certificates - women
12. Assignments of Mortgages and Leases - assignors
13. Assignments of Mortgages and Leases - assignees
14. Wills
15. Official Bonds
16. Mechanic's Liens
17. Transcripts and Judgment
18. Attachments
19. Notices of Actions
20. Separate Property of Married Women
21. Possessory Claims
22. Homesteads
23. Real Property Agreements
24. Mining Claims
25. Water Rights
26. General Index
27. Financing Statements (UCC)

Confused? You are not alone, especially when trying to research a specific parcel of land. So, consider an alternative; a title insurance company. Title insurance companies take all the information contained in the various indexes and apply the appropriate information to a particular parcel via tract books.

Tract Books

Tract books identify a specific parcel of property and then list every specific recorded document that affects that property. As one can see, it could take hours or maybe even days to research the county public records for the same information that could be gathered at a title insurance company in literally minutes.

Typically title insurance companies duplicate the same records that the county recorder has on a regular basis of actual recording, into their own tract records.

Before And After Priority

Priority Of Recorded Documents

Generally speaking, those documents first recorded take priority over subsequent recorded or unrecorded documents. However, it should be understood that some types of liens will in fact attach to property, even after the property has changed owners.

An example would be mechanic's liens. Another example could be property tax liens which attach to the property on January 1 of every year. These examples are another reason purchasers should seriously consider having an extended title insurance policy which covers liens not of public record at the time of recording.

Questions - Chapter 6

1. When one dies, proof of death is evidenced by providing:

    A. Newspaper obituary with date and time of death
    B. Funeral notice giving date and time
    C. Legible copy of death notice
    D. Authenticated copy of death certificate

2. If a married person dies without a will, how will the decedent's property be distributed?

    A. ½ community property of the decedent passes to the spouse
    B. All property passes to the spouse
    C. All property passes to the state
    D. Surviving family decides who gets what

3. When do the terms of a properly executed will of a married person take effect?

    A. When the will was signed and properly witnessed
    B. When the will was recorded
    C. Upon death of the married person
    D. When a divorce has been finalized

4. The definition of the ordinary high water mark is defined as:

    A. The normal water mark verified at any time during the year
    B. Sufficient periods water covers and depresses the soil to deprive soil of its vegetation
    C. The highest water mark publically recorded
    D. High water mark cannot be defined

5. What period of time must a person holding and possessing a property, hold the property to claim adverse possession?

   A. 5 years
   B. 10 years
   C. 20 years
   D. 40 years

6. An easement by prescription must be held and controlled for what period of time?

   A. 5 years
   B. 10 years
   C. 20 years
   D. 40 years

7. A water right can be lost if it is not used for how many consecutive years?

   A. 5 years
   B. 10 years
   C. 20 years
   D. Once properly obtained, a water right cannot be lost due to non use.

8. Eminent domain is an example of what type of transfer?

   A. Voluntary
   B. Involuntary
   C. Illegal
   D. Transfer for private use

9. The transfer of real property must be:

   A. Verbally agreed to in person
   B. Recorded at the county recorder
   C. Delivered through a title company
   D. Signed and in writing

10. Certain documents must be in writing to be enforceable to satisfy:

    A. Contract law
    B. Statute of Frauds
    C. Idaho Statutes
    D. Supreme Court decisions

11. 'Grant, bargain, and sell' transfers what type of ownership protection?

    A. The most protection to the buyer
    B. Warrants encumbrances for future owners
    C. Contains no covenants or warranties
    D. Implied ownership without warranty

12. 'Convey, release, remiss, and forever quit claim' transfers what type of ownership protection?

    A. The most protection to the buyer
    B. Warrants encumbrances for future owners
    C. Contains no covenants or warranties
    D. Implied ownership without warranty

13. How is a recorded instrument identified by priority of recording?

    A. Actual date and year of recording
    B. The year including date and hour
    C. Book where recorded
    D. Day, hour, and minute recorded

14. Along with state sales tax, what is the transfer tax in Idaho?

    A. 0.05 per cent of the value transferred
    B. 1.0 per cent of the value transferred
    C. Tax is based on property tax value
    D. There is no transfer tax

15. When is the transfer of a deed effective?

    A. When the deed is recorded
    B. When the grantee accepts delivery
    C. When the grantor signs the deed
    D. When the grantor delivers the deed

16. Any document required to be filed or recorded in Idaho shall be in what language?

    A. English only
    B. English or Spanish
    C. Any language
    D. English or certified Spanish

17. The title insurance industry is regulated by what government department?

    A. Department of Finance
    B. Department of Land
    C. Department of Insurance
    D. Department of Commerce

18. A title that is free from objectionable defects and encumbrances is deemed:

    A. Free and clear
    B. Contains no liens
    C. Saleable
    D. Marketable

19. The Uniform Commercial Code deals primarily with what type of transactions?

    A. Residential
    B. Farm land
    C. 2nd homes
    D. Business opportunities

20. What type of title insurance policy gives the most protection to a borrower?

    A. Mortgagee policy
    B. Owners standard policy
    C. Owners extended policy
    D. Extended lenders policy

21. The purpose of recording, beside giving constructive notice, is to provide:

    A. An immediate current history
    B. A history of county growth
    C. A brief history of the county
    D. A perpetual history of a parcel of land

Taxes and Liens

Property Valuation For Taxes

Based On Market Value

Taxes based On Market Value
Like most states, property taxes are collected to pay for the costs of local and county government services. In Idaho, property taxes are based on the *market* value of the property, real or personal.

How Property Is Valued
IC 63-201 (15)

How Is Property Valued?
Each year, all property, real or personal, is valued on January 1 at fair market value for tax purposes. Fair market value is determined by comparing similar properties that have sold to the subject property. Market value is supposed to be equivalent to a property exchange between a willing seller, under no compulsion to sell, and an informed capable buyer given a reasonable time to consummate the sale.

Even though the value is supposed to be on 'fair market' value, it is only an estimate of value, based on information that isn't necessarily verified for complete accuracy.

Fair market value may not be easily verifiable since Idaho is a 'non disclosure' state. Idaho statutes do not require disclosure of the price and terms of a real estate transaction like most states. If the price and terms of a real estate transaction are not made public, the accuracy of the county assessor's property values may or may not be accurate, especially with commercial transactions which may not be a part of a Multiple Listing Service that may allow public disclosure upon closing.

Annual Valuation
IC 63-314

Annual Property Valuation By The County Assessor
In order to promote uniform assessment of property in Idaho, taxable property shall be appraised or indexed annually to reflect current market value. All property in a county shall be appraised at least once every 5 years unless an extension is granted.

Idaho code also requires not less than 15% of taxable properties to be appraised the first year; 35% the second year; 55% the third year; 75% the fourth year; and finally 100% the fifth year. Thus, there is a partial ongoing physical appraisal each and every year. During the years an individual property isn't physically appraised, it will be indexed.

Mass Appraisal   Unlike the individual appraisal that is usually required to secure financing to purchase a property, the county assessors use a 'mass' appraisal concept. The 'mass' appraisal will include multiple properties located within a geographical area. All properties will be appraised within the specific area for a total value from the individual appraisals.

Indexing   The assessor will take the collective data of value to arrive at an index that would equate to the ups and downs of the real estate market from year to year. The index will be applied in the years the individual properties are not physically appraised in an attempt to keep the market value current and reflect the market trend that can go up or down from year to year.

For example, a property may be appraised at $300,000 on year one and may not be physically appraised for another 4 years. However, the law requires the property to be valued each and every year. The assessor has determined, via mass appraisal techniques, that the sales values of similar properties in the area increased 1.7% for the indexed year. Thus, the $300,000 valued property would increase to $305,100 the next year. If in the following year the mass appraisal was reduced, the index would go down proportionally.

Index Accuracy   This indexed value may or may not be correct. If the county appraiser hasn't physically appraised the subject property, the indexed value can be greatly skewed. In addition, Idaho code does not require the homeowner to give inside access of their property to the county appraiser. So, it is very conceivable that the original characteristics of the property could be in error.

The homeowner may have done extensive remodeling without a permit which would have increased the value. Or, a property sold at a very low price because the inside was trashed or had deteriorated below the original characteristics contained in the county appraiser files.

Because of all the variables, assessment values for tax purposes should not be used exclusively to determine market value. Remember, the values may be collectively indexed and may not be physically appraised except for once every 5 years.

Trend Accuracy   Value trends can also be incorrect. The data the county appraiser uses to assess each property on January 1 each year could already be a year old. If the market is increasing, it's a good bet that the assessed value could be low. If, on the other hand, the market is declining, the assessed value could be high since it takes time for the assessed value to catch up with the market.

Assessment Notices Sent To Property Owners

Notices Sent No Later Than 1st Monday In June
IC 63-308

Even though all assessments are based on January 1 of each year, the valuation assessment notice delivery to the taxpayer shall be no later than the *first Monday in June*.

The 5 month delay from January 1 to June is to allow the county assessor time to review, fine tune, and make adjustments to any or all the data they have for all properties. Thus, the value based on January 1 may or may not be the value contained in the assessment notice.

It is important to realize the assessment notice is *not* a tax notice. It is merely a notice of valuation of the property.

Assessment Notice And Appeal
IC 63-501A

What happens if a property owner doesn't agree with the assessed value? The property owner will receive the assessment notice no later than the first Monday in June but only has until *fourth Monday in June* to appeal.

Although a formal written appeal is good, a phone call to the assessors office may get a quicker result if a county appraiser can come to your home and reappraise. Be careful! If the appraiser finds your home to be of greater value than the assessment notice indicates, the appraiser *must* enter the new value into their records.

Most Idaho counties have websites that will give full instructions for the appeal process. Remember the appeal is based on the value as of January 1, not later. Thus, any sales data collected should predate January 1.

Property Taxes

Property taxes

Cost Of Operating The Government

Property taxes are based on the total cost of operating various parts of the government, divided by the total value of the properties. All the parts that make up a tax bill are known as tax districts. Each tax district operates within a boundary limit. Thus, your home could be exactly like the home across the street but the taxes could be different. Why? Because the home across the street may be in a different taxing district.

Tax Districts

Examples of different taxing districts could be:
    County
    City
    Fire
    School district
    Parks & Recreation
    Highway
    Special bonding
    Police
    Emergency bonding
    Ambulance
    Mosquito abatement
    Airport
    College
    Recreation center

As an example, if all the taxing districts where a home is located would total 0.01475 and the property value is $150,000. Multiply the tax rate times the property value and the property tax would equate to $2,212.50.

Assessed Value And Cost Of Operating Government

There's a misconception that if the assessed value of a property is increased, the taxes will also increase. However, if the cost of operating the government didn't change, the taxes would probably remain the same. Conversely, if all the property values decreased and the government kept the cost the same from one year to the next, the taxes would still be the same. Remember, the key is the cost of operating the government. Taxes only increase when the cost of the government (tax base) increases. Assessed value is only one part of the equation.

Tax Statements
IC 63-903

Tax Statements

All tax statements are to be sent to all property owners no later than the *fourth Monday in November*. The owner now has until December 20 to either pay the taxes in full or elect to make two equal payments without penalty or interest. The first half is due by *December 20* and the second half is due no later than *June 20* of the following year. Late payment or non payment will result in delinquency.

Tax Delinquency
IC 63-1001

Delinquency

Payment for delinquent taxes will be applied to the oldest delinquency on record. Interest on a delinquency will be charged at 1% per month calculated from January 1, following the year the tax lien attached.

Remember when we previously stated taxes can be paid in two installments? Don't be late on the second installment. The delinquency will start when the lien was first placed on the property. Let's say you were late by 2 days in making the second installment. The interest would revert back to and begin when the lien was placed; 1 year plus 5 months and 22 days; that equates to a little more than 17% interest!!!!

Important Dates

As one can see, it's very important to remember various dates involved with taxes. The following are helpful reminders:

January 1	Tax lien date each year
January 1	Annual assessment value on property
1st Monday in June	Assessment notice to owner
4th Monday in June	Latest date for assessment protests
4th Monday in Nov.	Tax notice to owner
December 20	1st half taxes due
June 20	(following year) - 2nd half taxes due

Occupancy Tax

An occupancy tax shall be levied upon all newly constructed and occupied residential, commercial and industrial structures, including manufactured housing. The occupancy tax shall be for that portion of the calendar year in which first occupancy occurs.

It is the obligation of the owner of any newly constructed improvement or manufactured housing to report to the county assessor that the improvement or manufactured housing has been occupied.

Upon completion of the appraisal by the county assessor, the owner will be notified of their right to apply for homeowner exemption. If done so within 30 days of receiving such notification, the exemption will be extended to the property.

In the event the owner fails to report to the county assessor that the property is ready for occupancy, the assessor shall notify the county board of equalization. The board may impose a penalty of an additional amount equal to 5% of the tax for each month following the date of first occupancy to a maximum of a 25% penalty.

The lesson to be learned is not to occupy, or allow to be occupied, any residential property without first notifying the county assessor.

As a side note, the owner will receive two tax bills for the first year; one for occupancy tax, and the other for the general tax on the land.

Tax Deed

If real property on which there is a delinquency is not redeemed within 3 years from the date of the delinquency, the county tax collector of the county wherein such property is situated must make, in favor of said county, a tax deed for such property. However, the county shall not be entitled to a tax deed for such real property until:

- A notice of pending issue of tax deed has been given; until
- An affidavit of compliance has been recorded.

The county tax collector of the county wherein the real property for which a tax deed may issue shall serve or cause to be served written notice of pending issue of tax deed upon the record owner or owners and parties in interest of record in the following exclusive manner:

- By serving or causing to be served a copy of such notice by certified mail with return receipt demanded upon the record owner or owners and parties in interest of record at their last known address, such service of notice to be made no more than 5 months nor less than 2 months before the time set forth for the tax deed to issue;

- In the event that such notice is served as above described and returned undelivered after attempting to locate and serve the record owner or owners and parties in interest of record, by publishing a summary of such notice in a newspaper having general circulation in the county wherein the real property is situated.

Such publication must be made at least once a week for 4 consecutive weeks, the last publication of which is to be no more than 2 months nor less than 14 days before the time set for the tax deed to issue.

The record owner or owners and parties in interest of record shall be liable and pay to the county tax collector all costs and fees in the preparation, service and publication of such notice and the tax deed process and such costs shall become a perpetual lien upon the property in favor of the county tax collector.

Property Tax Reduction Programs

Although there are many types of exemptions or reductions from taxation, we'll only discuss three available tax reduction programs related to home ownership.

Homeowner Homestead Confusion
IC 63-602G

Homeowner Exemption
Idaho code identifies property exempt from taxation as 'homestead' but shouldn't be confused with the federal homestead exemption that protects homeowners from unsecured creditors. Also, to add to confusion, the application for the property tax exemption is referenced as 'homeowner' exemption. So while the code refers to 'homestead' the form and format to receive the exemption will refer to 'homeowner' and not 'homestead'.

Primary Dwelling Exemption
IC 63-701

Idaho allows for an owner/occupant using a dwelling exclusively for personal use and as their primary dwelling, the ability to receive a reduction to the market value of the home. The land surrounding the dwelling will not exceed 1 acre for value purposes. The owner only has to make one application which will be good for the duration of ownership of the dwelling being used as the primary dwelling.

In order for the claimant to be eligible for the current year, the home must have been occupied and used as the primary dwelling place of the owner:

- At least 6 months during the prior year; or
- Majority of the time owned if less than 1 year; or
- Majority of time occupied if less than 1 year.

As a side note, if the claimant owned a duplex and occupied only one side as the primary dwelling, only ½ of the value would be use to calculate any reduction. The exemption does not include lessees, tenants, roomers or boarders.

Another word of caution. When a couple gets divorced and one of the spouses retains the home as their primary dwelling, ownership just changed. The 'new' owner needs to re-file for homeowner exemption, even though he/she never vacated the property. The divorced spouse/occupant is considered a new owner and thus has to be treated as such.

The exemption shall be effective upon the date of the application and must be taken before the reduction in taxes is applied.

Exemption History	In 1980, the first homeowner's exemption began with a maximum of $10,000. It remained at that level until 1983 when it was raised to $50,000. Again, in 2006, the Idaho Legislature raised the exemption to $75,000 and tied future limits to a House Price Index which is published annually by the Federal Housing Finance Agency.
Exemption Raised IC 63-602G	In 2021, the Idaho legislature raised the exemption to $125,000. The law has been simplified and currently reads 'for each tax year, the first $125,000 of the market value for assessment purposes of the homestead or 50% of the market value for assessment purposes of the homestead, whichever is lesser shall be exempt from property taxation'.
Calculation IC 63-602G	If a home has an assessed value of $415,900, 50% of the assessed value would be $207,950. Since $125,000 is less than the 50% number, $125,000 would be deducted from $415,900 - leaving $290,000 as taxable value.

Circuit Breaker
IC 63-701

Circuit Breaker

Another property tax reduction program is known as the 'circuit breaker' for a single family residence on less than one acre. The maximum amount of property tax reduction that can be claimed for 2022 can be as much as $1,500 based on 2021 income.

This program is designed primarily for lower income older people. For example, to qualify, the maximum income is currently capped at $32,230 or less after deducting unreimbursed medical expenses for 2021.

The applicant must meet one or more criteria as of January 1:

- Age 65 or older
- Widow(er)
- Blind
- Fatherless or motherless child under 18
- Former prisoner of war/hostage
- Veteran with 10% or more service disability
- Disabled as recognized by Social Security, Railroad Retirement, or Federal Civil Service

The applicant needs to contact the assessor in the county in which the owner and property is located to receive the application form. There will be a long list of what the income guidelines are, as well as explaining medical issues.

File the completed application between January 1 and April 15. This particular program must be applied for each and every year the owner is eligible. The deadline is April 15 and cannot be extended. If approved, the tax reduction will appear on the December tax bill.

The monies paid by the program come out of the Idaho state general fund and are paid to the county. Thus, the county does not suffer any loss of operating income.

New Construction Occupancy Tax
IC 63-317 (2) (3)

New Construction Exemption

New homes or improvements that have never been occupied are exempt from property taxation. Prior to having an occupancy permit signed off, the home is considered 'inventory' but the land will still be taxed. However, once residential improvements are occupied, the improvements shall be subject to occupancy tax.

Liens

General information About Liens

A lien is a financial claim on the property of another as security for a debt or obligation. In Idaho, liens are divided into two categories, general and special.

General Lien

A general lien is one which the lien holder is entitled to enforce the performance of *all* obligations which exist in the favor of the lien holder against all and real property of the owner.

Examples include judgments, inheritance taxes, debts of a decedent and unpaid taxes to the Internal Revenue Service (IRS).

Special Lien

A special lien is one which the holder is entitled to enforce the performance of a *particular* act or obligation and affects only a particular property.

The liens with earlier recording dates take priority over liens recorded at a later date. For example, a first mortgage takes priority over a second mortgage and so on.

However, if one subordinates their position to a later position, the earlier position gives the junior lien holder priority. An example would be when the holder of a 1st mortgage gives up their position to allow a 2nd lien holder priority, providing all lender(s) approve. This may happen when a lender behind a 1st mortgage requires a 1st position to make a loan to protect themselves.

Voluntary special liens are offered by the owner to allow another party to secure the property as collateral for a loan. Some examples include mortgages, vendor lien, and a bail bond lien.

Redemption
IC 11-401

Property sold subject to redemption, or any part sold separately, may be redeemed by the following persons or their successors in interest:
1. The judgment debtor, or his successor in interest, in the whole or any part of the property.
2. A creditor having a lien by judgment or mortgage on the property sold, or some share of part thereof, subsequent to that on which the property was sold. The persons are known as redemptioners.

Vendor Lien
IC 45-801

Vendor Lien

In Idaho, an example of a 'vendor lien' is where the owner/seller finances the property for the buyer and in essence becomes the 'bank'.

Although uncommon, the act is often known as 'seller financing' with an installment contract. A deed is not delivered by the seller until the contract has been fulfilled.

Bail Bond Lien
IC 19-2922 (1)

Bail Bond Lien

A bail bond lien attaches to the real estate of the person who posts bail. In Idaho, it should be noted that the lien will not be released until a verdict and sentencing has been approved by the court.

Homeowner Association Act
IC 55-3207

IC 55-3208
IC 55-3209

IC 55-3210

Homeowner Association Act

If a homeowner does not pay the homeowner assessments as agreed, the homeowner association (HOA) can lien the property for unpaid assessments.

No homeowner's association may add, amend, or enforce any covenant, condition, or restriction in such a way that prohibits the installation of solar panels or solar collectors on rooftop, or prohibit the display of political signs.

In addition a homeowner's association cannot prohibit the display the flag of the United States of America or any official or replica flag of any branch of the United States armed forces. The association may adopt reasonable rules subject to applicable laws or ordinances for display and pole requirements.

Statutory Liens

Statutory Liens

Statutory liens are liens imposed by statute or law. Statutory law is created by legislative action. These are involuntary statutory liens and can be placed on the property without the owner's consent. Several examples include mechanic's liens and property taxes.

Mechanics Lien
IC 45-501

Mechanics Lien

Anyone providing labor or furnishing materials to be used in the construction, alteration or repair in connection with any land or building development or improvement shall have the right to lien the property.

Included are: contractor, subcontractor, architect, builder, licensed surveyor, professional engineer or any person having charge of the construction in part or whole. The lien will attach to the property that the labor or services was delivered.

Claim Of Lien
IC 45-507

The filing of a claim shall be made within 90 days after the completion of the labor or services or furnishing of materials. The claim will identify the demand excluding all credits and offsets together with the name of the owner if known.

A true copy of the claim shall be personally served on the owner or mailed to the owner at his last known address no later than 5 business days following the filing of the claim.

Duration Of Lien
IC 45-510

Once filed, the claim will remain on the property for no longer than 6 months at which time the claim will expire.

Prior to expiration, a judgment can be filed to extend the debt. In Idaho, a recorded judgment becomes a lien on the property of the judgment debtor in the county the property is located, or acquired afterwards, at any time prior to the expiration of the judgment.

Judgment Lien
10 years
IC 45-510
IC 10-1110

The lien resulting from recording a judgment, other than child support, continues for 10 years from the date of the judgment. A judgment may be renewed every 10 years prior to expiration and then recorded. Each time the judgment is renewed, the judgment shall continue for another 10 years.

Priority Of Claim
IC 45-512

It's important to know and understand the order or priority in which claims will be processed.

1. All laborers, other than contractors or subcontractors
2. All materialmen including those furnishing, renting or leasing equipment, materials or fixtures
3. Subcontractors
4. The original contractor
5. All professional engineers and licensed surveyors

The liens of all laborers, other than the original contractor or subcontractor, shall first be paid in full or pro rated if the proceeds are insufficient to pay them in full.

Then, the materialmen including those furnishing, renting or leasing equipment, materials or fixtures other than the original contractor or subcontractor shall be paid in full or pro rated if the proceeds are insufficient to pay them in full.

Out of the remainder, if any, the subcontractors shall be paid in full or pro rated and the remainder, if any, shall be paid pro rated to the original contractor. The last to receive any proceeds will be the professional engineers and licensed surveyors.

Property Tax Lien
IC 63-1005

Property Tax Liens

A tax lien is placed on taxable property at the beginning of each tax year and is removed when the property taxes are paid. If they are not paid, the lien gives the county the right to force the sale of the property in order to collect the unpaid taxes if not redeemed within 3 years of the date of the delinquency.

Notice to locate and serve the owner(s) will be published in the county where the property is situated once a week for 4 consecutive weeks for no more than 2 months or less than 14 days before the time set for a tax deed to be issued to the county for non payment.

IC 63-1001

Interest on a delinquency will be charged at 1% per month calculated from January 1 following the year the tax lien attached, providing however, that the interest shall not be charged on collection costs.

Notice Of Lienholder - Manufactured Home Residency Act

Although technically not a lien, the landlord of a park can notify the lienholder or owner of the home if the resident becomes 60 days in arrears in rent. All costs shall become the responsibility of the legal owner or lienholder of the home.

The key is that the home cannot be *removed* from the lot without a signed written agreement from the landlord showing all moneys due and owing are paid in full. As stated, the landlord has control by not allowing the home to moved.

Additional Liens

Additional liens that can be filed with the Idaho Secretary of State's office include: 1. Financing Statement, 2. Commodity Lien, 3. Farm Products Financing Statement, 4. IRS Lien, 5. Labor Lien, 6. Seed Lien, 7. Utility Lien

More specific information governing Idaho lien filings can be obtained searching:
Uniform Commercial Code - (UCC)
Title 28, Chapter 9
Title 45, Chapters 3 and 18

Questions - Chapter 7

1. When is the dollar amount of the Circuit Breaker program reviewed?

   A   Semi annually.
   B. Annually
   C. At least once every 5 years
   D. January 1

2. At what age may one qualify for the Circuit Breaker program?

   A. 21 or older
   B. 55 or older
   C. 65 or older
   D. 72 or older

3. Occupancy tax applies to what type of property?

   A. Any occupied residential home
   B. Recreational housing for investment
   C. Newly constructed homes not previously occupied
   D. Investment properties

4. Newly constructed homes will receive how many tax statements in the year occupied?

   A. 1 for land value only
   B. 1 for land and dwelling value combined
   C. 2 with previous and current land value
   D. 2: one for land; one for dwelling value

5. Tax statements are sent to owners no later than:

   A. June 20
   B. July 1 (Idaho fiscal year)
   C. 4th Monday in November
   D. December 20

6. When is the first installment of property taxes due?

   A. June 20
   B. July 1 (Idaho fiscal year)
   C. 4th Monday in November
   D. December 20

7. What period of time does one have to bring delinquent taxes current and not be subject to a tax sale?

   A. 1 year
   B. 2 years
   C. 3 years
   D. 4 years

8. A bail bond lien won't be released until?

   A. A trial begins
   B. A verdict has been reached
   C. Upon court ordered sentencing
   D. The guilty party has served their sentence

9. A mechanics lien shall remain on the property no longer than:

   A. 1 month
   B. 6 months
   C. 12 months
   D. 24 months

10. Who has the highest priority in which mechanics liens will be processed?

    A. Original contractor
    B. Sub contractors
    C. Materialmen
    D. Laborers

11. How often are assessors required to make physical property valuations?

    A. At least once a year
    B. At least once every 2 years
    C. At least once every 3 years
    D. At least once every 5 years

12. All assessed property values are based on the value determined on:

    A. January 1
    B. First Monday in June
    C. Fourth Monday in June
    D. December 20

13. Homeowner Exemption is available for?

    A. Primary dwelling
    B. Agricultural purposes
    C. Second home in mountains
    D. Investment properties

14. What is the maximum time, excluding extensions, a HOA can lien a property?

    A. 1 year
    B. 2 years
    C. 3 years
    D. 4 years

15. A mechanic lien must be personally delivered or mailed to the owner within what period of time from making the claim?

    A, 1 business day
    B. 5 business days
    C. 14 business days
    D. 30 business days

Chapter 8

Appraisal and CMA's

Words of Wisdom

"Success is getting what you want; happiness is wanting what you get."

Dale Carnegie

Appraisal

Purpose And Function

Purpose And Function Of Property Appraisal
The Uniform Standard of Professional Appraisal Practice gives a general definition of appraisal as "the act or process of estimating the value". Two important appraisal concepts are incorporated in the terms - appraisal purpose and appraisal function.

The purpose is to estimate value of a property based upon a sale.
The function refers to the reason an appraisal is being made. Most often it is to help a lender decide if a property is suitable as security for a loan.

Both the purpose and function have to match in order to meet the qualifications of various financing programs.

Division Of Occupational And Professional Licenses

Appraiser Licensing
If one desires to become a licensed appraiser in Idaho, they can secure licensing information and application from the Idaho Real Estate Appraiser Board at the Division Of Occupational And Professional Licensing in Boise, Idaho.

License Requirements
IDAPA 24.18.01
Rules 300 & 350

Requirements For Licensure
A licensed residential appraiser can appraise 1 to 4 non complex residential units having a transaction value of less than $1,000,000 and complex. The applicant must document as an appraiser trainee and complete not less than 75 classroom hours of education related to real estate appraisal. Experience includes at least 1,000 hours of supervised experience in no less than 6 months.

A certified residential appraiser can appraise 4 units or less without regard to transaction value or complexity.

Possession of an Associate's degree in a field of study related to business administration, accounting, finance, economics or successful completion of specific college level courses.

Prior to taking the licensure examination, experience must include at least 1,500 hours of appraisal experience in no less than 12 months.

A licensed appraiser must take continuing education of at least 30 classroom hours in courses during the 24 months prior to renewal.

Appraisal License
IC 54-4103

Appraisal Regulations

Any federally related real estate loan requires an appraisal to be done by a properly licensed appraiser. Each state has its own criteria to regulate licensing and appraisers based on federal requirements including Idaho. Remember, if you are not an appraiser and cannot do an appraisal or use the term 'appraiser' unless you are a licensed appraiser.

Exceptions

Although it is illegal to practice appraisal unless one is licensed or certified by the Idaho Real Estate Appraiser Board, the law does offer a couple exceptions.

Price Opinion
IC 54-4105 (2)

1. Idaho Code does allow a licensed real estate salesperson to give an opinion of price for the purpose of securing a prospective listing or sale.

Broker Price Opinion (BPO)
IC 54-4105 (3)

2. In addition, the law shall not prohibit an active licensed real estate broker or associate broker to render a price opinion and may charge a fee. However, the broker price opinion shall be in writing and contain:

   - A statement of the intended purpose of the price opinion
   - A brief description of the property
   - Reasoning for conclusion including market data
   - Assumptions or limiting conditions
   - Disclosure of any contemplated interest of the broker
   - Name and signature of the broker
   - Disclaimer that opinion not intended to meet appraisal practice
   - Disclaimer that opinion is not intended to be an appraisal

A permitted broker price opinion may not be used as an appraisal, or in lieu of an appraisal, in a federally related transaction.

Basic Appraisal Concepts

Applying Basic Concepts Of Appraisal

Even though a real estate agent cannot perform an appraisal without an appraisal license, the agent can learn about and apply the same basic principles and concepts appraisers use in creating their own broker price opinion (BPO).

Some of the elements of value include: utility, scarcity, demand with purchasing power and transferability. In addition, knowledge and awareness of physical forces, economic forces, social forces, and political forces need to be carefully evaluated.

Perhaps one of the more important aspects of a market analysis revolves around the economic principle of value.

Does the property conform with the surrounding area? Does the property contribute to similar types of properties? Is the property being valued or being evaluated to include physical possible uses? What are the legally permissible uses allowed? In short, what is the highest and best use for the property being valued?

Once all the various elements of value are considered, one needs to use the cost approach, income approach, or market approach to determine which method will provide the most accurate value for the appropriate market place.

Cost Approach

Cost Approach

The cost approach is often used with new construction or perhaps unique properties in which there are no comparable properties available.

The cost approach is best used with new construction or recently constructed properties as a check and balance with the market approach. The cost approach is based on the cost to construct, minus depreciation, plus the value of the land to arrive at a final value. One of the difficulties with using cost approach, is that the cost can end up either higher or lower than what the market might bear.

However, sometimes the cost approach might be the only way a property can be valued, especially if the property is unique or comparable properties cannot be found to compare with the subject property. Examples are churches, hospitals or other types of unique manufacturing or applications that have few, if any, comparable properties. Another challenge revolves on how to apply accurate depreciation percentages, especially when the subject property is older.

Marshall & Swift Residential Cost Handbook

If the cost approach is used, an excellent resource is the *Marshall & Swift Residential Cost Handbook*. This handbook is updated quarterly and re-evaluated annually for all areas in the United States. It has incredible amounts of information and is used by most fee appraisers. In addition, the methods of valuation are accepted by many government backed programs including Fannie Mae, Freddie Mac, FHA, and VA.

The handbook can also offer great information to compare the component costs between the 6 different types of quality categories. Also, there is an extensive section about depreciation and how to make proper calculations.

Income Approach

Income Approach

The income approach is used to create value based on income and expenses. An in-depth analysis can however, require extensive knowledge to apply the appropriate formulas to arrive at an accurate value.

Basic information regarding the rental operation includes: the number of units, type of leases or rental agreements, what is included (utilities, etc) with the rent, condition of the property, tenant turnover, and other ancillary information.

Financial Information

In addition, necessary financial information to do an analysis should include at least 3 years or more of documentation including:

- Gross income - vacancy factor
- Detailed breakdown of operating expenses
- Capital expenditures
- Tax returns for subject property

Two types of analysis can be performed. One is known as the Gross Rent Multiplier (GRM) and the other is known as Capitalization Rate (Cap Rate).

GRM	The GRM is computed by dividing the sales price by the annual gross rent resulting in a number known as a multiplier in which one can compute a rough estimate of value.
Cap Rate	The Cap Rate analysis is far more accurate with complete accurate and up to date information. It is a method of providing a rate of return or yield on a real estate investment property based on the expected income the property will generate.
'IRV' Formula	The calculation is quick and easy to identify income, rate (return), and value and is often referred to as the 'IRV' formula based on annual data.

$$\text{Income} = \text{Rate x Value}$$
$$\text{Rate} = \text{Income} \div \text{Value}$$
$$\text{Value} = \text{Income} \div \text{Rate}$$

Real estate agents should really take the time to fully understand all that goes into creating a good investment property analysis before pursuing income properties.

Market Approach	**Market Approach** The market approach is the primary method used by appraisers to determine value for residential properties. The process involves getting characteristics and features about the subject property and then making the appropriate adjustments with the comparable sold properties that best meet the characteristics of subject property.
Non-Disclosure	Since Idaho is a 'non disclosure' state, appraisers may have a difficult time securing current data for sold properties. But if they are affiliate members of a multiple listing service (MLS), they will be able to obtain current comparable property data from the MLS.
	Appraisers try use comparable properties that have recently sold within the last 90 days to attempt to solidify accuracy due to a constantly changing marketplace.
	Location is an important factor, especially if similar properties are located along some busy roadways verses those that are located deep inside a platted subdivision.
	However no two properties are exactly alike so the appraiser must make the appropriate adjustments for the differences in construction quality, design, and other amenities.
	Financing concessions and/or requirements can also be a factor with selecting appropriate comparable properties to match the subject property, especially if there are loan programs that assist in the acquisition of property.
URAR Form	The appraisal form that appraisers will use is a universal form accepted by federally related lenders. The multi page appraisal form is known as the URAR (Uniform Residential Appraisal Report) Fannie Mae Form 1004 or Freddie Mac Form 70. The appraisal form is very comprehensive and includes:

- Neighborhood characteristics
- Housing trends

- Present land use
- Zoning compliance
- Utilities - water, sewer, elec, gas, streets, etc.
- FEMA Special Flood Hazard Area
- Exterior and interior condition
- Needed repairs, deterioration, deficiencies
- Value adjustments (including square footage)
- Source and dates of comparable sales

The appraiser must also adhere to the instructions of their client, which is usually a lender, to address specific loan program requirements including repair and inspection requirements. Particular attention must address property deficiencies that rise above the level of cosmetic defects, minor defects or normal wear and tear that could affect the safety of the occupants.

As an example, FHA standards require the appraiser to address inadequate access/egress from the bedrooms to the exterior of the home. Or, if a leaking or worn out roof contains 3 or more layers of shingles, all existing shingles must be removed before re-roofing.

An accurate valuation of property available for sale is the primary and first step to a successful real estate transaction. A properly priced property is already "half sold"; all that is needed is a ready, willing, and able buyer together with adequate financing to complete and close the sale.

If real estate agents become familiar and knowledgeable with appraiser requirements to value a property and the forms they use, then agents will be better equipped to do their own valuations with greater accuracy.

Competitive Market Analysis

Purpose Of CMA

The heart of the whole listing process starts with a competitive market analysis or sometimes referred to as a comparative market analysis. This analysis is known as a CMA. The CMA is designed to assist the seller in establishing a price in which the property will meet the sellers needs to sell and create demand for a ready, willing, and able buyer.

There are many formats to do a CMA from Multiple Listing Service forms to in-house brokerage company forms. Whatever format is used, be sure you can verify your information.

Although the cost or income approach could be used, the market approach is utilized most of the time for valuing residential real estate by real estate agents.

Broker Price Opinion
IC 54-2038 (3)

Broker Price Opinion
Idaho code allows an active real estate salesperson or broker to give an opinion of value (BPO) for the purpose of securing a listing or sale, but *does not allow* an associate broker or salesperson to charge for such service.

Only an actively licensed broker or associate broker can render a price opinion (BPO) and charge for the service. It is not uncommon for banks to request price opinions from real estate licensees and pay a fee without knowing Idaho law.

Again, only brokers or associate brokers can receive a fee. In addition, if an associate broker renders a BPO and receives a fee, the fee must be turned over to the designated broker. The code clearly states 'an associate broker who prepares and renders a price opinion shall notify the designated broker and the associate broker may not accept any fee except through the designated broker'.

Any licensee who renders a price opinion that does not comply with the requirements surrounding BPO's is subject to discipline for dishonest and dishonorable dealing by the Idaho Real Estate Commission.

Guideline 20

Guideline 20 offers some excellent section, Frequently Asked Questions, that address the 'what ifs' The better the understanding of BPO's the less risk of a licensee getting in trouble. The Idaho Real Estate Appraiser Board and the Idaho Real Estate Commission are more interested in obtaining compliance with the laws pertaining to BPO's than initiating discipline for violations.

CMA Characteristics

CMA Characteristics

When constructing a CMA, the first task is to get all the characteristics of the subject property (the property to be sold) for comparison with comparable properties that are either:

1. On the market;
2. Recently sold, or, as a last option;
3. Were on the market but expired.

The characteristics of the subject property that should be considered but not limited to, include:

- Type and age of neighborhood - single, multiple family
- Zoning and allowed uses - conforming
- Location of neighborhood - established, new, older, etc.
- Quality of neighborhood - well maintained, deteriorating
- Lot size - square footage, dimensions
- Age of home - new, 1-5 yrs, 6-10 yrs, 10-20, older, etc.
- Style of home - single story, multiple story, etc
- Habitable square footage
- Number of bedrooms
- Number of baths
- Condition and quality of construction - inside
- Condition and quality of construction - exterior
- Parking - size of garage, extra parking for RV's
- Landscaping - quality and quantity
- Amenities - view, extras, uniqueness, floor plan

Securing Comps

Securing Comparables

Once the subject property characteristics are obtained you will now find comparable properties that best match the characteristics of the subject property (the property to be sold). If an agent is a member of a Multiple Listing Service (MLS) the MLS will probably be the best resource available.

Internet Resources

The internet is another good resource but may have limitations. Generally speaking, you will only find those properties that are currently on the market and available for sale. 'Solds' are not easy to find on the internet. But with some deep searching you may even be able to find 'solds' through specialty sites.

To create accuracy and true comparisons, it's suggested you mirror what appraisers do and come up with a minimum of 3 comparable properties to work with. The goal is to find other properties that best match the subject property and then make appropriate adjustments to get as close as possible, for an accurate match.

Making Adjustments

Making Adjustments

Perhaps the most difficult challenge in constructing a CMA is making dollar adjustments where there are significant differences between the subject property and the comparable properties.

Market Trends

You really need to know and understand the current market trends and personal needs and desires of the buyer in the local market. For example, an outdoor in-ground pool may cost a lot of money but the local market may not support the cost equated with the demand. Thus, there may be no adjustment, or in some cases, there may even be a deduction for a pool.

Construction Quality

The quality of construction and condition of the property is another challenge. Let's say you find 3 comps that all match the subject. However, one of the comps has been 'trashed' but is the same floor plan, age, size, etc. Again, you must make a judgment call and decide what the dollar amount of adjustment will be made to the home that has been 'trashed' to make it equal to the subject home.

Adjustments Made To Comparable Home

Note, the adjustment is made to the comparable home; not the subject home. What we are trying to do, is make a like kind and similar comparable home mimic the subject home as close as possible with the least amount of adjustments.

Now comes the hard part; assigning a differential dollar value to the portion of the comparable that is substantially different from the subject property.

For example, you have found a comparable that virtually matches the subject property. However, the subject property has a 3 car garage and the comparable has a 2 car garage. The question is - how much adjustment will be made for the difference between a 3 car garage and a 2 car garage. This is where 'judgment' calls are made which could lead to questionable and subjective opinions.

Minimizing Variables

Minimizing Variables

To minimize opinion variables, agents can use different resources for various component values.

- Market trends based on supply and demand
- Actual cost to construct or reproduce
- Actual cost minus depreciation
- Builders and remodel contractors
- *Marshall & Swift Residential Cost Handbook*
- *Marshall & Swift Remodel Cost Handbook*
- Awareness of International Residential Code

Remember, most properties require financing of some sort which ultimately requires an appraisal. The closer real estate licensees can 'mirror' an appraiser, the closer the properties will approximate values utilized to meet various financing programs.

Use 3 Best Comps

Narrowing Down To The Best 3 Comparables

Generally speaking, the goal is to have 3 comparables, including adjusted differences, with the least amount of adjustments that will best equal the characteristics of the subject property.

Each of the three best comparables will arrive at a price. But there will be differences between each of the 3 comparables. Rather than arriving at a specific price for the subject property, a price range should be considered with maybe a $\pm$ 5% variable. Now the seller can choose somewhere from low to high.

Chances are, they will choose a higher price to leave room for negotiation. Bear in mind starting high could eliminate some potential buyers from making an offer because the property is out of their price range.

It's Sellers Decision

Much of the seller's decision will be based on their personal motivation. If they need to sell, they may start in the middle or even low. If they only 'want' to sell, chances are they might start with a higher price than the market might bear.

Agents Have Ability To Accept Or Reject.

Remember, you have the final say as to whether you want the listing or not. Will it sell within the listing period? How much time and effort will be required to service the listing? If it is listed 'high' will others sell against you? What will a 'over valued' listing do to your image and reputation? It's critical to know the motivation and a time frame the seller expects for performance.

Servicing Listing
IC 54-2053 (2)

Servicing The Listing

Once the listing is secured, the marketing plan springs into action.
When advertising, special attention needs to be made and rechecked to make sure the broker's licensed business name is included with any and all advertising or promotion.

IC 54-2053 (4)

Advertising a listed property with embellished or overstated information, including square footage, could be considered misleading.

Measuring Property

Nationwide Standard - ANSI

ANSI Z765

One area of practicing real estate that can be confusing is the proper way to measure single family houses. The American National Standards Institute (ANSI) developed a nationwide standard in 1996 with latest amendment in 2021.

The standard has been accepted by the National Association of Home Builders, The National Association of REALTORS®, Fannie Mae, Freddie Mac, and many other entities that deal with financing and appraisal methods.

ANSI Highlights

Highlights Of ANSI Z765-2021

Below are condensed highlights of how to properly measure homes with universal acceptance. Often appraisers use the MLS figures when they prepare their comparables so it's very important that everyone measure the same way

Measurement

- *Measuring*
  - Exterior dimensions only
  - Reported to nearest inch or tenth of a foot
  - Total measurement to the nearest whole square foot

Floor Openings

- *Openings to floor below*
  - Area of both stair treads and landings is included from which stairs descend
  - Staircases to unfinished basement included as 'finished'
  - Openings not supported by staircases are not included

Ceiling Height

- *Ceiling height requirements*
  - Must have a ceiling height of at least 7 feet
  - Under beams or other obstructions can be 6' 4"
  - Sloped ceilings
    At least ½ of finished footage must have vertical height of at least 7 feet
  - No portion can have height of less than 5 feet to be included as 'finished'

Garages And Unfinished Areas

- *Garages, unfinished, and protrusions*
  - No portion can be included as finished square footage
  - Chimneys, windows and other areas that protrude beyond exterior are not included if they do not have a floor on the same level
  - Finished areas above a garage are included only if connected to house by hallway

Converting Inches To Nearest 1/10ᵗʰ Of A Foot

Converting inches to 10^{ths} of a foot
1" = .0833
2" = .1667
3" = .25
4" = .3333
5" = .4167
6" = .5

$$7" = .5833$$
$$8" = .6667$$
$$9" = .75$$
$$10" = .8333$$
$$11" = .9167$$
$$12" = 1$$

Exterior Measurement

Measuring Exterior

Either get a surveyors tape (measures in 10th's or a regular tape that measures in 12ths) or, make the appropriate conversion.

Diagram the home on graph paper (to make it neater or easier to track). Line out squares to equal 1 foot. Then, measure and record your measurements for each length.

Once you have all the measurements make sure the home is 'square' with the parallel sides equaling each other. Once the outside dimensions are identified, break up the home into square and rectangular sections. Add up the square footage of each section. Then, total the sections to get the total square footage for the home.

Remember, measurements are based on 10th's. Most people do not know this and thus, inaccurate square footage is calculated. For example, 30' 6" is actually 30.5'; 42' 8" is actually 42.75'. The error is small but none the less an error. By the way, look at a plat map and you will see all linear measurements are in feet, tenths, and even hundredths of a foot. Interesting huh?

Most homes are not just squares and rectangles. They are made up with different angles. The math applications are:

Rectangles
   length x width

Triangles
   ½ the base x height

Trapezoid   (bay windows)
   Sum of the parallel sides ÷ in half x height

Passing along inaccurate or incorrect calculations of square footage based on 3rd party representation could lead to being charged with misrepresentation of a material fact.

A good way to avoid errors is to physically measure the home twice to make sure the total square footage equals each other with both measurements. It's not unusual to 'back in' values based on square footage or just get a 'feeling' of what the value would be based on square footage. It's also not unusual to see advertising relating cost per square foot.

Misleading Information
IC 54-2053 (4)

Remember, Idaho Code could come into play if advertised property is misleading or if such information will deceive the persons whom it is intended to influence which could include inaccurate square footage or cost per square foot information.

Issues That Can Lead To Errors

If agents don't physically measure either the subject home or comparables, errors can occur due to using inaccurate information. Examples include using assessor square footage, house plans, previous MLS information, owners information, and possible mis-measuring.

Whatever number the listing agent reports to MLS, the appraiser will eventually calculate the square footage. And, too many times the numbers do not agree. Let's just say that number is off by 200 sq.ft. and is taken from assessor data. When that agent determined a listing price for that home, they came up with an average price-per-square-foot for other homes that have sold in the same neighborhood. They take that average and multiply it by (what they decide to use for) the square footage of the home they are pricing. If a 200 sq.ft. error is priced at $150.00 per-square-foot, that equals a $30,000 mistake.

The errors are often much worse. That simple formula is used everywhere and works very well when you always have accurate square footage data. However, without national standards for measuring square footage, the MLS and square footage data will remain questionable.

If their square footage data is wrong, their price-per-square-foot average is wrong. Then you get a domino effect; changing one wrong number into two, three, and so on; until the final number they create is a long way from the actual current value.

Example: House "A" is listed at $359,900. The average price-per-square-foot of the last five sales in the neighborhood is $179.95. The 1st agent measured the house and found out it had 2,340 square feet. They placed the value at $421,000. The 2nd agent uses the square footage total listed in tax records of 2,112 square feet. The value they came up with was $380,000 making a *difference of $41,000*. Is that enough difference to matter? Who knows.

BEFORE ANSWERING QUESTIONS – Can You Define or Explain:

Cost approach	Purpose and function of an appraisal
Marshall & Swift Handbook	Income approach
Difference between market analysis and appraisal	CMA
Requirements for Broker's Price Opinion	Market approach
Application of basic concepts of appraisal	Who can accept fee for BPO
American National Standards Institute	How to calculate square footage
Capitalization Rate	Gross Rent Multiplier
'IRV' formula	Uniform Residential Appraisal Report

Questions Chapter 8

1. The purpose of a market analysis and giving an opinion of price is to:

   A. Secure prospective listing or sale
   B. Provide a price for a lender
   C. Verify price for financing
   D. Appraise property for the seller

2. Who can provide a price opinion for a fee?

   A. Any active real estate licensee
   B. Active or inactive real estate broker
   C. An active real estate salesperson
   D. An active broker or associate broker

3. A written price opinion for a fee must identify?

   A. Name and signature of salesperson issuing the opinion
   B. Purpose is to satisfy lender financing requirements
   C. Intended purpose
   D. Opinion does not have any limiting conditions or assumptions

4. The 'cost approach' is based on:

   A. Total cost to build or reconstruct
   B. Total cost plus land to build
   C. Cost minus depreciation
   D. Cost less depreciation plus land

5. The cost approach will provide the most accurate value when applied to:

   A. Older properties
   B. New construction
   C. Properties with high depreciation
   D. Historical renovated properties

6. The income approach is best used with:

   A. Residential properties
   B. Recreational 2nd homes
   C. Apartment complexes
   D. New home construction

7. How many hours of experience are required to become a licensed residential appraiser?

   A. 90
   B. 150
   C. 1,000
   D. 2,000

8. How many classroom hours are required to become a licensed residential appraiser?

   A. 75
   B. 100
   C. 1,000
   D. 2,000

9. Where can information be obtained to become a real estate appraiser?

   A. Idaho Real Estate Commission
   B. Bureau of Occupational Licensing
   C. Department of Commerce
   D. Secretary of State

10. What type of comparable properties are generally used as the basis of a CMA?

    A. On market
    B. Recently sold
    C. Expired listings
    D. For sale by owner properties

11. Based on ANSI Z765-2003, what is the minimum ceiling height excluding beams?

    A. 5'
    B. 6'
    C. 7'
    D. 8'

12. Based on ANSI Z765-2003, square footage is not calculated within any area that is less than:

    A. 5'
    B. 6'
    C. 7'
    D. 8'

13. What part of a home is included in calculating square footage?

    A. Stairways
    B. Garage
    C. Covered porch
    D. Unfinished basement

14. The use of the ANSI standard for various governmental agencies for measuring square footage is:

    A. Required
    B. Mandated
    C. Accepted
    D. Necessary

15. A broker price opinion can be rendered by:

    A. Sales associate
    B. Associate broker
    C. Designated broker
    D. Associate broker and/or designated broker

16. What is the appraisal form called that is accepted by Fannie Mae and Freddy Mac?

    A. Broker Price Opinion
    B. Competitive Market Analysis
    C. Certified Residential Appraisal Form
    D. Uniform Residential Appraisal Report

Real Estate Finance

Real Estate Finance

The majority of real estate purchases require financing of some sort for buyers who are unable or unwilling to pay cash for property. Because so many financing changes have taken place in recent years, a good overview into realm of real estate finance should be explained.

Overview
In the late 1980s the savings and loan industry ended up in a crisis and near insolvency and ended costing the U. S. taxpayers $150 billion. As a result, risk based capital standards were imposed with the passing of FIRREA (Financial Institutions Reform, Recovery, and Enforcement Act) in 1989.

1990s Market

In the 1990s the secondary market exploded with market giants Fannie Mae and Freddie Mac. Their charters were amended to include "....to have an affirmative obligation to facilitate the financing of affordable housing for low and moderate income families ....". The housing goals set by HUD ended up increasing from 30% of the total number of dwellings financed to over 55% in 2007.

2,000s Market

The 2000s brought additional relaxation of lending practices in order to help HUD and high risk loans were again counted toward meeting the housing goals of HUD in 2004. The subprime mortgage crisis began. The market also shifted away from regulated Government-Sponsored Enterprises (GSE) to Mortgage Backed Securities (MBS) issued by unregulated private label securitization conduits, typically operated by investment banks.

Shift Toward Deregulation

This shift from traditional, amortizing, fixed rate mortgages to nontraditional, structurally riskier, non-amortizing, adjustable-rate mortgages initiated a sharp deterioration in mortgage underwriting standards. With the lack of regulation, the market ended up with an oversupply of underpriced housing financing. Consequently, a number of borrowers, often with poor credit, were unable to pay their mortgage; especially those with adjustable rate mortgages.

Economy Declining

With the reduced standards, it was estimated that half of the U.S. home mortgage loans were of substandard quality and ended up with massive defaults. As foreclosures mounted to an already high housing inventory, housing prices declined which led to growing losses of the GSE's that backed the majority of U.S. mortgages. The U.S. Treasury Department and the Federal Reserve tried to shore up confidence in Fannie Mae and Freddie Mac by granting low interest loans and removing the prohibition on the Treasury Department to purchase GSE stock.

Recovery

Unfortunately "too little, too late" and Fannie Mae and Freddy Mac stock lost over 90% of its value in less than a year. In late 2008, Fannie Mae and Freddie Mac ended up being placed into conservatorship of the Federal Housing Finance Agency. This move ended up with the U.S. Treasury funding $187.4 billion of taxpayer funds to keep Fannie Mae and Freddie Mac afloat. With the economy rebounding, the U.S. Treasury was in the black until late 2019 but the Covid 19 pandemic has now added additional challenges for the U.S. Treasury.

Mortgage Reform Act

Regulations

As a result of the 'Great Recession', regulations surrounding the housing market have been strengthened with those portions dealing with housing in the Dodd-Frank Act signed into law in 2010. Title XIV of the Mortgage Reform and Anti-Predatory Lending Act addresses many of the issues that needed to be reviewed and overhauled, including subtitles such as:

A. Residential mortgage loan organization standards
B. Minimum standards for mortgages
C. High cost mortgages
D. Office of housing counseling
E. Mortgage servicing
F. Appraisal activities
G. Mortgage resolution and modification
H. Miscellaneous provisions

Regulatory agencies that play important roles in adhering to the Dodd-Frank Act lending environment include:

- Financial Stability Oversight Council
- Office of Comptroller of the Currency
- Federal Reserve System
- Federal Deposit Insurance Corporation
- National Credit Union Administration
- Federal Financial Institutions Examination Council
- Federal Housing Finance Agency
- Consumer Financial Protection Bureau

New standards of a 'Qualified Mortgage' Loan taken from the 804 page description of the Consumer Financial Protection Bureau include:

- No high fees - (generally less than 3% closing and related costs)
- Borrower's income and assets are verified
- Total monthly debt payments less than 43% of monthly gross income
- A maturity of no longer than 30 years

- Generally no prepayment penalties
- No balloon payments -(negative, zero, partial amortized loans are history)
- No artificially low 'teaser' interest rates in early periods

Because the Consumer Financial Protection Bureau considers an ARM (adjustable rate mortgage) risky, ARM's may go away unless the interest rate is fixed for a period of 5 years or longer.

Loan Programs

There are many different types of loan programs the buyer can choose from and not all lenders offer all programs. So, it's important the buyer realize that they may have to seek more than one lender to find the loan program that best fits the buyer's needs.

Also, loan program terms and requirements can change from time to time so it's important that the borrower seek up to date information.

Conventional Loans

Conventional
Conventional loans are not backed by the government and may or may not be conforming loans. However, conventional programs can allow for financing second homes or income residential properties. Many other loan programs (government sponsored) are restricted to owner occupied single family dwellings.

The Federal Housing Finance Agency (FHFA) has set conforming loan limits for mortgages acquired by Fannie Mae and Freddie Mac for single family dwellings to be $510,400 for 2020. A new ceiling limit for single family dwellings in most high cost areas (like Sun Valley) will be $625,500 but loan limits may be higher in specific locations.

A minimum of 5% down payment on a single family house or at least 20% on 2-4 family house is required. However, there are several special programs that could offer as low as 3% down payment.

Wait periods after a bankruptcy may require 2-4 years or more to qualify. With a minimum of 20% down, mortgage insurance is generally waived.

Seller contributions toward closing costs can range from 3% to 9% depending on buyer down payment.

FHA Insured Loans

FHA Insured Loans
The FHA insured loan program is government insured and will allow as little as 3.5% down to qualify. Loan rules state the borrower must use the residence as the primary occupant or as the 'principal' residence. Financing is available for up to and including 4 units as long as the owner occupies one of the units as his principal residence.

A credit score below 580 does not disqualify the applicant and wait periods after a bankruptcy can range from 1-3 years but may require a 10% down payment.

Mortgage insurance is required upfront as well as each month as part of the regular loan for the life of the loan.

The seller may contribute up to 6% of the sales price toward closing costs, prepaid expenses, discount points, and other closing costs.

VA Guaranteed Loans

VA Guaranteed Loans

VA-guaranteed loans are available to veterans as owner occupied residences. Eligibility includes good credit score, sufficient income, a valid Certificate of Eligibility (COE) and meet certain service requirements. If not active duty at the time of application, a DD Form 214 copy must show the character of the service and the narrative reason for separation.

VA-guaranteed loans are made by banks, savings and loan associations and mortgage companies and the program allows for 100% financing. However, it must be known that all banks may not offer VA financing.

A VA funding fee of 0 to 3.6% of the loan is also required but may also be financed thus allowing the veteran to borrow up to 103.6%! The funding fee is on a sliding scale; the lower the down payment, the higher the funding fee.

A seller may contribute up to 4% of the sales price plus reasonable and customary loan costs for VA loans. Total contributions may exceed the 4% because standard costs do not count toward the total.

USDA Rural Housing

Rural Housing Loans   (Section 502 loans)

A little known loan program is offered by the United States Department of Agriculture and known as 'rural housing loans' or 'USDA loans'.

Many small towns meet the 'rural' requirements of the agency, as do suburbs and exurbs of most major U. S. cities. No down payment is required and 100% financing is available. Homeowner counseling is not required and the loans can be used by first-time and repeat buyers alike for primary residences.

The program does require a 1.00% upfront mortgage insurance fee to be paid at closing and a small annual fee based on the remaining principal balance. However the upfront mortgage insurance needn't come out-of-pocket. It's an amount that is added to the loan balance.

USDA mortgage insurance rates are lower than FHA or conventional mortgages and USDA interest rates are also often lower. 15-year and 30-year fixed mortgages are available.

The seller may contribute up to 6% of the sales price toward the buyer's reasonable closing costs.

Private Money

**IDAPA 12.01.10
Rule 101**

Private Money

Typically unregulated by state or federal laws, there may still be some restrictions that need to be observed. In Idaho, one cannot engage in mortgage brokering, lending, modification, origination, contract loan processing or underwriting until one has received license approval through the Nationwide Mortgage Licensing System (NMLS).

Real estate loans made with private money, often referred to as 'hard money' loans, are typically issued by private investors or companies. A private lender could also be the seller or owner of the property being financed and is known as 'seller financing'.

The collateral is the property itself, whether real or personal, and usually requires substantial equity to help offset the risk. If the subject property does not have enough equity to secure a loan, additional properties may be used as additional collateral to provide the equity necessary to make a loan.

Because the loans are higher risk, they are usually for shorter periods of time and come with higher interest rates.

Most private money or 'hard money' loans are used in the commercial market where circumstances make it difficult to obtain conventional financing. These type loans are also used for as short term residential construction loans or 'bridge' loans to finance construction or home improvement with flexibility that traditional loans cannot provide.

**Idaho Real Estate
Loan Programs**

Idaho Real Estate Loan Programs

In addition to the general loan programs available nationwide, there are some additional loan programs available for Idaho properties.

**IHFA - Idaho
Housing And
Finance
Association**

Idaho Housing and Finance Association
Idaho Housing is a self-supporting corporation and does not use any state-appropriated funds for its operations.
It forms partnerships with banking and lending institutions throughout the state and functions as an agent for HUD.

Idaho has a great program offered only to residents of Idaho who must occupy the financed property as their primary residence within 14 days after closing.

Eligibility is limited to household income up to $90,000 in all counties (except Blaine County which is $110,000). The borrower must have acceptable credit and employment history.

**First Time Home
Buyer Savings
Account**
IC 63-3022V

First Time Home Buyer Savings Account
The purpose of this program is to pay eligible home costs of the account holder in connection with a qualified home purchase.

This Idaho state sponsored program allows a first time home buyer residing in Idaho to deposit up to $15,000 per year for individual or $30,000 for a married couple into a first time home buyer savings account. The account has a $100,000 life time cap.

Annual contributions and interest earned with this account may be deducted from the taxable income of the account holder. However, any withdrawals from the account for purposes other than eligible home costs shall be subject to taxes otherwise due.

Section 184 - Indian Housing Loan Guarantee

Indian Housing Loan Guarantee (Section 184)
Although Section 184 is a federal program, it is offered in 14 states in the U.S. Idaho is one of the approved states and all counties within the state are available to use the program.

Section 184 program offers Native American borrowers loans for new construction, rehabilitation, purchase of an existing home, or refinance. Because of the unique status of Indian lands being held in Trust, Native American home ownership has historically been underserved.

Section 184 home loans are guaranteed 100% by the Office of Loan Guarantee within HUD's Office of Native American Programs.

A low down payment of 2.25% on loans over $50,000 and only 1.25% under $50,000 make the program attractive with interest rates based on market rates and not the applicants credit scores.

A one time 1% up front guarantee is paid at closing and can be financed into the loan. There is no monthly mortgage insurance.

Security Instruments

There are two types of security instruments used to secure the property; a mortgage and a deed of trust.

Mortgage

Satisfaction Of Mortgage
IC 45-915

Mortgage
A mortgage can be used as a security instrument for any real property in Idaho. Once a mortgage has been satisfied (payed off) the holder must provide the purchaser (owner) a certificate of the discharge or 'satisfaction of mortgage' for recording.

Default

However, if the borrower defaults on the terms of the mortgage, the holder of the mortgage can file for foreclosure.

'Sheriff's Sale'

Mortgages must be foreclosed by judicial action and the court will direct the sale to be advertised. A notice of the 'sheriff's sale' must be published for 3 consecutive weeks in the county in which the property is located.

Auction
IC 11-304

All sales of property under execution must be made by auction, to the highest bidder between the hours of 9 a.m. and 5 p.m. on a normal county business day. After sufficient property has been sold to satisfy the execution, no more can be sold. When the sale is of real property, consisting of several known lots or parcels, they must be sold separately, or when a portion of such real property is claimed by a third person, and he requires it to be sold separately, such portion must be thus sold.

Certificate Of Sale
IC 11-310

The highest bidder will receive a Certificate of Sale and not a deed due to a statutory redemption period. When subject to redemption, it must be so stated. And when the judgment, under which the sale has been made, is made payable in a specified kind of money or currency, the certificate must also show the kind of money or currency in which such redemption may be made, which must be the same as that specified in the judgement. A duplicate of such certificate must be filed for record by the officer in the office of the recorder of the county.

Redemption
IC 11-402

Although anyone can bid at the sale, the lender will generally be the only bidder to protect their interest. Why? Because the holder of the Certificate of Sale cannot sell or market the property during the holding redemption period.

The statutory redemption period for a mortgage is:

- 1 year if the property is more than 20 acres;

- 6 months if the property is 20 acres or less or if the debtor releases their right of redemption.

If the property is redeemed, the original borrower must pay the *total* amount owing prior to the expiration of the redemption period. Upon redemption by the debtor, the person to whom the payment is made must execute and deliver to him a Certificate of Redemption, acknowledged and proved before an officer authorized to take acknowledgments of conveyances of real property.

Such certificate must be filed and recorded in the office of the recorder of the county in which the property is situated.

Sheriff's Deed

If the redemption has not been made, the successful bidder requests and receives a Sheriff's Deed from the sheriff conducting the sale that is then recorded in the county records where the property is located. The recording of the Sheriff's Deed concludes the foreclosure process unless additional matters are pending in the district court pertaining to the fixing any deficiency judgment against the borrowers.

Deed Of Trust

Deed Of Trust (aka Trust Deed)
The security instrument of choice by virtually all lenders will be a Deed of Trust. Why? There is no period of redemption and the foreclosure window is relatively short based on a nonjudicial foreclosure sale process.

Deed Of Trust Limitations
IC 45-1502 (5)

However, there are some restrictions to the use of a deed of trust and the use of a deed of trust shall be limited to:

- Any real property located within an incorporated city or village at the time of transfer.

- Any property not exceeding 80 acres, regardless of its location, provided that such real property is not principally used for the agricultural production of crops, livestock, dairy or aquatic goods.

- Any real property not exceeding 40 acres regardless of its use or location.

Reconveyance IC 45-1514	When a deed of trust has been paid off, a reconveyance will be issued which should be recorded to remove the lien from the public records.
Foreclosure IC 45-1505 (3)	However, if a deed of trust ends up in foreclosure, there are statutory laws that regulate the process as a nonjudicial foreclosure. The trustee must file a notice of default with the names of the beneficiaries and the book and page where the deed of trust is recorded. Notice will be sent registered or certified mail to: • Grantor (owner) or any person requesting notice • Any successor in interest to the grantor on record • Any person having a lien or interest subsequent
Notice Of Sale IC 45-1506 (2)	The notice of sale will identify the date, time, and place of sale in the county where the property is located.
IC 45-1506 (6)	The notice of sale must be published in a newspaper in each of the counties in which the property is situated (in case the property overlaps between 2 different counties) for 4 successive weeks with the last publication to be at least 30 days before the sale.
120 Days For Sale IC 45-1506 (2)	Once 'notice of sale' has been recorded the sale will take place in not less than 120 days from the date of notice. However, the sale can be postponed by the trustee up to 30 days at the time of the sale and postponed over and over; thus, delaying the actual sale.
115 Days To Cure IC 45-1506 (12)	Although there is no redemption period for a nonjudicial foreclosure in Idaho, the debtor can 'reinstate' themselves by bringing the past due payments current within 115 days from when the initial notice of default was recorded. The loan will now be restored to its original terms and conditions and the foreclosure is stopped. If, by chance, the debtor comes to the table between 115 and 120 days, the total balance of the loan must be paid to restore his position. If the real property goes to sale, anyone can bid at the auction except the officer holding the sale and his deputy. The high bidder will be issued a 'trustees deed' upon conclusion of the sale without covenant or warranty.
Proceeds IC 45-1507	Proceeds of the trustee's sale shall apply toward expenses of the sale, obligation secured by the trust deed, to any persons having recorded liens subsequent to the interest of the trustee and surplus, if any, to the grantor of the trust deed.

Financing Changes

Disclosure Requirements	Because mortgage fraud scandals have occurred over the past few years, two important disclosure changes regulating mortgage lenders became effective in October, 2015. The changes, known as TILA-RESPA disclosure rules, are meant to simplify and clarify mortgage disclosures previously established.
TRID Rule	TILA-RESPA Integrated Disclosure (TRID) Rule To help improve consumer understanding and promote industry compliance with initial and final disclosures, the Good Faith Estimate (GFE) and initial Truth-in-Lending Disclosure was replaced with a three page loan estimate. The HUD-1 Settlement Statement is replaced with a five page Closing Disclosure.

The forms must be used for most closed-end federally regulated consumer mortgages that are secured by a one to four unit dwelling attached to real property.

However, the rules do not apply to home-equity lines of credit, reverse mortgage loans, mortgage loans secured by a mobile home or by a dwelling not attached to real property, such as land, or creditors who write 5 or fewer mortgages a year.

Loan Estimate

Loan Estimate

A new Loan Estimate form combines the Good Faith Estimate and initial Truth-in-Lending statement into one form.

Your Home Loan Toolkit

In addition, Consumer Financial Protection Bureau (CFPB) requires lenders and brokers to provide borrowers with an easy-to-read booklet titled *Your Home Loan Toolkit* that is designed to answer key questions and includes interactive worksheets and checklists.

3 Business Days To Provide Loan Estimate

The Loan Estimate and *Your Home Loan Toolkit* is to be provided to the buyer within three business days of applying for a mortgage loan. Since the Loan Estimate is uniform from lender to lender, it can be used to compare and shop around for the best mortgage to fit the borrower's situation.

The Loan Estimate is a 3 page form designed to show the loan terms and settlement charges that will be incurred upon loan approval. It explains which charges can be changed before settlement and which charges will remain unchanged. It also contains a 'shopping chart' so the applicant can compare multiple mortgage loans and settlement costs.

Until a mortgage broker or lender gives the applicant a Loan Estimate, the loan originators are only permitted to charge the applicant for the cost of a credit report.

It should also be noted that under RESPA (Real Estate Settlement Procedures Act), the seller may not require the applicant, as a condition of the sale, to purchase title insurance from any particular title company.

There are three different categories of charges the applicant will pay at closing: charges that cannot increase at settlement; charges that cannot increase in total more than 10%; and charges that can increase at settlement.

With the Loan Estimate, the applicant can compare actual charges listed on the Closing Disclosure to ensure that the lender is not charging the applicant more than permitted.

10% limit

If the charges that cannot increase have increased, or the total of the charges that cannot increase more than the 10% have exceeded the 10% increase limit, the lender must reimburse the applicant at settlement or within 30 days after settlement.

Signing the Loan Estimate does not obligate the buyer to a loan; it only confirms the buyer has received the form

Closing Disclosure

Closing Disclosure

The borrower must be provided the Closing Disclosure three business days prior to the borrower committing to and signing loan documents.

The Closing Disclosure is a five page document designed to work with the Loan Estimate document so the borrower can easily compare the two documents to ensure they are getting the terms they were originally promised. The Closing Disclosure is not an estimate. It is the final terms of the loan.

Equal Credit Opportunity Act (ECOA)

Equal Credit Opportunity Act - (ECOA)

The ECOA prohibits discrimination by lenders to prospective borrowers based on race, color, religion, national origin, sex, marital status, and age if any or all of the applicant's income comes from any public assistance program.

If the lender requires an appraisal to verify the value to secure a loan, the ECOA allows the applicant the right to get a copy of the appraisal report.

If an application for a loan is denied, the ECOA requires the lender or mortgage broker to give the applicant a statement of the specific reasons why the application was denied.

Fair Housing Act

The Fair Housing Act is a little different from the ECOA which disallows discrimination based on race, color, religion, national origin, sex, disability or familial status. The key difference for marital status is based on the applicant receiving public assistance.

Charges of discrimination based on the Fair Housing Act will allow HUD to issue a Charge of Discrimination on the applicants behalf. A complaint based on discrimination of the ECOA will be with the Board of Governors of the Federal Reserve System. An applicant can always take private legal action and should consult with an attorney to understand their rights.

Offering Incentives
IC 54-2054
Guideline #10

Offering Incentives

Guideline #10 addresses incentives to buyers or sellers which could impact the legal aspects of securing financing. Idaho Code 54-2054 allows a broker to share any part of a commission, fee or compensation received with the buyer or seller in a real estate transaction.

However, no commission, fee or compensation may be split with any party to the transaction in a manner that would directly or indirectly create a double contract, as defined by IC 54-2004 (23), or would otherwise mislead any broker, lender, title company or government agency involved in the transaction, regarding the source of the funds used to complete the transaction or regarding the financial resources or obligation of the buyer or seller.

RESPA -Section 8
Kickbacks

In addition, Section 8 of the Real Estate Settlement Procedure Act (RESPA) specifically forbids any kickbacks or unearned fees to be tied to or connected with any federally related mortgage.

RESPA forbids any settlement provider from giving or receiving anything of value for the referral in connection with a mortgage or charging fees or markups when no additional service has been provided,.

Any person who violates Section 8 of RESPA may be fined up to $10,000 and imprisoned up to one year.

BEFORE ANSWERING QUESTIONS – Can You Define or Explain:

Title XIV of Dodd Frank Act	Conventional loan
FHA Insured loan	VA Guaranteed loan
Rural Housing loan (section 502)	Idaho Housing and Finance Association loan
Mortgage	Deed of Trust
Loan Estimate	Closing Disclosure
Offering Incentives	Satisfaction of mortgage
Certificate of Sale	Equal Credit Opportunity Act
Deed of trust notice of sale	Nationwide Mortgage Licensing System
FIRREA	Fannie Mae and Freddie Mac

Questions – Chapter 9

1. What does the highest bidder receive at a foreclosure sale of a mortgage?

   A. Certificate of Sale
   B. Sheriffs Deed
   C. Warranty Deed
   D. Mortgagee Deed

2. A 22 acre parcel secured with a mortgage ended up in foreclosure. What period of time is allowed for redemption?

   A. None, foreclosure secured with a mortgage is final
   B. 6 months
   C. 1 year
   D. Redemption period determined by a court decision

3. A 14 acre parcel secured with a deed of trust ended up in foreclosure. What period of time is allowed for redemption?

   A. None, foreclosure secured with a deed of trust is final upon sale
   B. 6 months
   C. 1 year
   D. Redemption period determined by a court decision

4. Once a 'notice of sale' has been recorded what period of time is given for the owner to bring the delinquency current?

   A. 60 days
   B. 90 days
   C. 115 days
   D. 120 days

5. What kind of deed does the successful bidder receive upon foreclosure of a deed of trust?

   A. Quit claim deed
   B. Trustee's deed
   C. Trustor's deed
   D. Sheriff's deed

6. When is the borrower supposed to receive *Your Home Loan Toolkit* booklet?

   A. Prior to making loan application
   B. Upon loan commitment
   C. Within 1 day of loan application
   D. Within 3 days of loan application

7. A real estate agent gave a purchaser $5,000 to assist with a down payment in the form of a private loan to be forgiven after the closing of a pending transaction. This could be considered as:

A. A nice 'gift'
B. A good business decision
C. An unenforceable loan
D. A 'double contract'

8. Upon receiving a complete loan application how long does the lender have to issue a Loan Estimate?

A. 1 business day
B. 3 business days
C. 5 business days
D. 1 week

9. How many days does the lender have to correct a violation found in a settlement statement?

A. 5 days
B. 21 days
C. 30 days
D. 45 days

10. Settlement charges between the Loan Estimate and the Closing Disclosure cannot change by more than:

A. 1%
B. 5%
C. 10%
D. 12%

11. The FHA loan program is:

A. Uninsured
B. Insured
C. Guaranteed
D. Secured

12. What residential financing program requires the borrower to be the owner/occupant?

A. Conventional financing
B. Seller financing
C. IHFA financing
D. Private financing

13. A 'Qualified Mortgage' loan can have a maturity time period for not longer than:

A. 15 years
B. 25 years
C. 30 years
D. 40 years

14. What type of short term loans are likely to go away?

A. 1-4 year ARM's
B. 1 year Construction loans
C. 10 year Seller financing
D. 15 year conventional financing

15. An applicant must be reimbursed for a settlement charge violation within:

A. 10 days
B. 15 days
C. 20 days
D. 30 days

Chapter 10

License Laws, Rules, and Guidelines

> **Words Of Wisdom**
>
> *"If you are doing something the same way you have been doing it for ten years, the chances are you are doing it wrong."*
>
> Charles Kettering

Regulated Conduct

Whether licensed or unlicensed, you need to be aware of the areas of regulated conduct involving the collection of fees or commissions that can lead to violations and disciplinary action by the Idaho Real Estate Commission (IREC).

Court Action
IC 54-2054 (1)

Court Action To Collect Commission Or Fee

A person must be actively licensed at the time of performing an activity that requires a license in order to use the court system to collect a commission or other forms of compensation.

Double Contracts
IC 54-2004 (22)
IC 54-2060 (8)

Double Contracts Are Prohibited

A double contract involves a situation in which there are 2 or more contracts for the purchase of real estate in which 1 is not made known to the prospective loan underwriter or loan guarantor. The intent is to enable the buyer to qualify for a loan in which he or she otherwise could not obtain.

IC 54-2054 (5)

No licensed broker or salesperson shall use, propose or agree to the use of, or knowingly permit the use of a double contract in connection with any regulated real estate transaction. Such conduct by a licensee is prohibited and shall be deemed as flagrant misconduct and dishonorable and dishonest dealing and shall subject the licensee to disciplinary action by the Commission.

Fee Splitting Prohibited
IC 54-2054 (2)

Fee Splitting With Unlicensed Persons

A licensee shall not share a fee involving compensation received in a regulated real estate transaction. This fee splitting action also includes unlicensed persons participating in a transaction in a manner a real estate license is required.

However, a licensee may pay part of a fee or commission directly to the buyer or seller in a real estate transaction providing such payment does not create a double contract or mislead any broker, lender, title company or government agency involved in the transaction.

Payment of any fee or commission to the buyer cannot be used as a source of funds used to complete a transaction or regarding the financial resources or obligations of the buyer unless such payment is in writing and approved by the lender and underwriter.

Finders Fee Prohibited

Finders Fee Prohibited
IC 54-2054 (3)

A licensee cannot offer anything of value to a unlicensed person to secure prospects to buy, sell, option or otherwise dispose of any interest in real property. Such action shall be considered as splitting fees with an unlicensed person and is prohibited.

IC 48-603 (15)

In addition, the Idaho Consumer Protection Act addresses unfair or deceptive acts or practices in the conduct of any trade or commerce as unlawful. Promising or offering to pay, credit, or allow to any buyer or lessee any compensation or reward in consideration of his giving to the seller or lessor in making a sale or lease to another person, if the earning of the rebate, discount or other value is contingent upon the occurrence of an event subsequent to the time the buyer or lessee agrees to buy or lease.

Kickbacks Prohibited
IC 54-2054 (6)

Kickbacks And Rebates Prohibited

A licensee shall not receive any kickback rebate or unearned fee for directing any transaction to a lender, escrow or title company as those practices are prohibited by the Real Estate Procedures Act (REPSA).

However, a licensee legally receiving any fee or rebate from any person providing direct services to either the buyer or the seller in connection with a regulated real estate transaction is required to disclose the licensee's intent to receive such fee, rebate or compensation in writing to all parties to the transaction prior to closing.

Compensation From More Than One Party
IC 54-2054 (7)

Compensation From More Than One Party

No licensed real estate broker or salesperson shall charge or accept compensation from more than 1 party in any 1 transaction, without first making full disclosure in writing of the broker's intent to do so, to all parties involved in the transaction.

Interference Prohibited
IC 54-2054 (4)

Interference With Real Estate Brokerage Agreement

It shall be unlawful for any person, licensed or unlicensed, to interfere with the contractual relationship between a client and broker.

Communicating a company's relocation policy or benefits to a transferring employee or consumer shall not be considered a violation so long as the communication does not involve advice or encouragement on how to terminate or amend an existing contractual relationship between a broker and a client.

After The Fact Referral Fees Prohibited
IC 54-2054 (8)

After The Fact Referral Fees Prohibited

Anyone seeking an 'after the fact' referral fee can not receive such fee unless:

1. The person seeking the referral fee has a written contractual relationship with the Idaho real estate broker for a referral fee or similar payment.

2. The contractual relationship providing for the referral fee exists at the time the buyer or seller purportedly referred by such person signs a written agreement with the Idaho broker for the lising of the real estate or for representation by the broker, or the buyer signes an offer to purchase the real estate involved in the transaction.

It shall be unlawful for any person including, but not limited to, a relocation company or company with a relocation policy or benefits, to directly or indirectly threaten to or actually reduce or withhold promised or expected employee or customer relocation benefits from a buyer or seller in a regulated real estate transaction based upon a broker's participation in payment of a referral fee or other fee.

All Fees Paid
Through Broker
IC 54-2054 (9)

All Fees Are Paid Through Broker

No sales associate shall accept any commission, compensation or fee for the performance of any acts requiring a real estate license from any person except the real estate broker with whom the sales associate is licensed.

However, if authorized by the broker, a sales associate may pay all or any portion of the accepted commission, compensation or fee to any other sales associate who is licensed with the same broker.

A broker may pay a former sales associate for services performed while the sales associate was actively licensed with that broker, regardless of the former sales associates's license status at the time the commission or fee is actually paid.

Idaho Real Estate Commission Authority

IREC Authority
To Investigate
IC 54-2058

IREC Authority to Investigate

The IREC has the authority to investigate the capacity of a broker, salesperson or anyone without a license acting as a licensee.

Upon receiving a written complaint, the executive director of the Commission shall initiate an investigation against the person of the alleged wrongdoings.

If the facts are deemed to be sufficient to proceed with formal action, the commission shall file an administrative complaint against the salesperson, broker or unlicensed person.

The person charged with wrongdoings shall answer all reasonable questions and make any and all records requested by the commission available to the Commission. The costs of providing records to the Commission shall be at the expense of the person charged.

Complaint & Investigative Process

The Commission is empowered to launch an investigation based on written complaints from the public and any information received by the Executive Director of the Commission.

The Staff will pursue disciplinary action only if the facts warrant such action. However, the final say remains with the Commission members to determine if the facts are sufficient.

If the gathered facts turn out to be insufficient, the Staff will issue a letter of 'no action' and the matter will be closed.

Investigation Process

Initiating The Investigation Process

If a complaint warrants investigation, the Commission investigator will inform the licensee in writing of the alleged allegations and request a written response. The licensee may also be requested to provide documents or other information in the licensee's response.

In addition, the investigator may request a personal meeting and if needed, more documentation from the licensee to clarify various issues.

1-3 Decisions

Completion Of Initial Investigation

Once the investigation is completed, the results and recommendations are forwarded to the Executive Director on how to proceed. The Executive Director will make 1 of 3 decisions.

1. Close the case and issue a 'no action' letter
2. Request additional information
3. Pursue disciplinary action

Disciplinary Process
IC 54-2058

Disciplinary Action Process

Before disciplinary action is pursued, the Executive Director will submit a written summary report with the relevant facts (excluding names, location or other identifying information) to the Commission members. If the Commission determines the facts are insufficient, the responding licensee will receive a written notification indicating a 'no action' determination.

If there are enough facts to proceed, the Commission will advise the staff to pursue formal disciplinary proceedings.

Licensee Disciplinary Notification

Licensee Notification For Disciplinary Action

The licensee will receive written notice from the Staff outlining the facts revealed by the investigation and violations the Staff believes occurred and can be proven.

Upon receipt of any notice, the Commission encourages licensees to consult with an attorney who can advise the licensee what to do. The licensee may seek legal advice from an attorney anytime during the investigation or hearing process.

Staff will provide the licensee, in writing, the option to informally resolve the matter through stipulation, or the licensee's right to a formal hearing. The licensee will have a set period of time to advise the Staff on how they choose to proceed. If a hearing is held, the parties shall be served notice of a hearing at least 21 days before the hearing is to be held.

IDAPA 33.01.02
Rules 600 - 849

Process To Reconsider Or Appeal Disciplinary Action

Should a licensee disagree with a disciplinary decision made by the Commission, the licensee may file a motion for reconsideration of a final order within 14 days of the decision.

The IREC will dispose of the petition for reconsideration within 21 days of its receipt, or the petition will be considered denied by operation of law.

IDAPA 33.01.02
Rules 850 - 851

Appeal To District Court

Any party aggrieved by a final order can appeal to a district court providing that person has exhausted all administrative remedies available. Petition for judicial review of a final order must be filed within 28 days of the service date of the final order by the IREC.

Grounds For Disciplinary Action

Grounds for
Disciplinary
Action
IC 54-2060

A licensee should be familiar with areas of misconduct which can result in severe disciplinary action. Some examples:

- *Making fraudulent misrepresentation*
Fraudulent misrepresentation is when a licensee knowingly makes a representation with intent to deceive and with the knowledge that it is false.

- *Continued course of misrepresentation*
A licensee continues to make false promises, whether done personally or through agents or salespersons, such as zoning uses or a prospective buyer being able to use a property for a specific use.

- *Failure to remit or account for money or property*
A licensee receives earnest money and retains it instead of promptly turning the earnest money over to the broker.

- *Failure to keep adequate records*
All property transactions, while acting in the capacity of a real estate broker or salesperson, must be complete with all paperwork and supporting documents intact.

- *Failure or refusal to disclose information to the Commission*
The Commission may request documents, books, or records for inspection within the person's knowledge. Refusal to cooperate would be considered misconduct.

- *Acting as a broker or salesperson under an assumed name*
An example could be a licensed salesperson who gives the illusion through advertising they are the broker instead of being the salesperson of a broker.

- *Unlawful means in applying for a real estate license*
Application for a real estate license is intentionally missing information through fraud, deception, misrepresentation or misstatement.

- *Using or proposing to use a 'double contract'*
Intentionally advising parties to a transaction with a side agreement not known to the underwriter is prohibited.

- *Seeking or receiving a 'kickback' or rebate*
A conditional agreement in which the licensee will receive something of value that would violate IC 54-2054 (6).

- *Violation of any provisions of the Idaho Real Estate License Law and Rules*
This could include any aspect of IC 54-2001 through 54-2097; or better put, the whole booklet!

- *Any other conduct which constitutes dishonest or dishonorable dealings.*
Conduct not specifically identified in sections 54-2001 through 54-2097 that would allow, and be subject to, disciplinary action.

- *Gross negligence or reckless conduct*
If conduct substantially fails to meet the generally accepted standard of care in the practice of real estate in Idaho, such conduct would be inappropriate and subject to discipline.

Additional Grounds For Discipline
IC 54-2061
IC 54-2062

Additional Grounds For Disciplinary Action
The IREC may also take action against a licensee where in a court of competent jurisdiction, the licensee:

- Has been convicted of a felony, or has been convicted of a misdemeanor involving fraud, misrepresentation, or dishonest or dishonorable dealing or which otherwise demonstrates the licensees lack of trustworthiness to engage in the real estate business
- Has been declared to lack capacity or to be incompetent
- Judgment against a licensee for fraud, misrepresentation, deceit, or gross negligence with reference to a real estate related transaction
- Has an order or determination of debarment, suspension, or any limitation on participation in government loan programs issued against the licensee for misconduct
- Has a real estate or other professional license suspended or revoked for a disciplinary violation involving fraud, misrepresentation, or dishonest or dishonorable dealings. A certified copy of the order of the administrative agency in the other jurisdiction shall be prima facie evidence of the suspension or revocation.

A licensee who is convicted, declared legally incompetent, has a judgment entered against him in civil action shall have 20 days of such action, conviction, declaration or judgment to remit to the commission a legal document evidencing the same.

IREC Disciplinary Powers
IC 54-2059

Disciplinary Powers

The IREC has the power to:

1. Temporarily suspend or permanently revoke licenses
2. Issue formal reprimand and issue formal penalty not to exceed $5,000
3. The Executive Director may issue informal letters of reprimand to licensees without civil penalty or cost assessment

If the Commission suspends or revokes a license, imposes a civil penalty, assesses costs and attorney's fees, the Commission may withhold execution of the suspension, revocation or civil penalty, or costs and attorney's fees on such terms and for such time as it may prescribe.

IC 12-117 (5)

Attorney's fees and expenses awarded in certain instances in any administrative proceeding or judicial proceeding involving as adverse parties a licensing authority and a licensee, the prevailing party shall be entitled to recover its reasonable attorney's fees and reasonable investigative or defense costs, as the case may be, necessarily and actually incurred.

If any amounts assessed against a defendant by final order of the Commission become otherwise uncollectible or payment is in default, and only if all the defendant's rights to appeal have passed, the Commission may then proceed to district court and seek to enforce collection through judgment and execution,

Civil penalties and attorney's fees collected may only be used for the exclusive use and purpose of developing and delivering real estate education to benefit Idaho real estate licensees.

Penalty For Acting Without A License
IC 54-2065

Penalty For Acting Without A License

A conviction as a misdemeanor for acting without a license, a broker or salesperson can be punished with:

- A fine not to exceed $5,000 for a natural person or
- A fine not to exceed $10,000 for a LLC or corporation
- Imprisonment in county jail not to exceed 1 year or
- Both fine and imprisonment

In addition, a court may assess a civil penalty not to exceed $5,000 against a natural person or $10,000 against a LLC or corporation.

Real Estate Recovery Fund

Purpose Of Fund
IC 54-2069
IC 54-2071

Purpose Of Recovery Fund

The purpose of the real estate recovery fund is to satisfy claims against real estate licensees. The fund provides a vehicle in which a party was damaged by a licensee on the grounds of fraud, misrepresentation or deceit in a real estate transaction. Such damages are determined when any person obtains a final judgment from any court of competent jurisdiction.

Fund Balance And Payout

Fund Balance
IC 54-2069
IC 54-2071

The fund is funded by portion of real estate applications or renewals of real estate licensees and replenished as needed with certification fees. A balance of no more than $20,000 shall be maintained in the fund with a maximum payment of not more than $10,000 per licensee per calendar year regardless of the number of persons damaged by any one licensee.

To obtain additional information regarding the procedure, grounds, hearing, and how the Commission may answer a petition and compromise of claims, payment from the recovery fund and recovery if fund balance is insufficient, and other information, one can refer to IC 54-2071 thru 54-2078 for complete detail.

Automatic License Suspension
IC 54-2074

Pursuant to court order, the Commission pays from the recovery fund any amount in settlement of a claim or towards satisfaction of a judgement against a licensed broker, associate broker, or salesperson.

The license of such broker, associate broker, or salesperson shall be automatically suspended without further order of the Commission upon the effective date of any order by the court as set forth authorizing payment from the recovery fund.

No broker, associate broker, or salesperson shall be granted reinstatement until he has repaid in full, the amount so paid from the recovery fund plus interest at the legal rate of interest allowable by law for judgments.

Real Estate Brokerage

Designated Broker

Designated Broker
IC 54-2038

All real estate companies must have a licensed real estate broker who is designated by the real estate company to supervise and manage the operation of the company including the activities of any associated licensees and associated unlicensed persons within the course and scope of their employment or agency.

Designated Broker Basic Responsibilities

Designated Broker Responsibilities
IC 54-2038

A designated broker is required to:

1. Supervise and control all office locations and the activities of all licensed and unlicensed persons associated with the brokerage company.

Unlicensed Activities
Guideline #17

Unlicensed persons should be educated and reminded about what activities they should and should not do. Guideline #17 gives a good overview for creating good office policies.

2. Review and approve all real estate agreements including, but not limited to:
   - Listing agreements (buyer or seller)
   - Selling or purchasing agreements
   - Brokerage representation agreements

3. Be reasonably available to manage and supervise the brokerage company during regular business hours.

Available To	When a broker is a regular full-time employee or engaged in a full-time activity at

Available To Supervise
54-2038 (1) (c)
Guideline #23

When a broker is a regular full-time employee or engaged in a full-time activity at a location other than where the broker is licensed to do business, a presumption will be made that the broker is unable to manage and supervise the brokerage company in accordance with the basic requirements. No sales associate shall be licensed under the broker until such assumption is overcome to the satisfaction of the commission.

An associate broker or salesperson can only be associated with one brokerage at a time. However, a designated broker can be a designated broker of more than one licensed entity providing all businesses operate their main offices at the same physical location. An example might be a real estate brokerage that also owns a separate licensed real estate referral or maybe a commercial real estate company.

Designated Broker License Suspension
Guideline #7 (3,5,6)

However, should the designated broker's license be suspended or revoked due to improper actions with one company, all companies having the same designated broker to manage would be affected. All licenses associated with all companies will be placed inactive.

Entity Has 10 Days
IC 54-2039 (2)
IC 54-2057 (1)

If the designated broker license of a licensed legal business entity (i.e. LLC or corporation) is suspended or revoked, the business entity shall have 10 business days to designate another qualified broker as designated broker before the entity's license is terminated and the licenses of all associated licensees are made inactive. The same requirements apply upon death or incapacity of a designated broker of a legal entity.

Business Location
IC 54-2040

Brokerage Business Location

A designated real estate broker shall have a definite, physical place of business on file at the IREC. No other place of business may be used as a main office until proper notice is acknowledged by the IREC.

A broker shall not conduct business under any name other than the one in which the license is issued. If notification of a change is not made to the IREC, the IREC shall automatically inactivate the license previously issued. The broker shall also notify the commission in writing of any change in the business telephone number.

Business Name

A broker shall not conduct business under any name other than the one in which the license is issued.

License Lending Prohibited
IC 54-2040 (5)

License Lending Prohibited

A broker cannot allow others to manage or have full control or allow anyone licensed or unlicensed to carry on a business for which a broker's license is required. This law is to prohibit someone using a broker as a designated broker in which the designated broker does not actively manage or have full control.

IC 54-2038 (1) (c)

For example, if a 'team' of real estate salespersons want to strike out on their own, they would need a 'designated' broker. If they found a broker to be their designated broker but the broker did not maintain adequate, reasonable, and regular contact with the sales associates, the broker would be in violation.

If there is a question of adequacy of supervision, the Commission will examine pertinent evidence such as:

- Was the designated broker physically able to supervise?

- What was the experience level of the sales associate?

- Has the designated broker contracted to avoid supervisory responsibility?

- What types of activity were licensed sales associates or unlicensed personnel engaged in?

- Has the designated broker established written or oral policies and procedures?

- Does the designated broker hold regular staff meetings and followup meetings to determine that policies and procedures are being properly implemented?

- What corrective or remedial action does the designated broker take if a misdeed of a sales associate or licensed personnel is discovered?

Brokerage Record Keeping

Record Retention
IC 54-2049

Record Retention

Certain records must be kept by a brokerage for 3 calendar years *after the year* in which the event occurred, the transaction closed, all funds disbursed, or the agreement and any expired written extension including:

1. Original or true copy of all accepted, countered or rejected offers
2. Listing or buyer representation agreements and 'consent to limited dual representation' forms
3. All transaction files and contents
4. Trust account ledger cards
5. All trust account reconciliation records

If a designated broker changes license status to less than being a designated broker, the IREC must be notified in writing the location where all trust account and transaction records will be kept during the time the broker was responsible for such records. The records shall be made available to the IREC for 3 years following the year in which each transaction was closed.

An example might be a brokerage that appoints a replacement designated broker, a brokerage that shuts down, a brokerage that is sold to another party, and a new designated broker is appointed.

Any transaction or trust account records located outside the state of Idaho shall promptly be made available to the IREC upon request at the licensees own expense.

Real Estate Trust Account

Trust Account
Responsibility
IC 54-2041

Trust Account Responsibility

A licensed real estate broker shall be responsible for all moneys or property entrusted to that broker or to any licensee representing the broker.

Unless instructed otherwise in writing, the broker shall deposit entrusted moneys relating to a real estate transaction in a neutral qualified trust account at an approved depository.

Approved
Depositories
IC 54-2042 (1)

Examples of approved depositories are:
- Federally chartered bank and trust companies
- State or federally chartered savings and loan companies
- Licensed title insurance companies
- Active licensed attorney at law

No Commingling
IC 54-2041 (2)

Commingling Prohibited

Only moneys relating to a regulated real estate transaction may be deposited in the broker's real estate account. Trust account moneys shall not be commingled with moneys of the broker, firm, or agent except for a minimum amount required to open and maintain the account. The balance of the maintenance funds cannot exceed $300.

IC 54-2041 (1)

However, if the parties to a transaction have instructed the broker or its licensees, in writing, to transfer moneys or property to a third party, the moneys or property shall not be considered entrusted property.

The broker shall be responsible for maintaining a record of the time and date that any money or property was transferred from the broker to a third party.

Examples of third parties might include but not be limited to title, escrow, or a trust company. Consequently the broker or its licensees have no right to exercise control over the safekeeping or disposition of the moneys or property.

Creating A Trust
Account
IC 54-2042
Guideline #15

Creating A Trust Account

Each trust account must be established at an approved depository and identified as 'real estate trust account' on checks, deposit slips, and with the depository and shall be a non-interest bearing account.

Notice of opening a trust account must be submitted to the IREC on an approved form giving the IREC permission to inspect the account. The form must be signed by the broker and an officer of a depository and returned to the IREC.

Each trust account must be established and maintained under the name of the licensed business name of the broker with a complete and separate set of records.

The records must consist of a monthly accounting, deposits, charges, and withdrawals even if moneys are deposited with a third party.

Funds from the broker to maintain the trust account (cannot exceed a balance of $300) can be used only to cover bank or depository charges of the account.

Interest Bearing
Trust Account
IC 54-2043

Interest Bearing Trust Account

An interest bearing trust account is possible but it can be used for 1 transaction only and cannot be combined with any other transactions. However multiple interest bearing trust accounts can be opened; each for a single transaction.

There must be a written agreement between the buyer and seller stating who will receive the accrued interest from any deposit. All deposits must be made into an approved depository.

The responsible broker will retain the agreement in the transaction file and give a copy to both the buyer and seller for their files.

An example of when an interest bearing account might be used, is when there is a large amount of earnest money deposited with an extended time to close a transaction.

Trust Account Record Keeping

Trust Account
Record Keeping
IC 54-2044

Each designated broker is required to maintain any real estate trust account to protect the financial interest of the consumers of Idaho.

The broker must reconcile and balance:
- Each trust account with all ledger records
- Check register and bank statement at least once each month

If an electronic record keeping system is used, a backup system should be in use at all times to protect data from being lost. As a precaution, the backup data should be stored in a safe place away from the main electronic system.

Ledger Records
IC 54-2044

Ledger Records

A separate ledger card or record, known as 'ledgers' and identified as 'trust account maintenance fund' shall be initiated when the broker's or firm's funds are initially deposited into the trust account.

Any time the broker receives earnest money, or other forms of consideration, an individual trust ledger card or record shall be created to track a pending transaction. Additions or deductions to trust account maintenance funds shall be posted to the ledger records as soon as the broker is given notice of the deposit or deduction.

It is the broker's responsibility to keep accurate records of each and every transaction to show the receipts and disbursements in and out of a real estate trust account.

As soon as the broker makes any additions to or deductions from a trust account, regardless where the trust account is located, the activity shall also be posted on the appropriate ledger card and kept current at all times.

IC 54-2042 (7)
IC 54-2044 (1)

As previously mentioned, funds for a broker to maintain a trust account (cannot exceed a balance of $300) can only be used to cover bank or depository charges attached to the account. The tracking of these maintenance funds must be initiated with a separate ledger card titled 'trust account maintenance fund'.

Depositing Funds With Another
IC 54-2044 (3)

Depositing Funds With Another
When a broker deposits funds with another broker, an approved depository, or directly to the seller or any other person as directed in writing by both parties to the transaction, a ledger record must be created by the transferring broker with a transaction number assigned.

Upon transfer of funds or consideration, a receipt for such deposit shall be obtained and retained in the transaction files of the transferring broker. The receipt must show the name of the payee and date of transfer.

Individual Ledger Records
IC 54-2044 (4)

Individual Ledger Records
Individual trust ledger records must be assigned a transaction number in chronological order and include:

- Chronological number for each transaction
- Names of both parties to the transaction
- Location of the property
- Date of each deposit or disbursement
- Name of the payor or payee
- Amount and check number of each disbursement
- Amount and nature of the deposit
- Current balance for pending or open transactions
- Final disposition of funds for closed transactions

Real Estate Trust Account Checks

Trust Account Checks
IC 54-2044 (5)

Trust Account Checks
The broker shall maintain consecutively numbered checks for each trust account and must contain:

- Broker's licensed business name and business address
- 'real estate trust account' imprinted on each check

Any checks drawn on a trust account shall have the transaction number noted on the face of the check. All checks must be accounted for including any voided checks which shall be clearly marked 'VOID' and retained in a numerical sequence with the other checks for the banking month.

Check Register
IC 54-2044 (6)

Check Register
A check register or journal must be kept current at all times (even if funds are held at a title company or other depository) and itemize deposits and disbursements in consecutive order. The register must clearly show:

- Date of deposit or disbursement
- The payee or payor
- Amount and purpose of deposit or disbursement
- Check number
- Transaction number
- Current cash balance remaining in that trust account

**Duplicate Bank
Deposit**
IC 54-2044 (7)

Duplicate Bank Deposit Record

Duplicate bank deposit slips shall be maintained for each trust account and imprinted with the broker business name and the words - 'real estate trust account'.

Each deposit record shall state:

- The name of the person or firm placing the money with the broker's office
- The date of the deposit
- A transaction number in the bank deposit records in proper chronological sequence and date stamped by the bank or the bank deposit receipt shall be attached to the duplicate deposit record in the deposit records.

**Trust Account
Deposits**
IC 54-2045

Trust Account Deposits

Earnest money received by a broker for a regulated real estate transaction shall be deposited into a real estate trust account at an approved depository.

IC 54-2045 (1)

All moneys received shall be deposited on or before the next *banking* day following receipt day of the funds unless written instructions signed by all parties direct the broker to do otherwise.

IC 54-2045 (2)

Checks held in an uncashed form must be accompanied by written instructions in the purchase and sale contract to withhold deposit until a certain time (date) such as acceptance of an offer by the seller.

IC 54-2045 (3)

If consideration is returned before it is deposited, it must be so noted with the date the consideration was returned on the purchase and sale agreement or other document dealing with the transaction. It should be noted that no consideration is to be returned without the knowledge and consent of the broker.

An example of why consideration could be returned prior to deposit, is if the buyer withdraws an offer prior to acceptance; or the seller rejected an offer prior to the earnest money being deposited into the broker's trust account.

**Ledger Card
Required**
IC 54-2044 (2)

Regardless of whether an offer is accepted or not, a ledger card must be created to track the transaction from beginning to end.

Other consideration, including but not limited to, promissory notes and tangible personal property must also be accounted for upon receipt. Remember, the broker is responsible for the safe keeping of such property that cannot be deposited into a real estate trust account.

Examples might include some earnest money together with a vehicle (with stated value). Even agricultural animals have been used as consideration!

All consideration, regardless of form, shall be immediately delivered to the broker or the broker's office. Although the term 'immediately' is not defined, the Idaho code, 54-2045 (1) does indicate 'all moneys to be deposited on or before the banking day following receipt'. Thus, 54-2045 (1) could be considered a good working 'default' time frame for 'immediate' delivery.

Trust Account Disbursements
IC 54-2046

Trust Account Disbursements

The broker who holds entrusted funds or like payments in lieu of cash received in a regulated real estate transaction is fully responsible for all such funds until a full accounting has been made to the parties involved. Failure to comply with trust account disbursement requirements is considered a violation of license law and will subject the broker to discipline.

No disbursements shall be made from a real estate trust account without written authorization signed by the parties or an order of the court.

Any disbursements made prior to closing or before the happening of a condition set forth in a purchase and sale agreement shall require written authorization of the parties of the transaction.

Nor shall disbursement of any portion of a broker's commission or fee take place without prior written, signed authorization from the buyer and seller or until copies of the closing statements, signed by the buyer and seller, have been delivered to the broker and until the buyer and/or seller has been paid the amount due as determined by the closing statement.

Disputed Earnest Money
IC 54-2047

Disputed Earnest Money

Any time more than 1 party to a transaction makes demand on funds or other consideration for which the broker is responsible, such as, but not limited to, earnest money deposits, the broker shall:

- Notify each party, in writing, of the demand of the other party
- Keep all parties to the transaction informed of any actions by the broker regarding the disputed funds or other consideration, including retention of the funds by the broker until the dispute is properly resolved

Based on the broker's interpretation of the terms of a purchase and sale agreement, the broker may disburse disputed funds or other consideration at the broker's own discretion providing the facts are not in violation of the law.

However, such disbursement may subject the broker to civil liability. If the broker does not believe it is reasonably possible to disburse disputed funds, the broker may hold the disputed funds until ordered by a court of proper jurisdiction to make disbursement.

Licensee Relationships

A licensee's license will be held in an inactive status with the Idaho Real Estate Commission until such time as the licensee decides to affiliate with a brokerage.

New Affiliation
IC 54-2056 (2)

New Affiliation
When a licensee selects a brokerage with which to affiliate, the broker shall submit written application to the IREC for each sales associate licensing with the broker. This application is made through the Commission's online services.

Dealing With Own Property
IC 54-2055
Guideline #24

Licensees Dealing With Their Own Property
An active licensee buying or selling Idaho property, or any interest in a property, in a regulated real estate transaction, must conduct that transaction through the broker with whom licensed whether or not the property is listed.

In addition, a licensee shall disclose to any buyer or seller no later than the presentation of a purchase and sale agreement that the licensee holds an active Idaho real estate license. This disclosure requirement includes if the active licensee acquires or *intends* to acquire any *interest* in real property or any option to purchase real property.

If a sales associate sold their own personal residence without listing the property for sale, the licensee would still be required to provide the broker all the details relating to the transaction. The same would be true if the licensee is purchasing unlisted property.

IC 54-2038

Remember, the designated broker is responsible for the actions of its licensees and unlicensed persons.

Sales Associate Termination
IC 54-2056 (1)

Sales Associate Terminating With Broker
If a sales associate terminates his licensed association with a broker, the sales associate shall provide to the broker written notice of the termination no later than 3 business days after the effective date. The same holds true in reverse if the broker terminates a sales associate.

Termination For Cause
IC 54-2056 (3)

Termination For Cause
If a broker terminates a sales associate for violating any of the provisions of sections 54-2059 thru 54-2065, the broker shall, within 10 business days of the termination, notify the IREC in writing of the termination and the facts giving rise to the termination.

Property Of The Broker
IC 54-2056 (5)

Property Of The Broker
When the sales associate terminates with a broker, the sales associate shall turn over all contracts and other property belonging to the broker including but not limited to listing and sales agreements, keys, and buyer brokerage information.

A sales associate shall not engage in any practice or conduct, directly or indirectly, which encourages or induces clients to terminate any legal business relationship with the broker is prohibited unless written permission from the broker is obtained.

Real Estate Guidelines

Real Estate Guidelines Purpose

Purpose

IREC guidelines are the Commissioners' explanation and guidance on the license law and rules.

The guidelines address day by day situations revolving around the practice of real estate. A licensee can have many questions answered with the information contained in the guidelines addressing specific situations.

Guidelines can be added or revised at any time during the year by the IREC so a licensee should periodically review the Guidelines for up-to-date changes.

List Of Idaho Real Estate Commission Guidelines

1. Cancellation Or Withdrawal Of Listings

2. Brokering Idaho Property Require3s An Idaho Real Estate License

3. Regular Employee Status Determination

4. Agency Disclosure Brochure ("THE BLUE BROCHURE") Record Keeping Requirements

5. Disclosure Of Transaction Fees - When Required

6. Offering Guarantees

7. Guidelines For "Suspended" Licenses

8. Off-MLS And Coming Soon Listings

9. Terms Under Which Rental Or Lease Fees May Be Split With Non Licensed Persons

10. Splitting Fees With Non Licensed Persons Prohibited

11. Failure To Account For Money And Property Of Others

12. RESERVED

List Of Guidelines

13. Real Estate Advertising

14. Disputed Earnest Money

15. Establishing Real Estate Trust Accounts

16. Presentation Of Multiple Offers By The Listing Agent

17. Use Of Unlicensed Assistants And Office Staff

18. Dealer In Options

19. RESERVED

20. Joint Guideline On Broker Price Opinions (BPOs)

21. RESERVED

22. Auctioneers Of Real Estate

23. Mandatory Duty Of The Brokerage "To Be Available" To Receive And Present All Written Offers And Counteroffers

24. Licensees' Personal Transactions To Be Conducted Through The Broker With Whom He Is Licensed

25. Short Sale Guidance

Double contract	Broker absences
Fee splitting	Record retention
Finders fee	Trust account responsibility
After the fact referral fee	Commingling
Grounds for disciplinary action	Interest bearing trust account
Penalty for acting without a license	Trust account check requirements
Recovery fund	Trust account ledger cards
Designated broker	Trust account deposit requirements
Disputed earnest money	IREC Guidelines

Questions - Chapter 10

1. An agent unconditionally gave his buyer a new riding lawn mower after a transaction closed as a 'thank you'. This activity is?

   A. O.k.
   B. Illegal
   C. Inappropriate
   D. Inducement

2. What is the maximum fine for an unlicensed person practicing real estate?

   A. $ 5,000
   B. $10,000
   C. $15,000
   D. $20,000

3. An active licensee buying or selling their own property must conduct all transactions through:

   A. Cooperating brokerage
   B. Idaho Real Estate Commission
   C. Broker with whom licensed
   D. A licensed title insurance company

4. If a licensee terminates with a broker, what is required?

   A. Nothing, the licensee just leaves
   B. Licensee must tell broker they are leaving
   C. Licensee must give written notice within 5 calendar days of leaving
   D. Licensee must notify in writing no later than 3 business days of effective date

5. If a broker terminates an agent for cause, the broker must notify the Idaho Real Estate Commission within:

   A. 3 business days from termination
   B. 5 calendar days from termination
   C. 5 business days from termination
   D. 10 business days from termination

6. Once a real estate commission investigation is completed, the results and recommendations are forwarded to:

   A. REALTOR® association legal counsel
   B. Attorney General
   C. Executive Director
   D. Chief Investigator

7. Company records must be retained by the broker for what period of time?

   A. 3 fiscal years after a transaction closes
   B. 3 calendar years after the year a transaction closes
   C. 3 calendar years after the year a transaction is initiated
   D. 3 fiscal years from the date company was created

8. What is the maximum amount of personal money allowed to maintain a trust account?

    A. $100
    B. $300
    C. $500
    D. $700

9. Trust account maintenance funds can be used for what purpose?

    A. Cover bank charges
    B. Cover NSF earnest money checks
    C. Cover general operating account charges
    D. Cover delivery of deposits to the bank

10. A trust account must be established under what name?

    A. Designated broker's name
    B. Licensed business name
    C. Name with State Tax Department
    D. Owner's name of the company

11. Who must be notified of opening a trust account?

    A. Secretary of State
    B. Idaho Tax Commission
    C. Idaho Real Estate Commission
    D. Internal Revenue Service

12. A broker transferred $500 from the general operating account to the trust account.

    A. It's O.K. to replace a missing check
    B. Is an example of commingling
    C. O. K as long as IREC is notified
    D. Used to maintain the trust account

13. A brokerage real estate trust account must be reconciled how often:

    A. Monthly
    B. Quarterly
    C. Semi-annually
    D. Annually

14. When is consideration received by a sales associate to be delivered to the broker or broker's office?

    A. Within 24 hours
    B. Within 1 day
    C. As soon as convenient
    D. Immediately

15. Trust account checks must be imprinted with the words:

    A. (Name of company) trust account
    B. Business trust account
    C. Real estate trust account
    D. Trust account

16. Unless otherwise stated, when must earnest money be deposited?

    A. Within 5 business days of acceptance
    B. Next banking day
    C. Next calendar day
    D. Next business day

17. Who is authorized to disburse disputed earnest money without written approval from the parties to the transaction?

    A. Cannot disburse without written approval from buyer and seller
    B. Escrow company
    C. The broker holding the earnest money
    D. Idaho Real Estate Commission

18. Who is considered the responsible broker in a cooperative sale?

    A. The listing broker
    B. The selling broker
    C. The broker holding entrusted funds
    D. Both the listing and selling brokers

19. Who is responsible for the accuracy of a closing (settlement) statement?

    A. Responsible listing agent
    B. Responsible selling agent
    C. Responsible escrow officer
    D. Responsible broker

20. How are rejected offers handled?

    A. Nothing is required
    B. Need to be marked as 'rejected'
    C. Given to seller for their records
    D. Marked and dated as 'rejected'

21. Sales associates can only accept fees, compensation, or commission from whom?

    A. The broker with whom licensed
    B. Directly from the buyer or seller
    C. From the escrow company
    D. Directly from the cooperating broker

22. Two competitive real estate companies were struggling and over lunch they each agreed to increase their fees so they could survive a down market. This would be an example of what?

    A. Cooperation
    B. Price fixing
    C. Good business practice
    D. Friendly competition

23. Who has/have the final say to invoke disciplinary action from a complaint?

    A. Department of Investigation
    B. Chief Investigator
    C. Executive Director
    D. Commission Members

24. If a judgment surrounding a real estate related transaction has been brought against a real estate agent, how long does the agent have to notify the Idaho Real Estate Commission?

    A. 10 days
    B. 20 days
    C. 30 days
    D. Not necessary, since civil action is outside the jurisdiction of the Idaho Real Estate Commission

25. Who is entitled to recover reasonable attorney's fees in an administrative or judicial proceeding?

    A. Plaintiff
    B. Defendant
    C. Prevailing Party
    D. The Court

Agency

Agency Principles

'Real Estate Agent'

When buyers and sellers seek the assistance of a real estate licensee, they refer to the licensee as their 'real estate agent'; similar to referring to a person with an insurance company contact as their 'insurance agent'.

However, in the real estate industry, the term, 'real estate agent' refers to our occupation but it does not define our duties or obligations to represent a buyer or seller in a transaction regarding who represents who.

In the early days and even up into the 1980's a lot of confusion surrounded agency and the overall representation between real estate agents and the public. Legislation was initiated and passed that clearly identified the duties and obligations of real estate licensees whether working with a buyer, seller or both.

All states throughout America now have legislated specific disclosure laws regulating agency relationships between the public and the real estate industry.

Because the legislated laws vary from state to state, it's very important that you know exactly how Idaho laws address agency representation.

Agency Principles

Basic Principles Of Agency

The basic principles of Agency revolve around representation based on different obligations and duties between the principal and the agent. When one person (principal) delegates to another person (agent) the right to act on behalf of the principal, an agency relationship is created.

3 Categories

Three Categories Of Agency

There are three different categories of agency: universal, general, and special.

* *Universal agency* is very broad and basically gives the agent unlimited power.

* *General agency* gives the agent power to bind the principal in a particular trade or business. For example, a real estate salesperson is an agent for the designated broker and represents that broker.

* *Special agency* is practiced in the real estate industry. The broker acts as a *special* agent. The principal (buyer or seller) authorizes the agent to perform activities over a specific period of time. A common example would be when an agent lists a property for sale for a property owner.

Idaho Real Estate Representation Act

Idaho Real Estate Representation Act
IC 54-2082 thru
IC 54-2097

The Idaho Real Estate Representation Act was created to clearly identify what duties and obligations exist between the consumer and a real estate brokerage. Any real estate transaction in which a real estate license is required will be governed by agency representation.

There are several steps and procedures to create an agency relationship between a licensee and a buyer or seller from the 'first initial business contact' to representation confirmation and acknowledgment of disclosure.

Although not required, many brokerages may have a written policy that identifies and describes the types of representation in which that brokerage and its associated licensees may engage with any buyer or seller, or both, as a part of the real estate brokerage services.

When a licensee affiliates with a brokerage, the licensee must adhere to whatever types of agency relationships are offered by the brokerage's office policies.

Agency Disclosure Brochure
IC 54-2085

Agency Disclosure Brochure (aka - Blue Brochure)
One of the first duties a licensee has is that a licensee shall give to a prospective buyer or seller at the *first substantial business contact* the agency disclosure brochure adopted or approved by the Idaho Real Estate Commission. Each brokerage shall keep a signed and dated record of a buyer or seller's receipt of the agency disclosure brochure.

It should be noted that signing the brochure by a buyer or seller *does not* obligate the signor to any contractual relationship with the licensee. It merely provides proof when the prospective buyer or seller received the disclosure brochure.

A licensee also needs to make sure they are using the most recent version (date on cover) of the disclosure brochure. From time to time, the Idaho Real Estate Commission may change the format or contents.

The agency disclosure brochure lists the various types of representation available to a buyer or seller in a regulated real estate transaction. In addition, the duties and obligations owed to a buyer and seller are also explained.

The disclosure brochure also contains a conspicuous notice that states *no* representation will exist unless there is a *written* agreement between the buyer or seller and the brokerage.

A brokerage must disclose its relationship to both buyer and seller in a transaction no later than the preparation or presentation of a purchase and sale agreement.

Many agents take extra time to personally go over the information contained in the brochure face to face with the buyer or seller to make sure the terminology is fully understood before the buyer or seller actually decides what type of agency will be selected.

Failure of a licensee to timely give a buyer or seller the agency disclosure brochure shall be a violation and subject to disciplinary action.

IC 54-2085 (6)   Neither the commission brochure nor the representation confirmation shall create a brokerage relationship. A separate, signed, written agreement is required for that purpose.

Creating Agency
IC 54-2084

Creating An Agency Relationship

In Idaho, there are 4 types of brokerage relationships.

- Nonagency
- Agency representation
- Limited dual agency representation
- Limited dual agency with assigned agents

A buyer or seller is *not* represented by a brokerage in a regulated real estate transaction unless the buyer or seller and the brokerage agree in a separate *written* document to such representation.

No type of agency representation may be assumed by a brokerage, buyer or seller or created orally or by implication. In other words, a client relationship that can only be created in Idaho with a separate, signed, written agreement. A nonagency relationship does not require any written agreement and the buyer or seller is known as a customer but there are still statutory duties.

Duties To A
Customer
IC 54-2086

Duties To A Customer (nonagency)

A customer is a buyer or seller who is *not* represented in a real estate transaction and the licensee is known as a nonagent. However, there are still duties and obligations that have to be followed. The following duties are mandatory and cannot be waived or nullified.

- Assist buyer and seller in sale or purchase

- Perform acts with honesty, good faith, reasonable skill and care

- Properly account for moneys placed in care of the brokerage

- Disclose to the buyer customer or seller customer, any adverse material fact actually known or reasonably should have been known.

A nonagent has no duty to conduct an independent inspection or verify the accuracy or completeness of any statement or representation made by the seller or source reasonably believed by the licensee to be reliable.

Nor is a nonagent required to conduct an independent investigation of the buyers financial condition or verify any statements made by the buyer.

If a buyer or seller elects to be a customer, the licensee should advise the customer that anything confidential in nature should not be disclosed to the licensee. Why? Because if the licensee does in fact end up representing the other party to a transaction the agent would owe duties to their client and may have to disclose such confidential information to their client.

Duties To A Client

If a buyer or seller enters into a written contract for representation, that buyer or seller becomes a client of the brokerage and its licensees. With the client relationship the following duties are owed:

1. Perform the terms of the written agreement

2. Exercise reasonable skill and care

3. Be available to timely present all written offers

4. Promote best interest of client in good faith, honesty, and fair dealing including but not limited to:

   - Disclosing any adverse material facts actually known or reasonably should have been known;

   - Seeking a buyer to purchase at a price, terms, and conditions acceptable to the seller and assisting in the negotiations;

   - Seeking a property and negotiating for purchase at a price, terms conditions acceptable to a buyer;

   - When appropriate, advising a buyer/client to obtain professional inspections and seek appropriate tax, legal, and other professional advice or counsel;

   - Upon written request from the seller, request reasonable proof of a buyer's financial ability to purchase property.

5. Properly account for moneys or property placed in the care and responsibility of the brokerage.

6. Maintain the confidentiality of specific client information:

   - Duty extends beyond termination of representation as long as information does not become generally known in the marketing community;

   - Confidential information by a licensee shall remain confidential even if the licensee later associates with a different broker;

   - Licensee shall inform a second client of any conflict of interest from a former client without first obtaining permission from a former client.

7. Unless agreed to in writing, no duty to verify accuracy or completeness of any statement or representation made regarding the property.

   Nor is there a duty to conduct an independent inspection to a client. In addition, unless in writing, there is not any duty to conduct an independent investigation as to the financial ability to complete a real estate transaction.

8. Duties are mandatory and cannot be waived or nullified.

9. Nothing prohibits the broker from charging a separate fee for each service provided in a transaction.

10. Imputed knowledge between multiple licensees will not result when neither has reason to have such knowledge.

11. A brokerage and its licensees may represent 2 or more buyers who wish to make an offer for the same property providing such buyers have been notified in writing of such offers. However, because of confidentiality, the terms and conditions of each offer is not required to be disclosed.

Adverse Material Facts
IC 54-2083 (1)
IC 54-2086 (1) (d)
IC 54-2087 (4) (a)

Adverse Material Facts

Whether a licensee represents a customer or client, the licensee has the duty and obligation to disclose to the customer or client 'all adverse material facts actually known or reasonably should have been known'.

Idaho code defines an adverse material fact as 'a fact that would significantly affect the desirability or value of the property to a reasonable person or which establishes a reasonable belief that a party to the transaction is not able to or does not intend to complete that party's obligations under a real estate contract'.

Areas that could lead to adverse material facts with some examples might be:

- Environmental hazards affecting the property - contaminated soils or water, meth, flood plains, air quality, etc;

- Material defects in the property - slide area, extreme soil conditions (clay), septic drain fields, poor drainage;

- Physical condition of the property - code violations (electrical, plumbing, or structural), peeling paint, broken windows, missing shingles, leaking roof, cracked foundation;

- Material defects in the title to the property - chain of title broken, missing owners, currently in foreclosure, tax liens, incomplete property survey;

- Facts that are in violation of the law - illegal use of the property (multiple family in single family zoning), violations of homeowners association rules, commercial use in non commercial zone, additions or alterations made without proper permits.

IC 54-2086 (5)	Idaho code also states that a nonagent brokerage or its licensees owe no duty to a buyer/customer to conduct an independent inspection of the property for the benefit of that buyer/customer and owe no duty to independently verify the accuracy or completeness of any statement or representation made by the seller or any source reasonably believed by the licensee to be reliable.
IC 54-2087 (7)	On a client basis, a brokerage and its licensees owe no duty to a client to conduct an independent inspection of the property and owe no duty to independently verify the accuracy or completeness of any statement or representation made regarding a property.
	But if the licensee has any knowledge about a 'adverse material fact', the agent is required to disclose to the buyer and seller regardless of their agency status. When in doubt, always consult with the designated broker or legal counsel.

Psychologically Impacted property
IC 55-2801

Psychologically Impacted Property

Real property could be deemed as being psychologically impacted if real property was at any time suspected of being the site of a suicide, homicide or commission of a felony which had no effect on the physical condition of the property.

Additional psychological impacts may include, but not limited to, an occupant or prior occupant had a disease to be highly unlikely to be transmitted through occupancy or that a registered or suspected sex offender occupied the property.

IC 55-2802

No cause of action shall arise against the owner for failure to disclose to the transferee or representative of the transferee that the real property was psychologically impacted.

Confidentiality
IC 54-2083 (6)

Confidentiality

Perhaps the biggest difference between an agent and a nonagent revolves around confidentiality. A client relationship requires confidentiality whereas a nonagent relationship does not.

Defined, confidential client information means information gained from or about a client that is:

- Not of public record;

- The client has not disclosed or authorized to be disclosed to 3rd parties;

- If disclosed, would be detrimental to the client; and

- The client would not be personally obligated to another person to the transaction.

Confidential information shall remain confidential even after representation has been terminated unless the confidential information becomes known in the public sector from a source other than the brokerage or its associated licensees.

Even though Idaho is not a full disclosure state, information generally disseminated in the marketplace is not confidential client information including a 'sold' price of real property.

If a licensee moves his license from one brokerage to another, confidential information given to the original brokerage shall remain with that brokerage unless it is released by the client in writing.

Buyer And Seller With Same Company
IC 54-2088

Buyer And Seller Clients With Same Company

So far we have discussed nonagency and single agency. But, what happens when a brokerage has a listing creating a client relationship with the seller and a buyer also wishes to be represented as a client with the same company? Can a buyer and a seller both be represented as clients within the same company?

The answer is yes, but with some conditions. When a brokerage represents both the buyer and seller in the same transaction, the agency relationship is known as Limited Dual Agency. Remember, in order for this type of relationship to occur, the brokerage must acknowledge approval in their written office policy. Let's explore the duties and obligations of a limited dual agent.

Limited Dual Agency
IC 54-2088

Limited Dual Agency

Only with an expressed written contract authorizing limited dual agency, can a brokerage represent both the buyer and seller. The key word is 'limited'. In order not to have conflict of interest, certain limitations will be imposed to not give one party an advantage over the other.

A brokerage acting as a limited dual agent may, at the option of the brokerage and with written consent, assign separate licensees to each client to represent and act solely for that client. Thus, the brokerage has basically allowed 'single' agency. This option could give both the client and their agent better communication without restrictions to make decisions that best meet each individual client.

The written consent to limited dual agency must have separate signatures of all clients involved in a transaction and must contain the following mandatory language:

CONSENT TO LIMITED DUAL REPRESENTATION AND ASSIGNED AGENCY

The undersigned have received, read and understand the Agency Disclosure Brochure.

The undersigned understand that the brokerage involved in this transaction may be providing agency representation to both the buyer and the seller.

The undersigned each understands that, as an agent for both buyer/client and seller/client, a brokerage will be a limited dual agent of each client and cannot advocate on behalf of one client over another, and cannot legally disclose to either client certain confidential client information concerning price negotiations, terms, or factors motivating the buyer/client to buy or the seller/client to sell without specific written permission of the client to whom the information pertains.

The specific duties, obligations and limitations of a limited dual agent are also contained in the Agency Disclosure Brochure.

Each client understands that a limited dual agent does *not* have a duty of undivided loyalty to either client.

Thus, a limited dual agent shall not disclose any of the following without express written consent:

- That a buyer is willing to pay more than the listing price for the property;

- That a seller is willing to accept less than the listing price for the property;

- Factors motivating the buyer to buy or the seller to sell;

- That a buyer or seller will agree to a price or financing terms other than those offered.

The parties to a transaction further acknowledge that, individual sales associates may be assigned to represent each client to act solely on behalf of the client consistent with applicable duties set forth in Section 54-2087, Idaho Code.

Assigned Agency

Assigned Agency
IC 54-2088

If a brokerage is acting as a limited dual agent and assigns separate sales associates to act on behalf of separate clients, <u>the designated broker continues to act as a limited dual agent</u> with the duty to:

- Supervise the assigned agents with their duties to their respective clients;

- Refrain from advocating on behalf of any one client over another;

- Refrain from disclosing, without permission, confidential information of any other client with whom the brokerage has an agency relationship.

If a designated broker determines confidential information of a client has been disclosed to another client and is a violation, the designated broker shall promptly provide written notice of the disclosure to the affected client.

As you can see, extra care needs to be taken when involved in a limited dual agency relationship whether assigned agency is utilized or not. Although tempting, do not disclose without written permission, any information that could be construed as confidential to anyone or anywhere including sales meetings. Remember, 'loose lips sink ships'.

Agency Confirmation - Purchase & Sale Agreement

Agency Confirmation
IC 54-2085 (3) (4)

A brokerage's agency relationship with a buyer and seller must be determined no later than the preparation of a purchase and sale agreement with copies confirming the agency relationship to both the buyer and seller.

In addition, a purchase and sale agreement, and any additional attachments which contain specific language and confirmation of the agency relationship regardless of whether the transaction involved representation or not.

Mandatory language that must accompany all real estate transactions involving real estate licensees is as follows:

REPRESENTATION CONFIRMATION AND ACKNOWLEDGMENT OF DISCLOSURE

1. Check one (1) box in Section 1 below and one (1) box in Section 2 below to confirm that in this transaction, the brokerage(s) involved had the following relationship(s) with the BUYER(S) and SELLER(S).

Section 1:

A. ☐ The brokerage working with the BUYER(S) is acting as an AGENT for the BUYER(S).

B. ☐ The brokerage working with the BUYER(S) is acting as a LIMITED DUAL AGENT for the BUYER(S), without an ASSIGNED AGENT.

C. ☐ The brokerage working with the BUYER(S) is acting as a LIMITED DUAL AGENT for the BUYER(S), and has an ASSIGNED AGENT acting solely on behalf of the BUYER(S).

D. ☐ The brokerage working with the BUYER(S) is acting as a NONAGENT for the BUYER(S).

Section 2:

A. ☐ The brokerage working with the SELLER(S) is acting as an AGENT for the SELLER(S).

B. ☐ The brokerage working with the SELLER(S) is acting as a LIMITED DUAL AGENT for the SELLER(S), without an ASSIGNED AGENT.

C. ☐ The brokerage working with the SELLER(S) is acting as a LIMITED DUAL AGENT for the SELLER(S), and has an ASSIGNED AGENT acting solely on behalf of the SELLER(S).

D. ☐ The brokerage working with the SELLER(S) is acting as a NONAGENT for the SELLER(S)

Each party signing this document confirms that he has received, read and understood the Agency Disclosure Brochure adopted or approved by the Idaho real estate commission and has consented to the relationship confirmed above. EACH PARTY UNDERSTANDS THAT HE IS A "CUSTOMER" AND IS NOT REPRESENTED BY A BROKERAGE UNLESS THERE IS A SIGNED WRITTEN AGREEMENT FOR AGENCY REPRESENTATION.

NOTE - The last paragraph of the above confirmation and acknowledgment disclosure contains an important clause in *ALL CAPITAL LETTERS*.

| IC 54-2085 (5) | Failure of a licensee to properly and timely give a buyer or seller the agency disclosure brochure or the failure of a licensee to properly and timely obtain any written agreement or confirmation shall be a violation and subject to discipline. |

Duration Of Agency Relationship
IC 54-2091

Duration Of Agency Relationship

If an agency relationship has been established, how long does it last? The agency relationship commences on the date indicated on the written agreement and will end at the earliest of:

- Performance or completion of the representation;
- Agreement by the parties;
- Expiration of the agency relationship agreement.

Broker Compensation
IC 54-2089

Broker Compensation

Payment of compensation or a written agreement for compensation does not create or constitute an agency relationship for representation.

Obligations After Termination Of Agency
IC 54-2092

Obligations After Agency Termination

Even after a transaction closes and the agency relationship terminates there are still several duties and obligations that continue after termination.

1. Accounting for all moneys and property received during representation;

2. Maintaining confidentiality of all information defined as confidential.

Within the real estate industry, one will hear the term, 'fiduciary' which is based on a common law system and originated in England in the Middle Ages and expanded to former colonies of the British Empire including the United States.

A fiduciary duty is the highest standard of care and revolves around trust, honesty, and good business practice. The judicial system in the United States is based on common law and the principle that it is unfair to treat similar facts differently on different occasions. To add to the complexity there can be interactions between common law, constitutional law, statutory law and regulatory law.

Like all other states, Idaho operates under the premise of common law. However, the practice of agency in real estate activities operates under statutory law.

Representation Not Fiduciary
IC 54-2094

Representation: Not Fiduciary In Nature

Therefore, it should be noted that representation is not fiduciary in nature. While it is intended to abrogate (cancel, nullify) the common law of agency as it applies to regulated real estate transactions, a brokerage is not prohibited from entering into a written agreement with a buyer or seller which creates duties and obligations greater than the statutory requirements.

Unless such duties are expanded beyond the statutory duties, the duties and obligations are not fiduciary in nature and are not subject to equitable remedies for breach of fiduciary duty. On the other hand, if a licensees duties were expanded their services beyond the statutory duties, then the licensee could be subject to both statutory and fiduciary duties.

Vicarious Liability Abolished
IC 54-2093

Vicarious Liability Abolished
Another law that may be different from other states is that vicarious liability is abolished. A buyer or seller shall not be liable for a wrongful act, error, omission or misrepresentation made by the broker or licensees.

On the other side, a brokerage or licensee representing a client shall not be liable for a wrongful act, error, or omission or misrepresentation made by the client unless the licensee should have known of the wrongful act, error, omission or misrepresentation.

BEFORE ANSWERING QUESTIONS – Can you define or explain:

4 types of brokerage relationships	Disclosure of adverse material facts
Agency Disclosure brochure	How long confidentiality exists
Agency Confirmation	Independent investigation requirements
When agency disclosure is required	Requirements after agency termination
Fiduciary vs. Statutory duties	Requirements of seller representation
Duties to a customer	Requirements of buyer representation
Duties to a client	Duration of agency relationships
Limited dual agency	Consent to Limited Dual Agency
Process to create assigned agency	Agency renewal requirements

Questions - Chapter 11

1. When is a prospective buyer or seller to receive the agency disclosure brochure?

    A. Upon the first meeting
    B. Prior to writing a contract
    C. Before closing a transaction
    D. First substantial business contact

2. What is the purpose of the buyer or seller signing the agency disclosure brochure?

    A. To establish a client relationship
    B. To create a customer relationship
    C. To acknowledge receiving the brochure
    D. To secure a real estate activity

3. If a buyer is a 'customer' and not a 'client', what duties must the agent extend to the 'customer'?

    A. None, unless there is a written contract
    B. Must collect fee or commission from another party to a transaction
    C. Disclose adverse material facts
    D. Verify accuracy of statements made by a seller.

4. A Exclusive Buyer Representation Agreement will:

    A. Be binding only when an offer and acceptance has been completed.
    B. Disallow the buyer from previewing property without their agent.
    C. Create a legally binding contract
    D. Bind the buyer for an unlimited time

5. A real estate agent would be classified with what type of agency?

    A Universal
    B. General
    C. Special
    D. Specific

6. The Idaho Brokerage Representation Act was created to identify obligations between the consumer and the:

    A. Buyer
    B. Seller
    C. Real estate licensee
    D. Real estate brokerage

7. How many types of agency can be practiced in Idaho?

   A. One
   B. Two
   C. Three
   D. Four

8. Signing the Agency Disclosure Brochure establishes what kind of agency relationship?

   A. None
   B. Client
   C. Customer
   D. Both customer and client

9. Where is the confirmation of an agency relationship contained?

   A. Agency Disclosure Brochure
   B. Purchase & Sale Agreement
   C. Buyer representation agreement
   D. Seller representation agreement

10. What is the primary difference between a customer and a client?

    A. Disclose adverse material facts
    B. Exercise reasonable skill and care
    C. Maintain confidentiality
    D Lender approval

11. When a buyer signs a representation agreement, who is the client relationship with?

    A. The agent the buyer is working with
    B. The real estate brokerage
    C. Idaho Real Estate Commission
    D. Idaho Association of Realtors®

12. When can limited dual agency with assigned agents be used?

    A. Only with written consent of all clients in a transaction
    B. Whenever a client desires
    C. Is allowed at anytime
    D. Only if Agency Disclosure Brochure states such relationship.

13. A signed and dated record of a buyer or sellers receipt of the agency disclosure brochure is kept by whom?

    A. Listing and selling agent
    B. Selling brokerage
    C. Each brokerage
    D. Both the buyer and seller

14. Each party not represented by a brokerage is classified as:

    A. Single buyer or seller
    B. Limited disclosed client
    C. Client
    D. Customer

15. Nonagent refers to working with or assisting a buyer or seller as a:

    A. Limited disclosed customer
    B. Client
    C. Customer
    D. Limited disclosed broker

16. Who cannot act as an assigned limited dual agent?

    A. A listing or selling agent
    B. A designated broker
    C. An associate broker
    D. A sales associate

17. An agent is working with a buyer client who makes an offer on another company's listing. The agent is practicing as:

    A. Limited dual agent
    B. Single agency
    C. Limited disclosed agent
    D. Nonagent

18. The practice of real estate and representation in Idaho is based on:

    A. Statutory law
    B. Common law
    C. Fiduciary law
    D. Federal law

19. A transaction closed and the agent represented the buyer as a client. When does confidentiality terminate?

   A. When agency confirmation signed
   B. At closing or representation cancelled
   C. Extends beyond termination until information becomes generally known in community
   D. Confidentiality never terminates unless agent changes brokerages

20. Adverse material fact(s) must be disclosed to:

   A. Customer
   B. Client
   C. Both customer and client
   D. Neither customer or client

Fair Housing & Ethical Practice

Fair Housing

Protected Classes
Idaho Fair
Housing
IC 67-5909 (2)

Protected Classes
Idaho basically mirrors Title VIII of the Civil Rights Act of 1968 known as the Fair Housing Act as amended. The Act prohibits discrimination in the sale, rental, and financing of dwellings. Prohibited discrimination includes:

- Race
- Religion
- Color
- Sex
- National origin
- Familial status
- Handicap

Most Fair Housing violations occur in the rental/property management arena. Anyone that rents should pay particular attention about advertising, steering, screening applications, occupancy standards and rules, reasonable accommodation/modifications, employee training, eviction, and record keeping.

Since Idaho does not regulate property management as far as real estate agents are concerned, this textbook will not go into detail surrounding Fair Housing and property management. Real estate agents should be very careful when it comes to potential steering or advertising violations.

Advertising

Fair Housing - Advertising
A key to successful marketing real estate for sale, is the use of various types of media advertising. One must be very careful about the selection of words contained in advertising. Advertising copy cannot lead toward or restrict from any of the protected classes in any advertising.

Most newspapers won't accept advertising that uses words that violate the Fair Housing Act by showing preference for a protected class. A good checklist of words that can and cannot be used is posted at the end of this chapter.

Steering

Fair Housing - Steering

The definition of steering is 'the illegal funneling of home buyers toward or away from a particular area based on the desire to influence the makeup of that neighborhood'.

A real estate agent should identify the housing needs of the buyer and locate those homes that meet the buyer's needs. Be careful to not use phrases such as 'good' neighborhood which is highly subjective. Or, 'you would not be comfortable or fit into a particular neighborhood'; it could be a lawsuit just waiting to happen.

Buyer Instructs Preference

On the other hand, when prospective buyers, on their own initiative, explicitly instruct their agent of a preference or a dis-preference for particular neighborhoods with reference to a classification based on a protected class status, the agent would not make housing unavailable and, thus, would not violate subsection 804(a) of the Fair Housing Act, merely by accommodating the clients' stated preference or dis-preference. It's a slippery slope and if there is any possibility of violating the Fair Housing Act, the agent should clearly document such buyer's instructions. In addition, the agent should have other houses available to show outside the specific area the buyer has shown preference.

The Fair Housing Act dos not interfere with an agent's delivery of services, as long as agents themselves do not indicate their own discriminatory preferences/dispreferences or, without instructions from their clients, limit the scope of the search, or otherwise make dwellings unavailable to them.

Sexual Orientation Gender Identity

Sexual Orientation Or Gender Identity Issue

Sexual orientation and gender identity are not protected classes under the Fair Housing Act. Law does not protect gays, lesbians, or other sexual minorities with discrimination in housing.

However, in 2012, the HUD office of Fair Housing and Equal Opportunity issued a regulation to prohibit LGBT (lesbian, gay, bisexual, transgender) discrimination in federally-assisted housing programs.

Anyone owning or operating a HUD-funded housing complex cannot inquire about an applicants sexual orientation or gender identity. 20 states prohibit housing discrimination based on sexual orientation and/or gender identity but Idaho is not among them.

Boise City Code
5-15-3 (C)

1-4-1 (B)

Some Idaho cities, including Boise, have passed ordinances prohibiting housing discrimination based on sexual orientation and/or gender identity in the sale, purchase, lease or rental housing accommodation. For example, under the Boise city code, the penalty for violation is a misdemeanor, punishable by a fine not exceeding $1,000 and imprisonment in the county jail not to exceed 6 months or both.

Illegal Activities

Illegal Activities

Under the Fair Housing Act, it is against the law to:

- Refuse to rent to you or sell you housing.
- Tell you housing is unavailable when if fact it is available.
- Show apartments or homes in certain neighborhoods only.
- Advertise housing to only preferred groups of people.
- Refuse to provide you information regarding mortgage loans.
- Deny you property insurance.
- Conduct property appraisals in a discriminatory manner.
- Refuse to make certain modifications for mental or physical disability including persons recovering from alcohol and substance abuse.
- Fail to design and construct accessibility for the disabled.
- Harass, coerce, intimidate, or interfere with anyone exercising or assisting someone with their fair housing rights.

Commission On Human Rights
IC 67-5809

The Commission on Human Rights was created to protect individuals and their interest in personal dignity. The Commission will hear complaints of alleged discrimination within 1 year of the alleged unlawful discrimination.

If one feels they have been discriminated against, they can also file a formal complaint with a HUD regional office. The Fair Housing Enforcement Center for Idaho is located with the U. S. Department of HUD in Seattle, Washington.

Additional fair housing resources in Idaho include:

- Idaho Legal Aid Services
- Idaho Human Rights Commission
- Intermountain Fair Housing Council

Care needs to be taken when working with any buyers or sellers, landlords or tenants when it comes to discrimination or perceived acts of discrimination.

Ethical Applications

'Doing It Right'

If used properly and practiced regularly, critical thinking and ethical application will be translated to adopting professionalism in the business world and the real estate industry. It's really nothing more than - 'doing it right'.

However, the need of consistent improvement with application modification takes effort. Understanding of changes in societal expectations, legislated regulations, constant increased education and economic changes, requires constant monitoring. Everyone dealing with real estate activities need to coordinate with each other with a common goal to arrive at a successful conclusion.

Moral Character

Ethical dealing with real estate can be interpreted as: taking moral character and applying fairness connected to good business applications. Positive experiences should occur for all participants to a real estate related activity. The process of fair dealing takes careful thought and critical thinking.

There are many resources available to assist with ethical applications, including but certainly not limited to:

- Idaho Real Estate License Law and Rules handbook
- National Association of REALTORS® - Code Of Ethics
- Federal Fair Housing Act
- *Doing The Right Thing*, 3rd Edition, Deborah Long
- *Real Estate Ethics*, 3rd Edition, William Pivar and Donald Harlan
- Daily interaction with other colleagues

IREC Booklet

Idaho Real Estate License Law And Rules Booklet
The handbook is the 'bible' of real estate law application to licensed real estate agents. There are references throughout the handbook that regulate activities of a real estate licensee including but not limited to:

IC 54-2038
IC-54-2085
IC-54-2053
IC 54-2055
IC-54-2060
IC-54-2065
IC-54-2059

- Broker responsibilities
- Agency disclosure
- Advertising
- Licensees dealing with their own property
- Grounds for disciplinary action
- Penalty for acting without a license
- License revocation, suspension or other disciplinary action

The Idaho Real Estate Commission is the regulatory agency that oversees licensed and unlicensed real estate activities. Their Education Department and Education Council constantly keeps the real estate industry updated on various laws affecting real estate licensees.

NAR Code Of Ethics

National Association of REALTORS® - Code Of Ethics
The National Association of REALTORS® has an excellent resource for ethical behavior and critical thinking with their Code Of Ethics. By creating standards of conduct to promote ethical practices by all real estate licensees, not just those who join the trade organization, the Code Of Ethics serves as the foundation of ethical real estate practice.

The Code Of Ethics is made up of Articles followed up with Standards of Practice that are reviewed and addressed annually.

- Articles 1 thru 9 - Duty to clients and customers
- Articles 10 thru 14 - Duty to the public
- Articles 15 thru 17 - Duties to REALTORS®

Members of the National Association of REALTORS® are required to take a mandatory ethics course every two years.

Fair Housing Act

Federal Fair Housing Act
The federal Fair Housing Act was created to make discrimination an illegal act based on a series of protected classes. In addition, the federal Fair Housing Act addresses activities associated with discrimination by using 'testers' to assist in the verification of violations that carry criminal penalties.

Doing The Right Thing

Author, Deborah Long, has specialized in ethics training of real estate practitioners for many years for both real estate regulatory agencies as well as the real estate industry at large. Her book, *Doing The Right Thing*, is an excellent practitioner's guide that addresses:

- Ethics and the practice of real estate
- Values, principles, and ethics
- The evolution of moral reasoning
- Ethical systems
- Models for ethical decision making
- Professional perspectives
- Applying ethics: agency
- Applying ethics: fair housing
- Applying ethics: environmental hazards
- Applying ethics: working with colleagues and employers
- Applying ethics: community and public concerns

Doing The Right Thing is designed to allow individual and group discussions alike with case studies and exercises. The lively book is designed to guide the reader to make clear and ethical decisions, not only in a professional setting, but also to inspire a fulfilling personal life.

Real Estate Ethics

Both authors, William Pivar and Donald Harlan, have been in the real estate industry for many years and have authored numerous books including *Real Estate Ethics* covering ethical conduct in such areas as:

- Understanding ethics
- Responsibilities to your principal
- Responsibilities to the buyer
- Responsibilities to the general public
- Responsibilities to other licensees
- Responsibilities to other licensees within your office
- Broker trust funds
- Advertising and ethics

Interaction With Other Colleagues

Nothing helps bridge ethical issues better than just good communication between anyone and everyone involved with real estate. If one isn't sure about how to handle a questionable situation, seek outside assistance from others. Get a '2nd opinion' and research.

Remember the law doesn't always agree or abide with ethical behavior. When in doubt, follow the golden rule and treat others as you would like to be treated. Don't compromise ethical behavior for personal gain by avoiding personal responsibility. You'll sleep better at night.

Fair Housing Advertising Word/Phrase List

This sample list is not all inclusive. Consult legal counsel if you have questions. As a rule of thumb, the listing agent should promote the features of the listing and not use any language for describing the type of buyer, tenant, or the type of neighborhood.

** May be used when housing requirements meet the Fair Housing Act criteria for "housing for older persons.

ACCEPTABLE	CAUTION	UNACCEPTABLE	UNACCEPTABLE
Credit Check Required	Active	Able-bodied	(Nationality)
Equal Housing Opportunity	Board Approval Required	Adult Living	Near Church(es)
Family Room	Close to _____	Adult Community	Near Synagogue
First Time Buyer	Desirable Neighborhood	Adults Only	Near Temple
Fixer Upper	Domestic Quarters	African	Newlyweds
Great for Family	Female(s) Only	Agile	No AIDS
Hobby Farm	Female Roommate	Asian	No Alcoholics
In-law Apartment	(Gender)	Bachelor	No Blacks
Luxury Townhomes	Gentleman's Farm	Bachelor Pad	No Blind
Near Mass Transit	Grandma's House **	Black Neighborhood	No Children
Near Golf Course	Golden Ager s**	Black Only	No Crippled
(Neighborhood Name)	Handyman's Dream	Catholic	No Deaf
Nice	Male(s) Only	Caucasian	No Drinkers
No Drinking	Male Roommate	Chicano	No Impaired
No Drugs	Man (Men) Only	Chinese	No Mentally Handicapped
No Drug Users	Membership Approval	Christian	No Mentally Ill
No Smoking	Nanny Room	Colored	No Play Area
Number of Bedrooms	Near	Couple	No Retarded
Nursery	Near Country Club	Couples Only	No Unemployed
Nursing Home	No Students	Empty Nesters	Not for Handicapped
On Bus Route	No Gays	(Ethnic References)	Older Person
Play Area	No Lesbians	Exclusive (Neighborhood)	One Child
Privacy	(Number of Persons)	Executive	One Person
Private Driveway	Prestigious	Filipino	Oriental
Private Entrance	Private	Healthy Only	Physically Fit
Private Setting	Quality Neighborhood	Hispanic	Polish
Quality Construction	Quiet Neighborhood	Hungarian	Protestant
Quiet	Retirees **	Indian	Puerto-Rican
Reference Required	Secure	Irish	Quiet Tenants
(School District)	Seniors **	Integrated	Sane Tenant Only
(School Name)	Senior Citizens **	Jewish	Shrine
Secluded	Senior Housing **	Landlord (description of)	Singles Only
Security Provided	Single Woman/Man	Latino	Single Person
Senior Discount	Sophisticated	Mature Couple	Stable
_____ Square Feet	Students	Mature Individual	Tenant (description of)
Starter Home	Two People	Mature Persons	White Neighborhood
Townhouse	Within Walking Distance	Mexican-American	White Only
Traditional Style	Woman (Women) Only	Mormon Temple	
Tranquil Setting		Mosque	
Verifiable Income		Must Be Employed	
View of _____			
With View			

BEFORE ANSWERING QUESTIONS – Can you define or explain:

Fair Housing Act

Examples of discrimination

Steering

Fair housing advertising

Protected classes

Sexual orientation & gender identity

Fair Housing illegal activity examples

Where to file a formal complaint

Questions - Chapter 12

1. The Fair Housing Act protected classes include:

   A. Marital status
   B. Gender
   C. Sexual orientation
   D. Sex

2. A Code of Ethics course is mandated by:

   A. Idaho Real Estate Commission
   B. Fair Housing Act
   C. Intermountain Housing Council
   D. National Association of REALTORS®\

3. The Commission On Human Rights will hear alleged discrimination complaints within what period of time?

   A. 1 year
   B. 2 years
   C. 4 years
   D. 5 years

4. Where is sexual orientation and gender identity approved as a protected class?

   A. In all states
   B. Cities with over 1,000,000 population
   C. Non federally assisted housing programs
   D. Some Idaho cities

Chapter 13

Working With Sellers And Buyers

> **Words of Wisdom**
>
> *"As long as man stands in his own way, everything seems to be in his way."*
>
> Ralph Waldo Emerson

Important Relationship

The relationship between a brokerage and a seller revolves around good communication, full understanding between the agent and the seller, and hopefully good decisions with rational thinking by all parties to a transaction. After all, successful real estate transactions begin with having a piece of property that will meet the needs of everyone, not just the seller or the buyer.

Most residential real estate is purchased with emotion (I want it) and verify with facts (appraisals).

Different Players

The buyer and seller are the primary players in a transaction but there are many sideline players such as: appraisers, lenders, inspectors, attorneys, accountants, and others who also play an important part in the real estate transaction process beginning with the seller and the property being offered for sale.

Appointments

Appointments For Listing

If possible, it is suggested that you make two listing appointments with the potential seller to demonstrate your professionalism and efficiency prior to securing the listing.

Inform the seller that the first appointment will take around 1-2 hours to get the necessary data and explain the marketing process. If everyone agrees, the second appointment will present the results of the data collected and secure a listing.

Make sure the seller understands that the purpose of the first appointment is to get acquainted and secure information to complete an accurate CMA (Competitive Market Analysis) and not to secure a listing.

Agency Disclosure Brochure
IC - 54-2085 (1)

Agency Disclosure

It's reasonable to assume that the first listing appointment would constitute a 'substantial business contact'. Therefore, the licensee needs to have the Agency Disclosure Brochure ready to give to the prospective seller at the first meeting.

When the brochure is given to the seller, the licensee should take the time to explain the different types of agency the brokerage offers so the seller fully understands the difference between a customer and a client.

It must also be remembered that each brokerage shall keep a signed and dated record of a buyer or seller's receipt of the agency disclosure brochure.

Listing Packet

Ordering A Listing Packet

Prior to meeting with the prospective seller at their home, it is advisable to order a 'property profile' or 'listing packet' from your chosen title insurance company. Generally you can order and get a listing packet within 1 day. If time doesn't allow, then get the listing packet prior to the 2nd meeting with the seller.

IDAPA 18.01.56
012.02

The listing packet can contain no more than 6 items below:

- Copy of last deed appearing of record
- Copy of deed of trust or mortgage appearing to be in full force or effect
- Plat map reproduction or locator map
- Copy of applicable restrictive covenants
- Tax information
- Property characteristics - number of rooms, square footage, etc.

Deed Information

The names on the deed should match the names of the people you will be meeting with. The financing document(s) will show what type of security instrument is used together with all the terms and conditions of such financing document(s).

Read the 'fine print' and again make sure of who exactly is liable for the obligation and if there are any clauses that could adversely impact the seller upon sale.

Subdivision Map

The 'subdivision' map will show roadways, easements, and the 'fine print' may indicate some general restrictions to meet local code or other issues not contained in the deed or other documentation. For example, there may be reference to noise abatement if the subdivision is near an airport. Or, perhaps there could be a comment regarding height restrictions to abide with special uses nearby.

Property
Dimensions

The map of the actual property the seller is thinking of selling will give actual property dimensions and show where all the corner pins are located.

CCR's

Finally, the CCR's (Covenants, Conditions and Restrictions) will provide the private restrictions that the homeowners are supposed to abide by. Again, read them carefully to see if there are violations, either with the subject property, or with other homeowners in the subdivision and that they conform with the original document together with the buyers intended use.

First Appointment

First Appointment

Arrive on time! The first impression is a lasting impression so you want to present yourself as a professional.

Once you and the seller become acquainted and get ready to gather information about the property, present and explain the Agency Disclosure Brochure and secure signatures.

Presentation Manual	To save time and to make sure you cover all the points necessary to secure and market a listing. Use of a presentation manual is an excellent method to keep everyone focused and make sure nothing is left out. A presentation manual will explain the process of listing property from the beginning through closing including all facets of marketing. The presentation manual could provide a 'check list' for both the seller and the agent for tracking.

After all the basic information is obtained, the next step is to get measurements of the home to apply to a CMA. Explain to the seller the time frame needed to create an accurate CMA and make an appointment for the second meeting and listing presentation.

Before leaving, you might consider leaving a partially completed sample of a listing agreement and Seller Property Condition Disclosure form. The seller can take time to carefully review the information and ask any questions when you meet with them on the second appointment.

Appointment For 2nd Meeting	When scheduling the time to meet for the 2nd.appointment, request that any and all owner(s) be present. Why? If both you and the seller decide to list the property, you will want all owner signatures on the listing agreement. The second appointment, like the first appointment, shouldn't take more than 1-2 hours to complete.

Red Flags	## Red Flags

When evaluating the marketability of a property, one needs to carefully consider issues that could adversely affect the value of the property. Issues to look for to make the appropriate adjustments include but are not limited to:

- Stigmatized issues - crime, noise, traffic, etc.
- Lead based paint
- Mold
- Sidewalks and foundations
- Drainage - soil instability
- Flood plains - or changes in elevations
- Roofs, windows, flashings
- Septic systems
- Recreational hazards
- Encroachments
- Easements
- Private restrictions
- Crawl spaces and basements
- House alignment
- Electrical, plumbing, HVAC systems
- Glass
- Smoke detectors

Second Appointment	## Second Appointment

Like the first appointment, arrive on time!

The 2nd appointment will focus on the explanation of the CMA together with any 'back-up' documentation to assist with your verification of value and securing the actual listing if agreed upon between you and the seller.

In addition, have a listing agreement ready and partially filled out, except for price and terms, to be signed.

Let the seller know exactly what happens once a listing is signed: MLS, advertising, marketing, any repairs needed, showings, negotiations, and closing.

Be patient and answer any questions or concerns the seller may have regarding all your services and the listing process. Be a good listener so you can build good communication, understanding and rapport.

Competitive Market Analysis

The heart of the whole listing process starts with a CMA. The CMA is designed to assist the seller in establishing a price in which the property will meet the sellers needs to sell. The CMA is discussed at length in Chapter 8.

CMA

There are many formats to produce a CMA from Multiple Listing Service forms to in-house brokerage company forms. Whatever format is used, be sure you can verify your information.

CMA Purpose
IC 54-4105 (2)

A CMA might be compared to, and used as, a condensed version of the basic features contained in a fee appraisal. Remember, you are not an appraiser and cannot do an appraisal unless you are licensed to do so. However, Idaho Code does allow you to give an opinion of price for the purpose of securing a prospective listing or sale, providing you have a salesperson or broker license.

A review of the chapter on Appraisal, offers the basics of appraisals and CMA's. Generally speaking, the market approach concept of appraisal will be used most of the time in developing CMA's to assist with valuing residential real estate.

Brokerage Representation Agreements
IC 54-2050

Brokerage Representation Agreements

All brokerage representation agreements, whether with a buyer or seller, must be in writing and contain required elements, whether exclusive or non-exclusive.

Required Elements

Seller
- Conspicuous and definite beginning and expiration date
- A property description that is sufficient to identify the property with understanding as to the location of the real property
- Price and terms
- All fees or commissions
- Signature of the owner or owner's legal, appointed and duly qualified representative and the date of such signature

Buyer
- Conspicuous and definite beginning and expiration date
- All financial obligations of the buyer or prospective buyer, if any, including, but not limited to, fees and commissions
- The manner in which the fee or commission will be paid to the broker
- Appropriate signatures and their dates

IC 54-2049 (2)	Copies of a brokerage representation agreement shall be given to the person or persons signing the agreement and also be retained in the broker files including electronically generated agreements. The broker is required to retain copies of the agreements for 3 calendar years after the year the event occurred.
IC 54-2050 (4) (5)	A broker or salesperson who obtains a written representation agreement shall give a legible signed copy to the person or persons signing such agreement. Agreements that are electronically generated shall be deemed as true and correct as the originals.
IC 54-2056 (5)	**Brokerage Representation Agreements Belong To broker**
	As a reminder, should a real estate agent terminate their affiliation with a broker, they shall immediately turn over to the broker all listing information, listing contracts, and other property belonging to the broker.
	Furthermore, a sales associate shall not engage in any practice or conduct that would encourage clients of the brokerage to terminate any legal business relationships with the broker unless there is written permission from the broker.

Seller Representation Agreement	**Seller Representation Agreement** (AKA - Listing Agreement)
	The Seller Representation Agreement, more commonly known as a 'listing agreement' is a contract between a real estate brokerage and the seller. Thus, the terms of the agreement belong to the broker, with the agent acting on behalf of the broker.
	There are many types of listing agreements, including an 'open listing' in which any brokerage that has an open listing contract is authorized to represent the seller. However, the seller also reserves the right to sell their property themselves without any compensation to any brokerage. However, if a brokerage secures an acceptable offer the brokerage would be entitled to compensation
Open Listing	The 'open' listing is rarely used since it offers no protection to any brokerage unless the brokerage is involved in a sale. 'Open' listings are also not allowed to be placed in a MLS (Multiple Listing Service) designed for real estate companies.
Exclusive Agency Listing	Another form of a listing is known as an 'exclusive agency' listing. This type of listing also allows the seller to sell their own property without any obligation to a brokerage. But if the brokerage initiates a sale, the brokerage will be compensated according to the terms of the contract. This type of listing may or may not be allowed in a MLS. Even though the brokerage is protected, the seller still has the right to sell their own property without the use of a broker.
Exclusive Right To Sell Listing	The most used and popular type of listing is known as an 'exclusive right to sell' listing since the brokerage is protected regardless of who sells the property. With this protection, the brokerage can invest in the marketing of the property with confidence regardless of who initiates an offer for acceptance.
	As the name implies, the brokerage has the 'exclusive' right to market the property.
	When preparing any kind of Seller Representation Agreement, the seller needs to understand exactly what an 'exclusive right to represent' really means. Once the agreement is signed the agreement becomes a binding contract.

Term Of Agreement	# Term Of The Agreement
	The term of the agreement should be indirectly based on the estimated time it takes to market and close a sale. Many variables enter into the equation including: broker policies, economic trends, supply and demand of customers/clients, and the cost.
Price Ranges To Consider	# Price Ranges
	Some price ranges sell quicker than others. Understanding where price point ranges break and change, may influence which price range the seller should consider to be most effective. Once a price range is identified that best suits the marketability of the property, a specific price can be determined by the seller.
	The agent should explain the pros and cons of 'list high and negotiate' verses 'list low and stay firm' theories to assist the seller in selecting what price best fits the timing desired to initiate an offer.
Finance Programs	# Finance Programs
	Different financing programs come with different requirements including additional closing costs to the seller. The agent should explain how different financing programs can affect supply and demand based on interest rates, etc. Also, some financing programs require different construction standards which could require additional costs.
	If the seller would consider 'seller financing', be very careful how the terminology is added into the agreement. You many consider adding the term, 'seller may consider ....'. This does not require the seller to accept the terms but rather 'consider' the terms. The seller should be encouraged to seek legal counsel if they do not fully understand the consequences of added language used within a contract; especially when it comes to financing.
Brokerage Fee	# Brokerage Fee
	The brokerage fee is based on the brokerage office policy. It may also give the sales associate latitude to negotiate a fee different from the brokerage office policy. The seller needs to know and understand what happens once a listing has expired. Someone who saw the property while it was listed, but makes an offer after expiration, may obligate the seller to still pay a fee.
Additional Fees	# Additional Fees
	Additional fees the brokerage may impose need to be fully explained to the seller so there are no surprises later. If the agent pays for some items, make sure it is explained how the agent will be reimbursed. Or, if additional fees for additional services are imposed, make sure everyone knows how such fees are calculated and paid.
Excluded Personal Items	# Excluded Personal Items
	If the seller desires to remove any items listed in the 'included items' section, such items should be so noted in the 'excluded items' section and make reference to the lines they were originally included.

Possible Tax
Consequences

Tax Consequences

If the seller is considering a short sale or even foreclosure, they should be encouraged to seek legal and accounting counsel before they make the decision. There can be major tax consequences, not to mention credit issues and other possible penalties.

Authorizations

Authorizations

Various authorizations for MLS, lockbox, internet options, inclusion into social media conduits and other types of advertising need to be explained to the seller. Educating the seller regarding some of the possible implications may result in the seller accepting or not accepting some of the authorizations.

Seller Property
Disclosure Form
IC 55-2508

Seller Property Disclosure Form

Whether using the state mandated Seller Property Disclosure Form or the Sellers Property Condition Disclosure form that can only be used by members of the Idaho REALTORS®, it is the responsibility of the seller to correctly fill in and complete the form.

Idaho Code requires that any person who intends to transfer any residential real property, including non-owner occupied rental property shall complete all applicable items contained in a property disclosure form. Residential property is defined as consisting of not less than 1 nor more than 4 dwelling units.

10 Day Delivery
IC 55-2509

Every transferor is to deliver a completed disclosure form to a perspective transferee within 10 calendar days of the transferors acceptance of the transferees offer. The perspective transferee shall acknowledge receipt of the form and shall return a signed and dated copy back to the transferor.

3 Day Procedure
To Rescind
IC 55-2515

If the transferee objects to the conditions of the disclosure form and plans to rescind, the transferee must state in writing to a specific objection and deliver a signed and dated document of rescission within 3 business days following the date the transferee received the disclosure form from the transferor.

Exemptions to Provide A Seller Property Disclosure Form

Exemptions
IC 55-2505

Exemptions to provide a Seller Property Disclosure form include:

1. Transfer pursuant to court order
2. Transfer by deed in lieu of foreclosure
3. Transfer to beneficiary of deed of trust in default
4. Transfer by foreclosure
5. Transfer under power of sale within 1 year of foreclosure
6. Transfer by mortgagee who acquired by 'deed in lieu of'
7. Transfer by fiduciary of a decedent's estate
8. Transfer from one co-owner to other co-owners
9. Transfer made by spouse to more lineal persons
10. Transfer between spouses or former spouses
11. Transfer to or from the state or another gov't entity
12. Transfer of new uninhabited residential real property
13. Transfer of occupant who has occupied for at least 1 year

14. Transfer by inheritance to non occupants within 1 year
15. Transfer by relocation company within 1 year
16. Transfer from a descendant's estate

Disclosure Requirements

The disclosure form is *not* a warranty and the purchaser is encouraged to obtain an independent professional inspection. The seller is relaying what they know to be true but does not possess any expertise in construction or any specific areas related to the construction or condition of the improvements on the property.

New Construction IC - 55-2508

Sellers of newly constructed residential real property shall disclose information regarding annexation and city services including:

1. Is the property located in an area of city impact, adjacent or contiguous to a city limits?

2. Does the property, if not within the city limits, receive any city services, thus making it legally subject to annexation by the city?

3. Does the property have a written consent to annex in the county recorder's office, making it legally subject to annexation by the city?

Required Disclosure By All Sellers

All sellers are required by Idaho law to disclose the following:

4. Appliances and service systems are functioning properly except (seller needs to list and explain).

5. Specify problems with
    Basement water
    Foundation
    Roof condition and age
    Well (type)
    Septic system
    Plumbing
    Drainage
    Electrical
    Heating

6. Describe any conditions that may affect ability to clear title (encroachments, easements, zoning violations, lot line disputes, etc.)

7. Are you aware of any hazardous materials or pest infestations on the property?

8. Have any substantial additions or alterations been made without a building permit?

9. Any other problems, including legal, physical or other not listed above that you know concerning the property.

The seller certifies the information is true and correct and both the buyer and seller acknowledge receipt of the disclosure.

The Idaho REALTORS® form is much more comprehensive than the mandated state form and is used by the majority of agents throughout the state. However, some offices choose to use their own disclosure form that matches the requirements of Idaho Code. Your broker can advise you on your office policy as to which form to use.

C.L.U.E. Report

FACT Act Disclosure (lexisnexis.com)

Comprehensive Loss Underwriting Exchange (C.L.U.E.)

Although not directly addressed in the state required Seller Property Disclosure form, the seller should consider ordering a LexisNexis CLUE report that shows all property insurance claims up to 7 years. This report can be an additional marketing tool especially if no claims have been made so the potential buyer is aware of possible future events that could occur.

For example, if a property is in a low lying area prone to water intrusion and has in fact been subject to water damage, the amount and cost of the damage will be reflected in the report. Or, if there has been a mold issue or maybe damage as a result of high wind, these issues would be shown in the C.L.U.E. report.

In spite of a preconceived notion of a negative impact from previous damage stated on a C.L.U.E. report, the prospective buyer would be able to see the damage was repaired to reduce future occurrences.

Of course a 'perfect' report would certainly put the prospective buyer at ease regarding damage claims.

Lead Paint Disclosure Form

Lead Paint Disclosure

If the home was built prior to 1978, the seller will need to agree to provide the Lead Paint Disclosure form to be signed by all parties to the transaction including the agent's acknowledgment.

Services Disclaimer

Services Disclaimer

A disclaimer should be understood by the seller that the agent is not an expert in all phases of real estate. In the event the seller requests the agent to secure products or services, the seller will reimburse the agent immediately when payment is due.

Limited Dual Agency Consent IC 54-2088 (1) (2)

Limited Dual Agency Consent

In order for an agent to represent both parties in a real estate transaction, there must be written consent. Such consent should be well explained and acknowledged by the seller so there are no questions regarding the use of Limited Dual Agency and the duties of the agent.

Seller Information

Seller Information

As a precaution for the agent, many contracts contain a clause that the information provided by the seller is warranted to be true and correct. However, the clause does not excuse the agent from disclosing to all parties when such information is known by the agent to be untrue or incorrect.

Although improbable, there should be a clause that identifies what happens should a law suit be filed including attorney fees to the prevailing party. If you are not using a pre-printed form contract, consult an attorney to help you draft appropriate language. *Do not practice law without a license.*

Discrimination
IC 67-5909

Discrimination Prohibited

A clause acknowledged by both the seller and broker should address that it is illegal to discriminate in the showing, sale, or leasing of the property based on race, color, national origin, religion, sex, family status or disability.

Time Is Of The Essence

Time Is Of The Essence

'Time Is Of The Essence' means strict time issues must be adhered to and can make a contract voidable or void if not done within the time frames agreed upon. Be aware of any and all issues that revolve around specific time frames.

Calculating Sellers Net Sheet

Calculating A Sellers Net Sheet

Obviously one of the key elements to selling a property is about how much money the seller will net after the sale closes. A rough estimate is to add around 3-4% to the listing fee and the total of both costs will be what the seller might expect to be the total selling costs will be to close. But, there are more items to take into consideration.

Basically the net proceeds will be the gross sales price, minus unpaid mortgage(s) balances, minus other selling costs. There could also be some 'hidden' costs such as overdue or unpaid bills not known or even judgments that have been attached to the property.

Some mortgages have penalties for 'pre-paying' a mortgage early or 'recapture', so it's important the seller be aware of and know exactly what the net proceeds will be upon sale.

Closing costs that the seller will have, or may incur, include:

- First mortgage
- Second mortgage (or more)
- Home equity loan
- Prepayment penalties
- Property taxes - current year (pro-rated)
- Property taxes - from previous year(s)
- Tax service fee
- Medical bills (secured by the property)
- Home improvement assisted grants
- Seller assisted closing costs
- Brokerage commission or fee
- Title insurance - owners
- Escrow fee (usually ½ of total escrow fee)
- Recording fees
- Overnight delivery (mortgage payoff)
- Homeowner Association Dues (HOA) - unpaid or prepaid
- Irrigation fees - unpaid or prepaid

- Unpaid public services - water and sewer
- Special assessments
- LID's (Local Improvement Districts)
- Judgments and IRS liens
- Mechanic's liens
- Fuel oil or propane

Guideline 1

Terminating A Listing Contract

Because of the confusion and possible legal ramifications, the Idaho Real Estate Commission has established a guideline to address cancellation or withdrawal of listings.

There may be circumstances in which a listing contract needs to be terminated either by the seller or the brokerage. Extreme care should be taken to make sure the seller understands the difference between the term 'withdraw' and the term 'cancel'.

There have been issues where the brokerage allowed the seller to withdraw the listing. The seller, in turn, listed with another company only to find the seller owed two commissions; one to the original listing company and the other to the new listing company.

Withdraw Listing

How could this happen? If the owner withdraws, the contract remains in full force and effect. Some listing agreements specify a penalty for early withdrawal of the property from sale by the owner. Even if no penalty is specified in the contract, the court might award damages to a broker if the seller has acted unreasonably and the broker acted in good faith.

Listing Cancellation

If the owner cancels a contract, they are essentially 'breaking' the contract. Unless the owner has sufficient legal justification to break the contract, he or she may be required to pay the losses or damages incurred by the broker. Such damages can include the out-of-pocket costs incurred by the broker.

Marketing

Before a seller is ready to commit to a listing, the seller wants to know how the agent plans to market the home once the listing is signed. Two questions the seller usually has are – "when and where will you advertise" and "when will you do an open house?". Interesting questions, but there is more to listing a property than just advertising and open houses.

In other words, the licensee needs to market their personal skills – "When you list with me, this is what I'll do for you." A good and complete check list in a presentation manual will address everything the agent will do for the seller including but not limited to:

- Communication - how and how often
- Preparing property to show and sell - 'curb appeal', repairs
- MLS input and lockbox - how system works
- Advertising - when where and how

- Safety and security - windows, doors, locks, etc.
- Open Houses - pre-planning preparation
- Showings - property preview and showing by other agents
- Listing review - how often for extensive in-depth review
- Offers - paperwork, inspections, timing
- Closing - paperwork, accuracy, timing

Although a CMA helps set the marketing tone around a listing, it is the ability of the agent to convey what services best fits the needs of the seller and everyone else involved for a successful sale. Getting a listing, putting a sign in the yard and praying just won't get the job done. Servicing a listing takes a well coordinated effort designed for success with a well executed plan.

Use of Unlicensed Assistants And Office Staff

Use Of Unlicensed Assistants And Office Staff

With the advent of 'team' groups of agents and high producing agents, there may be additional support staff needed to assist with the various marketing topics mentioned above.

Guideline 17

License law prohibits unlicensed persons from negotiating, listing or selling real property.

Unlicensed personal assistants or office staff may complete forms prepared and as directed by licensees but should never independently draft legal documents such as listing and sales contract. Nor should they offer opinions, advice, or interpretations for activities that require a license. In addition, they should not distribute information on listed properties other than that prepared by the employing broker or broker associate. As you can see, the use of unlicensed assistants at open houses could invite trouble if a licensee isn't available.

Remember, unlicensed personnel cannot get involved with offering, negotiating, selling or contracting. So what can unlicensed assistants and office staff do?

- Perform clerical duties which may include gathering information

- Provide access to a property to contractors, home inspectors, & appraisers with seller permission. However, they may not provide access to potential buyers

- Distribute prepared information at an open house, so long as no negotiating, offering selling or contracting occurs

- Answer simple questions on their own brokerage's listed properties with information from MLS printouts, property flyers, data sheets and marketing materials by the brokerage and/or employing licensee

- Deliver paperwork to other licensees

- Deliver paperwork to sellers or purchasers, if such paperwork has already been reviewed by a licensee and no offering of opinions, giving advice, or interpretations of such documents are given

- Assist in the preparation of market analysis for sellers or buyers under the direction and approval of the licensee

If a designated broker has a written office policy explaining the duties, responsibilities and limitations on the use of personal assistants, the policy should be reviewed by and explained to all licensed and unlicensed assistants.

Advertising
IC 54-2053

Advertising

One of the most important and key elements to creating interest in a listing is through advertising via yard signs, flyers, newspaper, MLS, Open Houses, social media, and even TV.

Because advertising plays such an important role in the marketing of real estate, the real estate salesperson or broker need to fully understand the regulations that address the advertising of real estate

All advertising of listed property shall clearly and conspicuously contain the Idaho broker's business name including licensed branch offices.

Only active Idaho licensees named by an Idaho broker, may advertise Idaho property in Idaho or may have a sign placed on a property.

No advertising shall provide any information to the public or to prospective customers or clients which is misleading in nature. Misleading is defined as information that when taken as a whole will deceive the person(s) whom it is intended to influence.

An example of deceptive advertising is advertising a listing that has expired or closed. Another example would be leaving a yard sign showing the property is for sale when in fact it the property listing expired.

Guideline 13

Any advertising that promotes a property with only the salesperson's name or 'team' name without having the broker licensed business name placed in the advertising could be interpreted as deceptive. Remember, *all* property advertising must include the broker's licensed business name (including internet and social media, car wraps, clothing, etc). Guideline 13 offers some frequently asked questions and answers.

Care needs to be taken with photos taken by others that are considered as copyrighted without some sort of copyright release.

As risk reduction, it is recommended that each brokerage develop and maintain a written policy regarding use of the internet and social media advertising by its sales associates and employees.

Periodic review of any advertising and marketing information should be taken to assure the information is correct and not misleading.

IC 48-603

The Idaho Consumer Protection Act addresses advertising goods or services with intent not to sell.

Guideline 8

IREC guideline 8 offers addresses the proper and improper uses of OFF-MLS and Coming Soon listings.

Working With A Buyer

One of the first issues that should be addressed when an agent meets with a prospective buyer is how financially the buyer plans to purchase a home. If the buyer elects to pay cash, the agent can start the home search immediately.

If the buyer needs financing to purchase a home, one of the first tasks the buyer needs to do is to get qualified or better yet, approved for financing. By knowing exactly what the buyer is able to purchase, the right homes can be sought to match the finance program the buyer is approved for.

Financing Approval

Need For Financing

As much as 85% of residential purchases involve financing. It's very important and good business to have the prospective buyer seek a lender who in turn can issue an approval letter indicating exactly what the buyer is qualified to do. This necessitates applying for loan approval and is another indication that the buyer is 'willing, able, and ready' to buy property.

It is not unusual for a buyer to want to postpone going to a lender until they actually find a home they wish to make an offer on. Although there isn't anything that disallows this to occur, the buyer should be aware there are literally hundreds of different loan programs; each with different requirements for qualifying to meet the specific needs of the buyer and property alike.

Without knowing exactly which program best fits the needs of the buyer, it is very difficult for the agent to locate a property that also fits within the parameters of the financing requirements.

Explain to the buyer, that it is in the best interest of everyone to get pre- approved first before looking at any property. It will save time, money, and possibly disappointment down the road.

When the buyer contacts a lender, it is suggested that the buyer inquire about Idaho specific loan programs both local and state sponsored with a lender. Bear in mind, not all lenders are approved for or work with many local and state programs available. So the buyer might need to shop around.

'Comfort Level'

However, just because a buyer is approved for a certain amount doesn't mean the buyer will feel comfortable for the amount approved. So ask the buyer what their 'comfort level' is when it comes to making a long term financial commitment. If the comfort level is for a lesser amount of financial obligations, then the agent should seek properties that match their financial 'comfort level'.

Once an agent and a prospective buyer decide to look for a home to buy and the buyer has met with a lender and knows the price and terms to purchase, the agent needs to address Agency and decide what type of agency will be utilized before the buyer discloses any additional information to the agent that could compromise a confidential disclosure of information.

Agency Representation For The Buyer

Agency Representation - Customer Or Client
When working with a prospective buyer, one of the first issues that needs to be addressed is Agency.

'Blue Brochure'
IC 54-2085

Idaho Code clearly states, "A licensee shall give to a prospective buyer or seller at the first *substantial business* contact the agency disclosure brochure (ake 'Blue Brochure') adopted or approved by the Idaho Real Estate Commission".

Always have the brochures available since one doesn't always know when a substantial business contact may occur.

As a safety precaution, it may be a good idea to read line by line, the contents of the brochure to the buyer before they sign the acknowledgment.

Another tip would be to have a copy of the brokerage office policy to show the purchaser regarding the types of agency the brokerage allows.

Duties To A
Customer
IC 54-2086

Working With The Buyer As A 'Customer'
If there is no written agreement, the prospective buyer will be treated as a customer. Without any agreement, the buyer is free to work with any and all agents to meet their real estate needs.

However, there are still statutory duties the agent must comply with when working with a buyer-customer. The chapter on Agency extensively identifies the duties for both a customer and client.

As a precaution, the agent may desire to utilize a compensation agreement with the buyer to assure the brokerage it will receive an agreed upon compensation should the buyer purchase a property with the aid and assistance from an agent with the brokerage.

Such agreement needs to be carefully read and understood by all parties since it is a binding contract.

Duties To A Client
IC 54-2087

Working With A Buyer As A 'Client'
If a buyer signs a representation agreement with a brokerage, the buyer becomes a 'client' of that brokerage and is committed to that brokerage based on the terms and conditions of the agreement.

The statutory duties to a client are different that those duties owed a customer including the duty to maintain the confidentiality.

Limited Dual
Agency
IC 54-2088

It's also important that the client know and understand that if they choose 'limited dual agency' for representation, the agent is representing both parties in a transaction in which the listing and sale is with the same broker. That being said, the agent cannot legally disclose to either client certain confidential information such as motivating factors or price negotiations without written permission to whom the information pertains.

Single agency type relationships might be possible with a dual agency situation in which the broker will assign individual agents to represent solely one client. However, the designated broker still remain as a limited dual agent. Maintaining confidentiality is critical for all parties.

Buyer Representation Agreement

Buyer Representation Agreement Requirements

If there is a written and properly executed Buyer Representation Agreement, a client relationship has been established.

It's extremely important that the agreement (contract) is carefully and completely read and understood by the buyer before the buyer signs the agreement.

Because many real estate licensees are members of the Idaho Association of REALTORS®, the Buyer Representation Agreement (RE-14) is used by the majority of the membership which makes up the majority of all licensees in Idaho.

So, let's go over some of the basics of the form. In small print, the top of the agreement identifies the form as a 'legally binding contract' and the buyer needs to fully understand possible implications that may be contained within the body of the agreement.

'Exclusive' Right To Represent

The agreement also identifies it as being an 'exclusive' right to represent, followed with bold print re-emphasizing and defining the conditions of 'exclusive' representation and the type and location of the property sought.

Term

The term of the agreement has specific beginning and ending dates.

Services

The broker identifies what brokerage services will be used to locate and negotiate property for the buyer. However, the agreement also states those services the brokerage may not be qualified to advise the buyer on certain real estate matters.

Financial information

Financial information, the handling of other potential buyers, and the limits of confidentiality of offers should be discussed to reduce potential conflicts or misunderstandings.

Consent To Limited Dual Representation

A detailed explanation for consent to limited dual representation and assigned agency is given and cites Idaho Code in the explanation. To make sure there isn't any misunderstanding, the agreement addresses and seeks buyer acknowledgment with consent to release the broker from conflicting agency duties. To make sure the buyer understands, the buyer will need to initial acceptance of limited dual representation or retain single agency.

Non-discrimination

A non-discrimination clause is included in the agreement to address potential fair housing issues and acknowledges the brokerage will not discriminate against any prospective buyer, seller or lessor.

Some legal disclosures are addressed including: severability, singular and plural defined, and default/attorney's fees, should the buyer default under the terms of the agreement.

Compensation   The area of compensation offers various options for the brokerage to receive compensation. Not all brokerages will offer all the options available. The brokerage should let the licensees know what is acceptable and supported with a written office policy.

It is equally important that the buyer know what could happen after the Buyer Representation Agreement expires as far as compensation or penalties are concerned.

Addendum   Other terms and conditions not covered in the Buyer Representation Agreement can be added into the agreement. If space is not sufficient, an Addendum can be added but make sure the Addendum is addressed in the original agreement with wording such as 'see attached Addendum #1'.

Facsimile transmission is o.k. but law does require such use be approved in writing so the issue is addressed in the agreement.

Signatures   The authority of signatory together with 'time is of the essence' helps bind the agreement into a legal binding contract. All that is left are the proper signatures and date.

Seller Property Disclosure Form

Seller's Name and Address_____

　　　　Section 55-2501, et seq., Idaho Code, requires Sellers of residential real property to complete a property condition disclosure form.

　　　　PURPOSE OF STATEMENT: This is a statement of the conditions and information concerning the property known by the Seller. Unless otherwise advised, the Seller does not possess any expertise in construction, architectural, engineering or any other specific areas related to the construction or condition of the improvements on the property. Other than having lived at or owning the property, the Seller possesses no greater knowledge than that which could be obtained upon a careful inspection of the property by the potential buyer. Unless otherwise advised, the Seller has not conducted any inspection of generally inaccessible areas such as the foundation or roof. It is not a warranty of any kind by the Seller or by any agent representing any Seller in this transaction. It is not a substitute for any inspections. Purchaser is encouraged to obtain his/her own professional inspections. Notwithstanding that transfer of newly constructed residential real property that previously has not been inhabited is exempt from disclosure pursuant to section 55-2505, Idaho Code, Seller of such newly constructed residential real property shall disclose information regarding annexation and city services in the form as prescribed in questions 1., 2., and 3.

1. Is the property located in an area of city impact, adjacent or contiguous to a city limits, and thus legally subject to annexation by the city? _____Yes _____No
2. Does the property, if not within city limits, receive any city services, thus making it legally subject to annexation by the city? _____Yes _____No
3. Does the property have a written consent to annex recorded in the county recorder's office, thus making it legally subject to annexation by the city? _____Yes _____No
4. All appliances and services systems included in the sale, (such as refrigerator/freezer, range/oven, dishwasher, disposal, hood/fan, central vacuum, microwave oven, trash compactor, smoke detectors, tv antenna/dish, fireplace/wood stove, water heater, garage door opener, pool/hot tub, etc.) are functioning properly except: (please list and explain)
_____
5. Specify problems with the following:
　　Basement water _____
　　Foundation _____
　　Roof condition and age _____
　　Well (type) _____ Problem _____
　　Septic system (type)_____ Problem _____
　　Plumbing _____
　　Drainage _____
　　Electrical _____
　　Heating _____
6. Describe any conditions that may affect your ability to clear title (such as encroachments, easements, zoning violations, lot line disputes etc.) _____
_____
7. Are you aware of any hazardous materials or pest infestations on the property_____
_____
8. Have any substantial additions or alterations been made without a building permit? _____ _____
_____
9. Any other problems, including legal, physical or other not listed above that you know concerning the property?
_____

　　　　The Seller certifies that the information herein is true and correct to the best of Seller's knowledge as of the date signed by the Seller. The Seller is familiar with the residential real property and each act performed in making the disclosure of an item of information is made performed in good faith.

　　　　I/we acknowledge receipt of a copy of this statement.
Seller:　　　　　　　　　　　　　　　　　　　　Buyer:

_____　　　　　　_____
Date:_____　　　　　　　Date: _____

_____　　　　　　_____
Date: _____　　　　　　　Date: _____

BEFORE ANSWERING QUESTIONS – Can You Define or Explain:

Importance of 2 listing appointments	Required elements of a contract
Listing package	Misleading information
Deed information	Seller Representation Agreement terms
CCR's	Seller Property Disclosure requirements
Competitive Market Analysis (CMA)	Lead Paint disclosure
Making adjustments on a CMA	Calculating a sellers net sheet

Questions – Chapter 13

1. What's the purpose of the first listing appointment?

    A. Gather information
    B. Present a listing packet
    C. Secure the listing
    D. Discuss MLS requirements

2. What type of comparable properties are generally used as the basis of a CMA?

    A. On market
    B. Recently sold
    C. Expired listings
    D. For sale by owner properties

3. What information must be included with all advertising of listed properties?

    A. Agent's name
    B. Broker's name
    C. Seller's name
    D. Brokerage business name

4. The Sellers Property Disclosure must be completed by the:

    A. Agent
    B. Buyer
    C. Seller
    D. Lender

5. Sellers of newly constructed residential real property shall disclose information regarding:

    A. Annexation
    B. Contractor licensing
    C. Mechanic's liens
    D. Occupancy tax

6. Covenants, Conditions, and Restrictions (CCR's) impose what kind of restrictions?

    A. Public
    B. Private
    C. Personal
    D. Popular

7. When must the Agency Disclosure brochure be given to a prospective seller?

    A. Prior to writing a contract
    B. Before Property Condition completion
    C. At first substantial business contact
    D. Prior to closing

8. A listing packet or property profile from a title company cannot contain more than how many items?

    A. 4
    B. 5
    C. 6
    D. 7

9. A Seller Property Disclosure Form definition of 'residential real property' is?

A. 1 to 4 dwelling units
B. All residential dwellings
C. Residential dwellings built before 1978
D. Any residential property up to 10 plex

10. Brokerage representation agreements must:

A. Be submitted to the MLS
B. Be completed by sellers only
C. Be in writing
D. Be orally approved

11. An agent had a seller sign a representation agreement for 90 days with a automatic 30 day extension if the property didn't sell within the 90 days. The agreement is:

A. Legal
B. Illegal
C. Acceptable
D. Prohibited

Real Estate Contracts

Contract Definition

Contract Definition

A contract is an agreement between two parties or entities with an obligation to do or not to do something in return for a benefit known as consideration.

The real estate industry is founded upon the use of contracts which can involve variations of circumstances and complexities.

The Idaho Real Estate Commission encourages real estate agents to advise the parties to a transaction to seek legal counsel for any questions arising on any area of contract law. This concept is acknowledged with statutory duties - 'when appropriate, advising the client to seek appropriate tax, legal, and other professional advice or counsel when legal advice is desired or necessary'.

Rule 303

Furthermore, Rule 303 of the Idaho Real Estate License Law and Rules specifically states on the subject of legal opinion - 'A broker or sales associate will *not* discourage any party to a real estate transaction from seeking the advice of an attorney'.

Contract Requirements

6 Essential Elements

Contract Essential Elements
In order to create a valid real estate contract to purchase real estate in Idaho, there are six essential elements.

1. Legally competent parties

2. Offer and acceptance with a meeting of the minds

3. Lawful objective

4. Enforceable legal description

5. Valuable consideration

6. Written document, signed by all parties to the contract

Competent Parties
IC 32-101

Legal Capacity

In Idaho, a person must be 18 years old or older to have the legal capacity to enter into a valid contract. Persons younger than 18 years old are considered as minors.

Although minors do not have the legal capacity to contract, a minor may make a contract and live up to it. The contracts created by a minor are not void, but they are voidable. This means the minor may renounce or dis-affirm as long as they are still minors or within a reasonable time after they have reached 18 years old.

Incompetency

If a person has been declared by a court to be of unsound mind, any contract made by that person would be void. The reason is that such persons do not comprehend the consequences or obligations of a contract. However, an incompetent person could be represented by a parent or legally appointed guardian to assume the obligations of a contract.

Parole Board Approval

If a person has been convicted of a serious crime and enters into a contract, the contract could be considered void unless such a person has obtained expressed permission from the state parole board.

Contracts To Be In Writing
IC 9-505 (4)

Idaho Statute Of Frauds

The Idaho Statute of Frauds statesa an agreement for the sale or interest therein of real property is invalid unless it is in writing. Also, leases for longer than 1 year must be in writing.

Commissions To Be In Writing
IC 9-508

The Idaho Statute of Frauds also clearly states that no contract for the payment of any sum of money or thing of value (i.e. real estate commission) shall be valid unless the contract shall be in writing. Examples would include seller or buyer representation agreements, where a fee or commission is involved between the consumer and the brokerage.

"Meeting Of The Minds"

Mutual Agreement

The term mutual agreement may also be known as the 'meeting of the minds'. It means that there is a willingness by all parties to enter into a contract. However, mutual agreement cannot exist if the terms are ambiguous, vague, or undisclosed. Nor can a mutual agreement exist if the offer does not clearly state the obligations of each party involved.

Also a meeting of the minds cannot be achieved if there is an intent to deceive or failure to disclose important information such as an adverse material fact. Lastly, the offer and acceptance must be without duress or undue influence giving unfair advantage to one party over the other.

Lawful Objective

A contract cannot be made for the purpose of breaking the law or violating public policy. An example could be purchasing a property for a use such as a day care center in a residential neighborhood that violates local use code. Such a contract is void or if already in operation, it is unenforceable in a court of law.

Enforceable Legal Description

The legal description should be sufficient enough that no other property will encroach or duplicate the subject property. A recorded record of survey will verify the description.

Valuable Consideration

If consideration is lacking from any party to a transaction, the contract fails to be legally binding. Both parties give something of value to a real estate contract. Consideration does not always involve money. It can also be a promise, other property or services.

Written Document Signed By All Parties

It's not unusual to have additional documents accompany a offer to purchase such as: amendments, addendums, counter offers and possible required disclosures. ALL documents must be signed by ALL parties to a transaction.

Purchase and Sale Agreements

Purchase And Sale Agreement

Although real estate licensees cannot draft a contract, they are allowed to 'fill in the blanks' of a pre-printed contract or agreement. The state of Idaho does not endorse the use of, or require any specific contract form or format to be used in the practice of real estate. But a generally known contract for acquiring or selling residential real estate in Idaho is known as a Real Estate Purchase and Sale Agreement (RE21) created by the Idaho REALTORS®.

Approximately 90% of all active licensees in Idaho are members of the Idaho REALTORS®. Most licensees use the forms created by this trade organization for their real estate business since they are well drafted and have been reviewed by legal counsel. However, there may separate agreements drafted by member boards used by their local members.

Suggesting Legal Counsel

Disclaimer To Seek Counsel

At the top of the Purchase and Sale Agreement, a disclaimer should clearly suggest the agreement is a legally binding contract and if any party has questions, an attorney or accountant should be consulted. It's not a bad idea for an agent to read the total disclaimer to both buyer and seller as a reminder that outside counsel could be sought.

Unauthorized Practice Of Law

It's really important that real estate licensees work hard on giving lots and lots of information instead of advice. Every contract is a legal document which adds to the confusion of whether an issue results in information or advice. Taking instructions from the buyer and/or seller and converting those instructions into the contract can create a fine line. Did the agent make the recommendation to do something or did the agent merely transcribe the desires of the buyer or seller into the contract?

The penalty for someone practicing law without a license includes a fine not to exceed $500, or be imprisoned for a period not to exceed 6 months, or both! Again, let the buyers and sellers make legal decisions based on information you can provide, not the other way around.

In addition, a real estate licensee could lose his/her real estate license, commission, and even face a law suit for damages.

Fill In The Blanks

Sample contracts created by private sources or trade organizations are designed to 'fill in the blanks'. Remember, not all contracts contain the same information. If one is unfamiliar with a contract, it is highly suggested that each and every line be read by the agent, buyer and/or seller.

Some rules to use when completing a contract that will help assure a 'meeting of the minds' between the parties include.

1. Fill in all the blanks
If some of the blanks are not applicable, then fill in the blank with NA or DNA which means 'not applicable' or 'does not apply'. The key is to make the contract complete and not ambiguous.

2. Dates
If dates are called for, try to work with specific dates. If an activity is tied to a situation occurring and not a specific date, the interpretation of the situation timing could be contested, especially if 3rd parties are involved.

3. Categories
Address all the categories contained within the contract to make sure all parties are aware of and understand the printed material. If any category involves activity that is date specific, make sure the dates to perform are reasonable and achievable. An overlooked category may lead to trouble later on after a contract has been accepted by all parties.

4. Personal Property
If there are personal property items included, make sure there is a complete identification of each item, including model and serial numbers if possible. Specific identification eliminates the possibility of substitution of items.

5. Mandatory disclosures

If there are mandatory disclosures required, either state or federal, make sure they are included in the contract. As an example, lead paint disclosure is required if the residence was built prior to 1978. Another example would include the Idaho required Seller's Property Condition Disclosure which is to be completed by the seller.

6. Addendums and attachments

Identify each and every addendum and/or attachment with numbers in a sequential order. Do not skip numbers or mix numbers and alphabet letters.

7. Signatures

Make sure all parties to a transaction sign and date all of the documents relating to a transaction. Avoid using initials whenever possible, especially if they aren't accompanied by a date. This can lead to question as to who signed what and when.

Representation Confirmation
IC 54-2085 (4)

Representation Confirmation

Care needs to be exercised to make sure the agency representation is accurate and correct. Whether there is representation or not, Idaho code requires representation confirmation to be included with any purchase and sale contract and must contain the following language:

REPRESENTATION CONFIRMATION AND ACKNOWLEDGMENT OF DISCLOSURE

1. Check one (1) box in Section 1 below and one (1) box in Section 2 below to confirm that in this transaction, the brokerage(s) involved had the following relationship(s) with the BUYER(S) and SELLER(S).

Section 1:

A. ☐ The brokerage working with the BUYER(S) is acting as an AGENT for the BUYER(S).

B. ☐ The brokerage working with the BUYER(S) is acting as a LIMITED DUAL AGENT for the BUYER(S), without an ASSIGNED AGENT.

C. ☐ The brokerage working with the BUYER(S) is acting as a LIMITED DUAL AGENT for the BUYER(S), and has an ASSIGNED AGENT acting solely on behalf of the BUYER(S).

D. ☐ The brokerage working with the BUYER(S) is acting as a NONAGENT for the BUYER(S).

Section 2:

A. ☐ *The brokerage working with the SELLER(S) is acting as an AGENT for the SELLER(S).*

B. ☐ *The brokerage working with the SELLER(S) is acting as a LIMITED DUAL AGENT for the SELLER(S), without an ASSIGNED AGENT.*

C. ☐ *The brokerage working with the SELLER(S) is acting as a LIMITED DUAL AGENT for the SELLER(S), and has an ASSIGNED AGENT acting solely on behalf of the SELLER(S).*

D. ☐ *The brokerage working with the SELLER(S) is acting as a NONAGENT for the SELLER(S).*

Each party signing this document confirms that he has received, read and understood the Agency Disclosure Brochure adopted or approved by the Idaho real estate commission and has consented to the relationship confirmed above. EACH PARTY UNDERSTANDS THAT HE IS A "CUSTOMER" AND IS NOT REPRESENTED BY A BROKERAGE UNLESS THERE IS A SIGNED WRITTEN AGREEMENT FOR AGENCY REPRESENTATION.

Time Is Of The Essence

Time Is Of The Essence

If 'time is of the essence' is incorporated into a contract, performance of one party is necessary to enable that party to require performance by the other party within the time period specified in the contract.

Failure to comply within the required time frame constitutes a breach of the contract. When time is not of the essence, courts generally permit parties to perform their obligations within a reasonable time. It's important to understand what is 'reasonable' to one party may not be 'reasonable' to the other.

There can be many different time frames contained in a purchase and sale agreement; not just a closing date. Dates for financing, inspections, repairs, appraisals and possession need to be known by all parties concerned.

Contract Changes

Contract Changes

It's not unusual for a purchase and sale agreement to incorporate changes after acceptance but prior to closing. Addendums, amendments, counter offers, exhibits, and other items can flow in and out of a transaction. The key to maintaining a 'meeting of the minds' is to accurately keep all changes in numerical sequence and dated. There needs to be a 'paper trail' with no voids.

If changes are made, it is important to know the difference between an addendum and an amendment.

Addendum

Addendum

It might be noteworthy to know that an addendum adds to or supplements an existing contract. For example, the original contract called for and was contingent upon a property inspection by a certain date. The inspection was completed and acknowledged with an addendum.

Amendment

Amendment

An amendment, on the other hand, is a later modification to the terms of an already accepted contract. Should it be necessary to change the contract it would require the approval of *all* parties to the contract. An example would be to extend a closing date from the original accepted date. Both parties would need to agree. If one of the parties does not agree, then the original closing date would be the binding date for all parties to close the transaction.

Counter Offer

Counter Offer

A counter offer is a response to a previous offer that has not yet been accepted. Making a counter offer automatically rejects the original offer or prior counter offer. Because the original offer becomes 'dead' with a counter offer, sellers need to be aware that the buyer is no longer bound by the terms of the original offer.

Caution needs to be taken when a seller makes minor changes on the original offer and initials and dates the changes. Bear in mind, the seller 'changed' the original document and the changes now constitutes a counter offer requiring buyer acceptance.

Although not that unusual, these 'short cuts' are not recommended. Why?

- 1ˢᵗ - where is the time limit for the buyer to accept?
- 2ⁿᵈ - in what manner is the buyer expected to accept?
- 3ʳᵈ - do changes change other parts of the original agreement?

If so, how? Are the changes (usually handwritten) legible? Initialing and dating changes on the original contract can be dangerous indeed. For example, changing a price could have implications surrounding the buyers ability to finance by changing the terms of financing.

By using a separate counter offer form, confusion as to who did what and when is greatly reduced or eliminated. The counter offer form allows plenty of space to make whatever necessary changes are needed to address unanswered issues in the original offer.

With a properly executed counter offer, signatures and dates are well documented to eliminate what changes and when changes were actually made. It is very important that the counter offer makes specific reference to the original offer so all the original terms and conditions are connected to and incorporated into the counter offer.

As a precaution to make sure all paperwork is incorporated, it is a good idea to have the counter offer stapled (not paper clipped) to the original offer and addendums, if any.

Also, do not use an addendum form and scratch out the word 'addendum' and add 'counter offer'. The sequence for acceptance and dates of an addendum are not adequate unless specifically referenced. Just use the counter offer form; it's much safer!

If a counter offer has specific language that incorporates it into the original agreement, it is not mandatory that the seller sign both documents. The seller may sign the counter offer only. However, if there isn't any specific incorporation language, the seller must sign both the counter offer and the original purchase and sale agreement.

Rejected Or Terminated Contract

Rejected Offers
IC 54-2048 (3) (d)

If a purchase and sale contract is not accepted or is rejected, there still needs to be a record of the 'sale fail'. The original or a true copy of all rejected offers must be retained in the files of the selling broker.

Although Idaho code does not identify who is to date and identify as 'rejected', it may be a good idea to have the seller actually date and sign as 'rejected' in their own handwriting as proof that the offer was actually presented to the seller. This would serve as proof that the rejection came from the seller and no one else.

Rejected Offers
Record Keeping
IC 54-2049

All offers accepted, countered or rejected, are to be kept by the broker for 3 calendar years *after* the year in which the event occurred, the transaction closed, all funds were disbursed, or the agreement and any written extension expired.

Double Contracts

Prohibited Double
Contracts
IC 54-2004 (23)

Double contracts, sometimes known as 'creative' financing, are prohibited, period!! You will find the term, 'double contract' used several times throughout this text as a constant reminder of this illegal activity.

No licensed broker or salesperson shall use, propose the use of, agree to the use of, or knowingly permit the use of a 'double contract'. Such conduct by a licensee shall be deemed flagrant misconduct and dishonorable and dishonest dealing and shall subject the licensee to disciplinary action by the Commission.

Simply put, a 'double contract' means 2 or more written or unwritten contracts of sale, purchase and sale agreements, loan applications, or any other agreements, 1 of which is not made known to the prospective loan underwriter or the loan guarantor, to enable the buyer to obtain a larger loan than the true sales price would allow, or to enable the buyer to qualify for a loan which he or she otherwise could not obtain.

Again, this is why it is so important that all addendums and amendments be included in sequential order. No side agreements are allowed without written disclosure to the loan underwriter.

Earnest Money Delivery
IC 54-2045 (4)

Handling Earnest Money

One of the required elements of a purchase and sale agreement includes earnest money (consideration). Idaho code requires all consideration, including cash, checks held in an uncashed form and promissory notes, received by a sales associate in connection with a real estate transaction shall be *immediately* delivered to the broker or the broker's office.

Earnest Money Transfer To 3rd Party

If the parties to a transaction have instructed the broker or its licensees, in writing, to transfer moneys or property to a 3rd party including but not limited to, a title, an escrow or a trust company, the broker or its licensees have no right to exercise control over the safekeeping or disposition of said moneys or property.

However, the broker shall be responsible for maintaining a record of the time and date that said moneys or property was transferred from the broker to a 3rd party.

Whoever delivers the earnest money or property to an approved 3rd party needs to get a receipt in exchange for the deposit. It's suggested that the receipt contain a date including hour and minute received. This will serve as evidence in case documents are either misplaced or lost.

Questions – Chapter 14

1. Subject area of legal opinions, Rule 303 states a broker or sales associate shall:

   A. Encourage the use of legal counsel
   B. Seek opinion from a title insurance company to verify their own opinion
   C. Not discourage any party from seeking advice from an attorney
   D. Obtain legal opinion from the Idaho Real Estate Commission

2. Leases must be in writing if they are longer than:

   A. 1 month
   B. 3 months
   C. 6 months
   D. 1 year

3. What's the maximum time a real estate salesperson can be imprisoned for unauthorized practice of law?

   A. 1 year
   B. 6 months
   C. 3 months
   D. Can receive a fine but not imprisoned

4. Representation Confirmation and Acknowledgment must be included with:

   A. Agency Disclosure Brochure
   B. Buyer Representation Agreement
   C. Seller Representation Agreement
   D. Purchase and Sale Agreement

5. What does a counter offer do to the original offer.

   A. Makes original offer voidable
   B. Voids the original offer
   C. Extends the terms of the original offer
   D. Makes original offer valid

6. All rejected offers must be:

   A. Maintained in broker's file for 5 years
   B. Removed from the broker's files
   C. Marked and signed as 'rejected'
   D. Marked and dated as 'rejected'

7. The use of a 'double contract' is:

   A. Encouraged
   B. Discouraged
   C. Prohibited
   D. Used as a back-up contract

8. When does earnest money need to be delivered
   to the broker or broker's office?

   A. Immediately
   B. Within 24 hours
   C. Within 48 hours
   D. Prior to closing

9. Who is responsible for record keeping of
   earnest money transferred to a 3rd party?

   A. 3rd party
   B. Bank or trust company
   C. Escrow or title company
   D Broker or broker's office

Chapter 15

Writing And Presenting Offers

Words of Wisdom

"We are what we repeatedly do. Excellence, therefore is not an act but a habit."

Aristotle

Preparing To Make An Offer

Preparing To Purchase

When the prospective buyer has made the decision to make an offer on a property, the next step is to prepare a Purchase and Sale Agreement providing the buyer is ready, willing, and able.

Both the agent and the buyer need to set aside enough time so the contract can be completed in it's entirety with plenty of time to explain and answer any questions.

Use Current Version

If using a pre-printed Purchase and Sale Agreement and other incorporated forms, make sure the most recent version is used. Occasionally changes in the law require changes in various forms.

The Idaho REALTORS® carefully reviews all their forms annually and any revisions usually are accompanied with new forms around June or July. Unless a law is declared an emergency in Idaho, legislated law changes take place on July 1 of the year the law was passed.

Only active members of the Idaho REALTORS® can use their forms and use by any other person is prohibited. Separate member boards may also have their own forms which also can only be used by the respective members of the board.

Good Business Practices

Good Business Practices

Some good business practices regarding the completion of the Purchase and Sale Agreement or any other incorporated forms include:

- Write legibly
- Refrain from using ambiguous language or phrases
- Refrain from using abbreviations

- Fill in all the blanks

- Use 'na' or 'dna' for 'not applicable' or 'does not apply'

- Use reasonable time frames to complete contingencies

- Use reasonable dates to meet 3rd party requirements

- Double check that stated dollar amounts are correct

- Properly identify included addendums or amendments

- Include agency representation confirmation - IC 54-2085

- Secure signatures of *all* parties to the transaction

Real Estate Purchase And Sale Agreement

Purchase And Sale Agreement

This text book will address some of the items that should or could be included in any Purchase and Sale Agreement.

However, many real estate licensees are members of the Idaho REALTORS®, may use forms created by this trade organization or member boards and cannot be used by non members.

Disclaimer

Disclaimer

Regardless of what form(s) are used, it should be clearly noted that the Purchase and Sale Agreement is a legal binding contract and if anyone has any questions, an attorney or accountant should be consulted before signing.

Buyer

Buyer

Identify the buyer(s) by a full name. If more than one buyer will be purchasing, separate each buyer from the other. Example: John L. Jones and Mary Sue Jones, not John and Mary Jones.

Purchase Price

Purchase Price

Make sure the filled in blanks are very legible, both numerically and spelled out.

Earnest Money

Consideration

There isn't any rule regarding the amount of consideration or better known as earnest money. However, the amount of earnest money should be sufficient enough to compensate the seller should the contract be cancelled or not completed by the buyer.

Earnest Money Delivery

IC 54-2045 (4)

Generally speaking, the buyer will tender a personal check which will be deposited either upon receipt or upon acceptance as stated in the Purchase and Sale Agreement as well as who will hold the earnest money.

Time Of Deposit

IC 54-2045 (1)

All consideration (earnest money) received shall be immediately delivered to the broker or broker's office.

All moneys received by a broker for another in a real estate transaction are to be deposited on or before the banking day immediately following the receipt day of such funds, unless written instructions signed by the party or parties having an interest in the funds direct the broker to do otherwise.

If the broker or associate receives a check to be held for later deposit, a ledger card needs to be created upon receiving the check in an uncashed form.

Return Of Earnest Money

IC 54-2045 (3)

If the earnest money is returned before deposit, a ledger record must also be created. A written and dated notation must be placed on both the Purchase and Sale Agreement, offer or other document dealing with the consideration, and on the ledger record. No consideration is to be returned without the knowledge and consent of the broker.

Financial Terms

Financial Terms

If the purchase requires financing, it's important to make sure all the dollar blanks add up to the purchase price. If they don't, there isn't a 'meeting of the minds'.

The financing terms and conditions need to be carefully reviewed to make sure all the 't's' are crossed and the 'i's' dotted, especially when it comes to the time frames.

A Purchase and Sale Agreement should state, in part, that the seller is to receive *written* confirmation that funds are sufficient to close and if such written confirmation is not received by the sellers within the *strict* time allotted, the sellers may at their option *cancel* the agreement. Sloppiness or failure to adhere to the language contained in the Purchase and Sale Agreement can lead to great disappointment.

Additional Terms

Additional Terms And Conditions

If additional terms or conditions are needed, this clause allows insertion such terms and conditions. It helps avoid using a separate addendum or amendment and keeps everything nicely contained in the original Purchase and Sale Agreement. Make sure whatever is inserted is legible and unambiguous.

Addendum

If there is not enough room on the Purchase and Sale Agreement, then use an addendum that makes reference to the Purchase and Sale Agreement.

Escalation Clause	A buyer may use a price escalation when the buyer believes there will be multiple offers on a property. An escalation clause states if a competing offer is made on the property, the bid will automatically increase by a certain amount of money to surpass the new offer to a predetermined limit.
Included/Excluded Items	## Included And Excluded Items There are pre-printed items that are included with the transaction and the seller and the buyer need to know and understand what goes with the property. If there are additional items to be included, they need to be inserted to include model and/or serial numbers if possible. Model and serial numbers help eliminate any confusion regarding specific items that accompany a sale.
Bill Of Sale	It's also a good business practice to get a bill of sale for any personal property that will be included in the sale; especially if the personal items are of great value. Examples might be expensive riding lawn mowers, tractors, refrigerators, washers and dryers, swing sets, etc. If, on the other hand, items are to be excluded or replaced, they should also be so noted and even tagged, to eliminate any confusion upon closing about what items are or are not included with the sale.
Title Insurance	## Title Insurance Provider Typically the buyer chooses the title insurance company when making an offer but then the seller changes the title company to their choice. This can happen when the seller could receive a discount or perhaps a builder has their own favorite title insurance company to work with.
RESPA Procedures	RESPA procedures and regulations to the United States Code include: Title 12 - Banks and banking, Chapter 27 - Real Estate Settlement Procedures, Section 2608 - Title Companies; liability of seller
RESPA Section 9 12 U.S.C. §2608 **Regulation X** §3500.16	(a) *No seller of property that will be purchased with the assistance of a federally related mortgage loan shall require directly or indirectly, as a condition to selling the property, that title insurance covering the property be purchased by the buyer from a particular title company.*
Violation Penalty 3 Times All Charges	(b) *Any seller who violates the provisions of subsection (a) of this section shall be liable to the buyer in an amount equal to three times all charges made for such title insurance.*
	Because the title insurance is for the benefit of the buyer (regardless of who pays), it's reasonable that the buyer should be able to choose the title insurance company of their choice. However, if both parties agree otherwise, then whatever title insurance company is chosen by both parties shall meet the law by agreement of both parties.

Inspections

Inspections

If the buyer chooses to have a home inspection, the time frame to conduct the inspections should be reasonable for not only the initial inspections but also for any time necessary to repair any defects.

It's also important to make sure everyone knows who is paying for what. If multiple inspections are agreed upon, each specific inspection should be identified separately with a statement about who is responsible for any required repairs. Make sure all time frames are adhered to and completed as agreed.

Lead Paint Disclosure

Lead Paint Disclosure

If the home was built prior to 1978, make sure the buyer has been provided the pamphlet, 'Protect Your Family From Lead in Your Home' and agrees to waive or not waive the right to have the property tested for lead based paint. It is not required to have any property tested; it is an elective choice.

Square Footage Verification

Square Footage Verification

Even though there may be a disclaimer that it is the buyer's responsibility to verify square footage if it is a material fact for the purchase, there could still be liability should the square footage be grossly misrepresented. However, the disclaimer is to remind the buyer of their responsibility.

Property Condition Disclosure Form
IC 55-2504
IC 55-2509

Sellers Property Condition Disclosure Form

Based on Idaho Code, the Sellers Property Disclosure Form (previously discussed) shall be delivered to the buyer or buyer's agent within 10 days of execution of an agreement.

CC&R's

Covenants, Conditions, and Restrictions

The buyer is responsible for obtaining and reviewing and approving the CC&R's. Some CC&R's are very lengthy and the agent needs to encourage the buyer to take the time to do a close review and look for any items that could adversely affect the buyer.

HOA information
IC 55-115
IC 45-810

Homeowner's Association Information

It's also important that the buyer review the declaration and by-laws of the homeowner association if there is one. Included is the financial stability of the HOA as well and pending law suits. The buyer should also fully understand what the HOA fees are and what they include. When was the last time the HOA increased fees and are there any future plans for future increases?

Who Pays Costs?

Who Pays What Costs?

Although some loan programs require the seller to pay specific costs, most loan programs allow for closing costs to be negotiable between buyer and seller. Whether the Idaho REALTORS® Purchase and Sale Agreement is used or some other form of Purchase and Sale Agreement is used, various costs should be addressed as to who pays what - including:

✓ Appraisal fee

    ✓ Appraisal re-inspection fee

    ✓ Closing escrow fee

    ✓ Lender document preparation fee

    ✓ Tax service fee

    ✓ Flood Certification and tracking fee

    ✓ Lender required inspections

    ✓ Attorney contract preparation or review

    ✓ Title insurance - standard owners policy

    ✓ Title insurance - standard owners extended policy

    ✓ Title insurance - lenders policy (mortgagee)

    ✓ Fuel oil or propane in tank

    ✓ Well test

    ✓ Septic inspection

    ✓ Septic pumping

    ✓ Survey

Occupancy

Occupancy

It's important that the buyer fully understand the Occupancy clause in that if it is to be the buyer's primary residence, it will be the buyer's primary residence. If the buyer doesn't plan to occupy, the buyer should say so.

The purpose of this disclosure is to verify how the financing will be arranged. There are different rules for occupied and non-occupied residences.

Walk Through

Final Walk Through

The primary purpose of the final walk through is to make sure any repairs scheduled were properly completed and that the property is in substantially the same condition as the acceptance date of the Purchase and Sale Agreement. It should be noted that it is the responsibility of the seller to make sure the utilities are turned on in the event the property is vacant. This takes pre-planning and needs to be addressed before the walk through is scheduled. However, the final walk through cannot be used as justification to cancel a contract or a closing.

Risk Of Loss

Risk Of Loss

All risk of loss will be borne by the seller. This is another indirect reason that early occupancy is risky. If the property is materially destroyed prior to closing, the buyer has the option to void the contract.

Foreclosure Notice
IC 45-1602

Foreclosure Notice

If the property is involved in foreclosure, a Notice Required By Idaho Law must be in writing and be accompanied with the Purchase and Sale Agreement. The RE-42 Property Foreclosure Disclosure Form is available to members of the Idaho REALTORS® for acknowledgment. If there are questions relating to the foreclosure process, an attorney or financial professional should be contacted.

Foreclosure
Short Sale
REO's

Foreclosures, Short Sales And REO's

With the 'Great Recession' of 2008, the U.S. housing market was hit hard with extreme drops in housing values nationwide.

Adding to the economic crisis of our nation, many homeowners owned homes in which more money was owed than the property was worth. As the unemployment numbers increased, more and more homeowners were unable to meet their housing obligations.

As a result, many homeowners lost their homes and the banks re-acquired the properties for resale known as REO's (real estate owned). These bank owned property inventories added to the economic recession that began around 2009.

Economic Changes

However, the housing market started to improve around 2015 until the start of the Covid epidemic around 2018 which greatly reduced new construction and housing sales. But around 2020, the marked started to reverse again. Adding fuel to the fire the housing market became so heated, bidding wars were initiated due to demand exceeding supply.

But like most recessions, when the market cools down due to lack of demand and/or increased interest rates, or economic downturns, the housing market can result in foreclosures, short sales, and bank owned properties.

Unfortunately, due to constant changes to the banking laws, the process of foreclosure or executing short sales can be cumbersome and complicated. There are many different programs such as the Home Affordable Foreclosure Alternatives or the Foreclosure Sales Program and the Home Affordable Modification Program have very specific guidelines that have to be followed to qualify for such programs.

To add complications to the issues, short sale payoffs can trigger potential tax implications that can adversely impact the owner for years to come.

Anti-Flipping Rule

In addition, buyers planning on securing HUD owned properties financed with FHA insured mortgages need to be aware of the anti-flipping rule.

Any resale of a property may not occur 90 or fewer days from the last sale to be eligible for FHA financing and for resales that occur between 91 and 180 days where the new sales price exceeds the previous sales price by 100% or more, FHA will require additional documentation validating the property value.

Buyers, sellers, and real estate licensees should seek legal and accounting expertise before making any decisions to buy or sell any properties that have been the result of a foreclosure, short sale, or REO.

General Contractor Disclosure

IC 45-525

General Contractor Disclosure
If a General Contractor plans to enter into construction or make improvements to real property in an amount exceeding $2,000 or for the purchase and sale of newly constructed property, a Disclosure Statement must be given to the homeowner prior to entering into a contract. The Disclosure Statement must contain:

- Homeowner or purchaser has the right at reasonable expense to require that the General Contractor obtain lien waivers from any subcontractors providing services or materials to the General Contractor;

- Homeowner or purchaser has the right to receive proof of general liability insurance including worker's compensation insurance for the General Contractor employees;

- Homeowner or purchaser's right to require at homeowner or purchaser's expense, a surety bond in the amount of the construction project;

- Homeowner or purchaser has right to purchase an expanded title insurance policy covering certain unfiled or unrecorded liens.

Sales Price Information

IC 54-2083 (6) (d)

Sales Price Information
Idaho, not being a 'full disclosure' state, does not require sales information to be of public record. Even though 'sold' prices are not required to be disclosed, but if disclosed, such 'sold' information is not considered confidential client information.

Business Or Calendar Days

IC 73-108

Business Days Or Calendar Days
A business day is defined to be Monday through Friday between 8:00 A.M. and 5:00 P.M. in the local time zone where the subject property is physically located.

This can be important when doing business between northern Idaho and southern Idaho where there are two different time zones; especially for recording purposes. Business days also do not include legal holidays recognized by Idaho Code 73-108.

A calendar day is defined as Monday through Sunday, midnight to midnight in the local time zone where the subject property is located. If business and calendar days are not pre-printed in a Purchase and Sale Agreement it is suggested they be included in an addendum to avoid confusion.

Default

Default

What happens if the buyer defaults? What happens if the seller defaults? A detailed default clause should be included in the Purchase and Sale Agreement so everyone knows what consequences and possible penalties might occur should one party, default against the other party, including brokerage fees.

Representation Confirmation

Representation Confirmation

Idaho Code mandatorily requires Representation Confirmation to be contained in any Purchase and Sale Agreement regardless of the type of property being sold.

IC 2050 (4)

Don't forget, if a sales associate obtains a signed brokerage representation agreement of any kind, the sales associate shall provide a true and legible copy to the designated broker or broker's office prior to the next business day.

Closing Date

Closing Date

There are many different definitions of what closing means. Closing means the date on which all documents are either recorded or accepted by an escrow agent and the sale proceeds are available to the seller. Closing does not always mean when one or the other party signs their respective documents.

The scheduled closing date can be very important especially if the transaction cannot close on or before the specified date. A written, not verbal, extension needs to be approved by all parties if the closing date is to be extended. Remember, 'Time Is Of The Essence'!

Also be careful with having the closing date at the end of the month. If for some reason the closing extends over to the beginning of the following month, all kinds of things happen; all new pro-rates have to be calculated and the buyer could have to come up with additional closing costs, which they may not have!

Possession

Possession

Another critical area of the Purchase and Sale Agreement involves a possession date. Some forethought needs to be taken to meet the needs of both the buyer and seller.

For example, when does the seller need to make their move? Is the seller going to use a moving company to move their belongings? How much advance notice is required?

Try to coordinate between buyer and seller so both aren't moving at the same time.

Also, if possible, try to allow time for the seller to 'reclean' the home after they have moved so the buyer won't have to clean before they move in.

Early Possession

No pun intended - never, never, never allow early possession unless there is an emergency. All kinds of challenges can occur including the buyer demanding more things to be fixed or cleaned. Or, last minute issues that could cancel the transaction and now the buyer is in possession. Liability issues could fall back on the seller since they are still in title.

If, for some reason, early possession is allowed, it is suggested both parties seek legal counsel to address important issues like personal liability, homeowner insurance coverage, default by either party, and damages, just to name a few concerns before actual possession is allowed. If early possession is allowed, confirmed written approval must be acknowledged by both buyer and seller.

Presenting The Offer

IC 54-2051 (1)

Presenting The Offer

Once an offer has been completed and signed by the purchaser(s) the offer must be delivered to the seller. A broker or sales associate shall, as promptly as practicable, tender to the seller every written offer to purchase obtained on the real estate involved, up until the time of closing.

Copy To Designated Broker

IC 2051 (3)

Upon obtaining any document, signed by the buyer or seller, the sales associate shall provide a true copy to the designated broker or broker's office prior to the next business day.

If the document is a fully executed offer to purchase, counter offer, or addendum, true and legible copies shall be provided to both buyer and seller

There are many ways to get the offer to the seller. The usual way is to deliver the offer to the listing agent and have them deliver the offer to the seller. The selling agent may or may accompany the offer to the seller via the listing agent.

If the offer is faxed or electronically delivered to the listing agent, care should be taken to assure the confidentiality of the buyer.

Multiple Offers

Guideline #16

Multiple Offers

Should multiple offers be made on the subject property, the listing agent should be diligent in informing the seller about any offers on the property that might materially affect the seller/client's decisions about the sale of the property. It's advisable to have the listing agent discuss the possibility of multiple offers prior to or upon securing the listing.

On occasion, a seller who has accepted an offer is presented with a better offer from a different buyer at a later time. In such cases, the licensee should advise the seller to seek legal advice before attempting to terminate the existing contract, and before becoming obligated under the second contract. The licensee may not give the seller legal advice; but the licensee can state that failing to perform the terms of the contract, or obligating oneself under two contracts, can have serious legal consequences for the seller.

If issues arise on any area of contract law, such as if and when effective acceptance or revocation of an offer or counteroffer will take place, it is in the agent's best interest to advise the seller or buyer to seek legal counsel.

<table>
<tr><td>**Seller Options**</td><td>

Seller Options

When an offer is presented to the seller, the seller has 3 options: accept, reject, or counter the offer.

</td></tr>
<tr><td>**Acceptance**</td><td>

Acceptance
If the offer is accepted, the acceptance needs to be immediately conveyed to the agent representing the buyer who will in turn, relay it to the buyer. Remember, the buyer can withdraw an offer anytime prior to acceptance by the seller. So, Time Is Of The Essence.

</td></tr>
<tr><td>**Rejected Offers**

IC 54-2048 (3) (d)</td><td>

Rejection
All rejected offers must be retained in the files of the selling broker.

All accepted, countered or rejected offers must be kept by the broker for 3 calendar years after the year in which the event occurred.

</td></tr>
<tr><td>**Counter Offer**</td><td>

Counter Offer
A counteroffer can be made when the seller likes most of the offer but dislikes something. So the seller prepares a counter offer to present back to the buyer. In an effort to avoid illegible alterations on the Purchase and Sale Agreement, 'counter offer' forms should be used to make any changes to the original offer.

Do not confuse the addendum form with a counter offer form. An addendum is just that; adding to an existing contract.

</td></tr>
<tr><td>**Counter Offer Voids Original Offer**</td><td>

The counter offer form voids the original offer and creates a brand new offer from the seller to the buyer but may or will incorporate the terms and conditions of the original offer except for what is changed in the counter offer.

Once a counter offer is made, the buyer is under no obligation to accept and may in fact, make a second counter offer.

It should be noted that when a counter offer is made and the price is modified, a written statement should be inserted into the counter offer to have the buyer and seller acknowledge. The down payment and/or loan amount could change if the purchase price is changed. Once the counter offer is signed and accepted by all parties, a legally binding contract is now in place.

</td></tr>
</table>

Follow-Up

Follow-Up After Acceptance

After acceptance, all parties need to keep on top of all the terms and conditions of the Purchase and Sale Agreement and attachments. Make a list of everything that needs to be accomplished prior to closing and take immediate action if something isn't going according to the terms of the agreement.

Once a preliminary title report is provided, check for any discrepancies. If something shows up that needs attention, notify all parties of the issue and take action.

Keep in constant contact with escrow and make sure all tasks are being resolved within the time frames indicated in the agreement.

Keep a good check list for contingency related activities or other items that are date related. Remember, 'time is of the essence'. Keep in good communication with everyone for a team effort to make everything happen withing the time frames agreed to.

Questions – Chapter 15

1. Unless there's an emergency bill, when do legislative law changes take place?

   A. January 1

   B. April 15

   C. July 1

   D. December 20

2. When earnest money is received, it should be delivered to:

   A. Selling agent

   B. Seller

   C. Title company

   D. Broker's office

3. If earnest money is returned before it is deposited, where must a written and dated notation must be placed?

   A. Purchase and Sale Agreement

   B. Ledger card

   C. Both Purchase and Sale Agreement and ledger card

   D. Trust account record

4. What's the penalty to the seller who requires the buyer to use a particular title insurance company against the buyers choice for a federally related mortgage?

   A. Total amount of the title insurance

   B. Buyer has no recourse

   C. 3 times all charges for title insurance

   D. No penalty to the seller

5. When is the Sellers Property Disclosure form required to be delivered to the buyer?

   A. Prior to writing a contract

   B. Within 1 day of execution of a contract

   C. Within 10 days of execution of a contract.

   D. Within 5 days of loan commitment

6. When must a disclosure statement be given to the homeowner by a general contractor making improvements exceeding $2,000?

    A. Prior to entering into a contract

    B. Prior to being paid for the job

    C. Within 10 days of completing a job

    D. The contractor is not required to give a disclosure statement

7. A business day is defined as:

    A. Monday thru Friday, midnight to midnight

    B. Monday thru Saturday, 8:00 am to midnight

    C. Monday thru Friday, 8 am to 5 pm

    D. Monday thru Saturday, 8 am to 5 pm

8. Once an offer has been completed and signed by the purchaser(s), the offer must be delivered to:

    A. Escrow

    B. Selling brokerage

    C. Seller

    D. Title insurance company

9. How long are signed offers, counter offers and rejections to be retained in the broker files?

    A. 1 year

    B. 1 calendar year

    C   3 years

    D   3 calendar years

Chapter 16

Closing The Transaction

<table>
<tr><td>Words of Wisdom

"The highest form of ignorance is to reject something you know nothing about."

Dr. Wayne W. Dyer</td></tr>
</table>

Closing Procedure

Prior To Closing

Prior to closing, both the buyer and seller should be in close contact and communication with their respective agent and be available to assist with inspections, access for appraisal, repairs, financing requirements, and any other issues that need attention.

Checklist

It's especially important for everyone including the agent(s) involved to take extra care to make sure anything attached to a date is fulfilled within the time frame agreed upon in the Purchase and Sale Agreement. A date related check list is a good reference. As a precaution, review your check list at least a day or two before specific actions are to be completed.

If something can't be completed as agreed, try to get an extension so the contract won't become void or voidable.

Walk Through

One of the primary reasons for the buyer to do a walk through is to make sure the property is in substantially the same condition as when the property was originally visited. Another reason for the walk through is to verify any scheduled repairs have been properly completed. Usually the walk through is scheduled 2-3 days prior to closing to make sure the condition of the property is acceptable.

Homeowner Insurance

It's also a good idea to have the buyer initiate the homeowner insurance application soon after acceptance of the Purchase and Sale Agreement so the insurance will be in place upon closing. In the event the property is located in a flood plain, the buyer needs to be advised of the additional cost for flood insurance coverage.

C.L.U.E. Report

Previous insurance claims (up to 7 years) on the subject property identified by the Claim Loss Underwriting Exchange (CLUE) could also impact the cost of homeowner insurance for the new owner. The property losses can include recent surge in water, mold, or wind related claims that could suggest the possibility of returning claims and increasing the risk factor for insurance companies.

The result could be catastrophic to the point that the buyer may not be able to secure homeowner insurance. To make matters worse, the insurer may not take action until after a transaction has closed; leaving the insured without insurance and at risk of default based on mortgage loan requirements.

RESPA

RESPA - Real Estate Settlement Practices

The Real Estate Settlement Practices Act (RESPA) covers settlement rules associated with federally related residential loans. However, cash, commercial, private financing and non-federally related loans, are not regulated by the Real Estate Settlement Practices Act.

Consumer Protection Rules

The Consumer Financial Protection Bureau has rules that combine mortgage disclosures into a single rule (TRID)on how lenders handle settlement services for any federally related residential loan including:

- Lenders must provide borrowers with a standard origination charge for the loan which must include all points, appraisal, credit, and application fees, administrative, lender inspection, wire, and document preparation. Lenders have the option of providing borrowers with a list of approved service providers such as closing attorneys and title insurance companies.

  - A tolerance range has been specified for various types of loan/closing costs to prevent unnecessary escalation of promised vs. actual charges.

    - Fees quoted for lender origination charge cannot change.

    - Fees for title and closing costs where the lender selects the provider or where the borrower selects the provider from the lender's approved list cannot change by more than 10%.

    - Fees that borrowers can shop for themselves can increase (or decrease) by any amount.

  - The final page of the Loan Estimate contains charges to compare different loans and terms that the borrower can use to shop pricing.

  - The charges quoted on the Loan Estimate are then carried over to the Closing Disclosure to ensure that the prescribed tolerances are met.

3 Day Rule

Borrowers must receive the Closing Disclosure at least 3 business days before consummation. The loan product changes if the Annual Percentage Rate (APR) becomes 'inaccurate' or a prepayment penalty is added, a new Closing Disclosure must be provided and an additional 3-business-day waiting period after receipt of the new Closing Disclosure is required before the loan can close.

By having the escrow/closing officer and real estate agent(s) review the closing documents before the actual closing, errors may be detected and corrected before the actual closing takes place. Most errors can be corrected prior to closing and both the buyer and seller will have a more pleasant experience during closing with error free closing statements.

Generally speaking, there may be two different types of closing statement formats; one with debits (minus) and credits (plus) designed by the escrow department of a title insurance company and the other utilizing the 5 page Closing Disclosure statement. Both show the same exact numbers but are presented with two totally different formats.

A real estate licensee should become familiar with each format so whatever form the escrow officer uses to explain the closing statement to the buyer or seller, it will be fully understood.

Planning For Closing And Signing Documents

Planning For Closing And Signing

The escrow/closing officer will usually plan the day and hour to conduct the closing for both the buyer and seller. Usually one party signs in the morning and the other in the afternoon.

A little known tip is to have the buyer sign first. Why? Because if any errors are found in the closing statement they are most often found on the buyer's side. If the error can be easily corrected, there will only have to be one signing by each party and the seller won't have to sign twice.

If the seller signs first and an error is found with the buyer's settlement statement, the seller will have to sign again with a 'new' closing statement to acknowledge the error. The less the buyer and seller have to deal with errors, the better. That's why it is such a good idea to have the agent and escrow review the closing statements before the buyer and seller are brought to closing.

Responsible Broker

Responsible Broker

IC 54-2048 (1)

The 'responsible broker' shall be responsible for the transaction, transaction records, funds and closing. The responsible broker shall ensure the correctness and delivery of detailed closing statements which accurately reflect all receipts and disbursements for the respective accounts to both the buyer and seller in a transaction.

Even if the closing is completed by a real estate escrow closing agent, title company, or other authorized 3rd party, the responsible broker is still responsible for the accuracy and delivery of the closing statement.

Therefore, it may be prudent for the real estate agent to request a copy of the closing statement before attending closing with their customer/client. By reviewing the closing statement, the agent can double check for any errors.

Potential Errors   Some areas where errors can occur include:

- Closing date pro-rations

- Tax pro-rations

- Mortgage pro-rations

- HOA pro-rations

- Rent pro-rations

- Missing items that should have been included

- Items that should have been excluded

Many errors are not the escrow/closing officer's fault. Sometimes addendums or changes are made during the transaction process in which the escrow officer did not receive the appropriate documentation. If everyone works together, team work can accomplish and solve most issues without delaying or slowing down the closing process.

Agent Responsibilities

Agent Responsibilities

If possible, the agent should attend all closings; if for no other reason, to be a 'security blanket' for the buyer and/or seller. Closing can be a very intimidating experience for buyers and sellers. The closing is perhaps the first time they have met a escrow/closing officer. Having a 'friendly face', like their agent, helps bridge the anxiety that is normal.

The agent is primarily a bystander; just sit back and observe. Let the escrow/closing officer do their job. However, the agent might be able to assist and answer questions the escrow/closing officer may ask to clarify different issues.

Remember, statistically speaking, buyers and sellers will be involved in buying or selling homes around 5-7 homes in their whole lifetime. Each event is somewhat traumatic. The closing is where the agent can really build rapport for future business.

Follow-Up

Follow-Up After Closing

As a courtesy and good business practice, a good real estate licensee will plan on contacting their customer/client within a week after the closing to make sure everything went according to plan. Besides, the follow-up offers an additional opportunity to build rapport and seek additional business or referrals.

Sample Closing Statement

Sample Closing Statement

Every closing will be different with different numbers specific to the circumstances for purchase.

The following sample closing statements are examples with the buyer putting 5% down and financing the balance of $190,000.

Figures 1 thru 10	Pay particular attention to the various pro-rations and line items of various items such as taxes, mortgage interest, tax service, endorsements, appraisal fee, etc. Also note those items that the borrower must pay up front such as: mortgage insurance, hazard insurance, hazard insurance reserve, and tax reserve. Because the down payment is less than 20%, the lender is requiring that the lender handle the payment of taxes and insurance to assure the lender the charges for these items are paid as agreed and kept current.

You will note there are also additional charges to the buyer for Homeowner Association transfer fee and prepaid expenses including insurance and HOA dues.

There are additional fees for recording, title company work (title insurance), and lender required endorsements.

The buyer closing statement from the title company will mirror the Buyer Disclosure statement that is required for federally related loans.

It's very important to carefully review the closing statements prior to closing and fix any errors that show up. This way the final closing and signing of documents will be efficient and without excess anxiety.

Record Retention

IC 54-2049

Don't forget, the responsible broker is responsible for the accuracy of the signed closing statements and must retain copies of the closing statement(s) in the transaction file records for 3 calendar years after the year the transaction closed and all funds have been disbursed.

Figure 1 — Seller Closing Statement

Pioneer Title Company of Ada County
8151 W. Rifleman Street
Boise, ID 83704
(208)377-2700

SELLER(S) FINAL CLOSING STATEMENT

File Number:	000001
Sales Price:	$363,000.00
Close Date:	3/6/2020
Disbursement Date:	3/6/2020
Date Prepared:	3/6/2020 2:39:11 PM

Certified True and Correct Copy

_____
Pioneer Title Company of Ada County

Type: Purchase
Property: 9876 Fireside Drive
MERIDIAN, ID 83646 (ADA)
(01-1 R0000000000)

Seller(s): SUE AND JOHN MITH

Lender: Acme Bank
3456 Anywhere Boulevard, Meridian, ID 83646

Description	P.O.C.	Debit	Credit
Deposits, Credits, Debits			
Sale Price of Property			$363,000.00
Seller Credit Towards Buyer Closing Costs		$4,420.00	
Deposit of Exchange Funds from Jane Doe			
Prorations			
County Taxes 7/1/2019 to 3/6/2020 @ $2,446.64/Year		$1,669.08	
HOA 1/1/2020 to 3/6/2020 @ $360.00/Year		$64.11	
Payoffs			
Net Payoff to Mortgage Company		$174,846.66	
Commissions			
Real Estate Commission, 3% to Super Great Realty Group		$10,797.00	
Real Estate Commission 3% to Super Great Realty Group		$10,797.00	
New Loans			
Appraisal Fee to Appraisals-R-Us		$600.00	
Title Charges			
Title - Lender's Title Insurance to Pioneer Title Company of Ada County			
Title - Owner's Title Insurance to Pioneer Title Company of Ada County		$1,477.00	
Title - Settlement or closing fee to Pioneer Title Company of Ada County		$500.00	
Additional Settlement Charges			
Irrigation, 2nd 1/2 2019 to Nampa and Meridian Irrigation District $44.00		$44.00	
Final Utility Billing- Seller Paid Outside Closing to City of Meridian			
Electrical Correction Billing to Sample Electric Inc. $300.00		$300.00	
HOA Set up Fee to HOA, Inc.		$225.00	
HOA Dues- Late Fees for 2020 Dues to ABC Subdivision Homeowners' Association, Inc.		$32.20	
Totals		$205,772.05	$363,000.00

Balance Due TO Seller: $157,227.95

File Number: 000001   1 of 1

Figure 2 - Seller Closing Disclosure - Page 1 of 2

Closing Disclosure

Closing Information		Transaction Information	
Date Issued	3/6/2020	Borrower	Jane Doe
Closing Date	3/6/2020		54321 Anywhere Street
Disbursement Date	3/6/2020		Boise, Idaho 83702
Settlement Agent	Pioneer Title Company of Ada County	Seller	Sue Smith and John Smith
File #	000001		
Property	9876 Fireside Drive Meridian, ID 83646 (01-1 R0000000000)		
Sale Price	$363,000		

Summaries of Transactions

SELLER'S TRANSACTION

M. Due to Seller at Closing	$363,000.00
01 Sale Price of Property	$363,000.00
02 Sale Price of Any Personal Property Included in Sale	
03	
04	
05	
06	
07	
08	

Adjustments for Items Paid by Seller in Advance

09 County Taxes 3/6/2020 to 1/1/2021	
10 County Taxes	
11 Assessments	
12	
13	
14	
15	
16	

N. Due from Seller at Closing	$205,772.05
01 Excess Deposit	
02 Closing Costs Paid at Closing (J)	$23,648.20
03 Net Payoff to Mortgage Company	$174,846.66
04 Payoff of First Mortgage Loan	
05 Seller Credit Towards Buyer Closing Costs	$4,420.00
06	
07	
08	
09	
10 Title Premium Adjustment	$1,124.00
11	
12	
13	

Adjustments for Items Unpaid by Seller

14 County Taxes 7/1/2019 to 3/6/2020 @ $2,446.64/Year	$1,669.08
15 HOA 1/1/2020 to 3/6/2020 @ $360.00/Year	$64.11
16 Assessments	
17	
18	
19	

CALCULATION

Total Due to Seller at Closing (M)	$363,000.00
Total Due from Seller at Closing (N)	-$205,772.05
Cash to Close ☐ From ☑ To Seller	$157,227.95

Contact Information

Real Estate Broker(B)

Name	Super Great Realty Group
Address	100 Realty Way Boise, ID 83706
ID License ID	SGRG0001
Contact	Bill Broker
Contact ID License ID	
Email	billbroker@email.com
Phone	(208) 555-1000

Real Estate Broker(S)

Name	Super Great Realty Group
Address	200 Real Estate Broker Way Meridian, ID 83642
ID License ID	SGRG1000
Contact	Rudy Realtor
Contact ID License ID	
Email	rudyrealtor@email.com
Phone	(208) 555-0001

Settlement Agent

Name	Pioneer Title Company of Ada County
Address	8151 W. Rifleman Street Boise, ID 83704
ID License ID	5685
Contact	Order Desk
Contact ID License ID	
Email	orders-ada@pioneertitleco.com
Phone	(208)377-2700

Questions? If you have questions about the loan terms or costs on this form, use the contact information below. To get more information or make a complaint, contact the Consumer Financial Protection Bureau at www.consumerfinance.gov/mortgage-closing

Closing Disclosure

Page 1 of 2

Figure 3 - Seller Closing Cost Details - Page 2 of 2

Closing Cost Details

Loan Costs	Seller-Paid	
	At Closing	Before Closing
A. Origination Charges		
01		
B. Services Borrower Did Not Shop For		
01 Appraisal Fee to Appraisals-R-Us	$600.00	
C. Services Borrower Did Shop For		
01 Final Utility Billing- Seller Paid Outside Closing to City of Meridian		
02 Irrigation, 2nd 1/2 2019 to Nampa and Meridian Irrigation District $44.00	$44.00	
03 Title - Lender's Title Insurance to Pioneer Title Company of Ada County		
04 Title - Settlement or closing fee to Pioneer Title Company of Ada County	$500.00	

Other Costs	Seller-Paid	
	At Closing	Before Closing
E. Taxes and Other Government Fees		
01		
F. Prepaids		
01		
G. Initial Escrow Payment at Closing		
01		
H. Other		
01 Electrical Correction Billing to Sample Electric Inc. $300.00	$300.00	
02 HOA Dues- Late Fees for 2020 Dues to ABC Subdivision Homeowners' Association, Inc.	$32.20	
03 HOA Set up Fee to HOA, Inc.	$225.00	
04 Real Estate Commission 3% to Super Great Realty Group	$10,797.00	
05 Real Estate Commission, 3% to Super Great Realty Group	$10,797.00	
06 Title - Owner's Title Insurance to Pioneer Title Company of Ada County	$353.00	
J. TOTAL CLOSING COSTS	$23,648.20	$0.00

Certified True and Correct Copy

Pioneer Title Company of Ada County

Figure 4 - Buyers Closing Statement - Page 1 of 1

PioneerTitleCo.
GOING BEYOND

Pioneer Title Company of Ada County
8151 W. Rifleman Street
Boise, ID 83704
(208)377-2700

BUYER(S) FINAL CLOSING STATEMENT

File Number:	000001
Loan Number:	123456789
Loan Amount:	$263,000.00
Sales Price:	$363,000.00
Close Date:	3/6/2020

Disbursement Date: 3/6/2020
Date Prepared: 3/6/2020 2:39:02 PM

Certified True and Correct Copy

Pioneer Title Company of Ada County

Type: Purchase
Property: 9876 Fireside Drive
MERIDIAN, ID 83646 (ADA)
(01-1 R0000000000)

Buyer(s): Jane Doe
54321 Anywhere Street
Boise, Idaho 83702

Lender: Acme Bank
3456 Anywhere Boulevard, Meridian, ID 83646

Description	P.O.C.	Debit	Credit
Deposits, Credits, Debits			
Sale Price of Property		$363,000.00	
Deposit			$3,500.00
Seller Credit Towards Buyer Closing Costs			$4,420.00
Deposit of Exchange Funds from Jane Doe			$98,900.00
Prorations			
County Taxes 7/1/2019 to 3/6/2020 @ $2,446.64/Year			$1,669.08
HOA 1/1/2020 to 3/6/2020 @ $360.00/Year			$64.11
New Loans			
Loan Amount			$263,000.00
1.2500% of Loan Amount (Points) to Acme Bank		$3,616.25	
Credit Report to XYZ Company	$12.00	$110.50	
Administration Fee to Acme Bank		$995.00	
Processing Fee to Acme Bank		$295.00	
Wire Transfer Fee to Acme Bank		$10.00	
Prepaid Interest (32.8800 per day from 3/6/2020 to 4/1/2020)		$854.88	
Homeowner's Insurance Premium (12 mo.) to Acme Insurance Companies		$587.00	
Homeowner's Insurance $48.92 per month for 4 mo.		$195.68	
Property Taxes $308.19 per month for 6 mo.		$1,849.14	
Aggregate Adjustment		-$195.68	
Title Charges			
Title - Lender's Title Insurance to Pioneer Title Company of Ada County		$435.00	
Title - ALTA 22 Location Endorsement(s) to Pioneer Title Company of Ada County		$10.00	
Title - ALTA 8.1-06 Environmental Protection Lien Endorsement(s) to Pioneer Title Company of Ada County		$10.00	
Title - ALTA 9-06 ORT4344 Endorsement Restrictions, Encroachments, Minerals – Loan Polic Endorsement(s) to Pioneer Title Company of Ada County		$30.00	
Title - ALTA 5.1-06 Planned Unit Development Assessments Lenders Endorsement(s) to Pioneer Title Company of Ada County		$40.00	
Title - Courier Fee to Pioneer Title Company of Ada County		$50.00	
Title - Doc Download Fee to Pioneer Title Company of Ada County		$25.00	
Title - E-File Fee to Pioneer Title Company of Ada County		$9.00	
Title - Settlement or closing fee to Pioneer Title Company of Ada County		$500.00	
Title - Wire Fee to Pioneer Title Company of Ada County		$25.00	
Government Recording and Transfer Charges			
Recording fees: Deed $15.00		$15.00	
Mortgage $45.00		$45.00	
Additional Settlement Charges			
Final Utility Billing- Seller Paid Outside Closing to City of Meridian			
HOA Dues - 2020 to ABC Subdivision Homeowners' Association, Inc.		$360.00	
Mobile Notary Fee to Certified Signer Nationwide $175.00		$175.00	
HOA Transfer Fee to ABC Subdivision Homeowners' Association, Inc.		$150.00	
HOA Dues to ABC Subdivision Homeowners' Association, Inc.		$100.00	
Totals		$373,296.77	$371,553.19

Balance Due FROM Borrower: $1,743.58

Figure 5 - Buyer Closing Disclosure - Page 1 of 6

Closing Disclosure

This form is a statement of final loan terms and closing costs. Compare this document with your Loan Estimate.

Closing Information

Date Issued	3/4/2020
Closing Date	3/5/2020
Disbursement Date	3/6/2020
Settlement Agent	Pioneer Title Company
File #	000001
Property	3456 Anywhere Boulevard Meridian, ID 83646
Sale Price	$363,0000

Transaction Information

Borrower	Jane Doe 54321 Anywhere Street Boise, ID 83702
Seller	Sue Smith and John Smith
Lender	Acme Bank

Loan Information

Loan Term	30 years
Purpose	Purchase
Product	Fixed Rate
Loan Type	☒ Conventional ☐ FHA ☐ VA ☐ _____
Loan ID #	123456789
MIC #	ABCDEC654321

Loan Terms

		Can this amount increase after closing?
Loan Amount	$263,000	**NO**
Interest Rate	4.5%	**NO**
Monthly Principal & Interest *See Projected Payments below for your Estimated Total Monthly Payment*	$1,332.58	**NO**
		Does the loan have these features?
Prepayment Penalty		**NO**
Balloon Payment		**NO**

Projected Payments

Payment Calculation	Years 1-30
Principal & Interest	$1,332.58
Mortgage Insurance	+ 0
Estimated Escrow *Amount can increase over time*	+ 357.11
Estimated Total Monthly Payment	**$1,689.69**

		This estimate includes	In escrow?
Estimated Taxes, Insurance & Assessments *Amount can increase over time* *See page 4 for details*	$387.11 Monthly	☒ Property Taxes	YES
		☒ Homeowner's Insurance	YES
		☒ Other: Homeowner's Association Dues	NO
		See Escrow Account on page 4 for details. You must pay for other property costs separately.	

Costs at Closing

Closing Costs	$10,296.77	Includes $6,335.75 in Loan Costs + $3,961.02 in Other Costs - $0 in Lender Credits. *See page 2 for details.*
Cash to Close	$100,643.58	Includes Closing Costs. *See Calculating Cash to Close on page 3 for details.*

Figure 6 - Buyer Closing Disclosure - Page 2 of 6

Closing Cost Details

Loan Costs		Borrower-Paid		Seller-Paid		Paid by Others
		At Closing	Before Closing	At Closing	Before Closing	
A. Origination Charges		**$4,916.25**				
01 1.375 % of Loan Amount (Points)		$3.616.25				
02 Administration Fee		$995.00				
03 Processing Fees		$295.00				
04 Wire Fee		$10.00				
05						
06						
07						
08						
B. Services Borrower Did Not Shop For		**$1,244.50**				
01 Appraisal Fee	to Appraisals-R-Us			$600.00		
02 Credit Report Fee	to XYZ Company	$110.50				(L) $12.00
03 Title - Courier Fee	to Pioneer Title Company	$50.00				
04 Title - E-Doc Fee	to Pioneer Title Company	$25.00				
05 Title - E-Recording Fee	to Pioneer Title Company	$9.00				
06 Title - Endorsements	to Pioneer Title Company	$90.00				
07 Title - Escrow Fee	to Pioneer Title Company	$500.00				
08 Title - Lender's Title Insurance	to Pioneer Title Company	$435.00				
09 Title - Wire Fee	to Pioneer Title Company	$25.00				
10						
C. Services Borrower Did Shop For		**$175.00**				
01 Title - Notary Fee	to Notary Company	$175.00				
02						
03						
04						
05						
06						
07						
08						
D. TOTAL LOAN COSTS (Borrower-Paid)		**$6,335.75**				
Loan Costs Subtotals (A + B + C)		$6,335.75				

Other Costs		Borrower-Paid		Seller-Paid		Paid by Others
E. Taxes and Other Government Fees		**$60.00**				
01 Recording Fees	Deed: $15.00 Mortgage: $45.00	$60.00				
02						
F. Prepaids		**$1,441.88**				
01 Homeowner's Insurance Premium (12 mo.) to Acme Insurance Companies		$587.00				
02 Mortgage Insurance Premium (0 mo.)						
03 Prepaid Interest ($32.88 per day from 3/6/20 to 4/1/20)		$854.88				
04 Property Taxes (0 mo.)						
05						
G. Initial Escrow Payment at Closing		**$1,849.14**				
01 Homeowner's Insurance $48.92 per month for 3 mo.						
02 Mortgage Insurance per month for 0 mo.						
03 Property Taxes per month for 6 mo.						
04						
05						
06						
07						
08 Aggregate Adjustment		– $146.76				
H. Other		**$610.00**				
01 HOA Dues	to ABC Subdivision	$360.00				
02 HOA Setup Fee	to ABC Subdivisoin	$250.00				
03 Invoices	to Sample Electric Inc.			$300.00		
04 Real Estate Commission	to Super Great Realty Group			$10,797.00		
05 Real Estate Commission	to Super Great Realty Group			$10,797.00		
06 Title - Owner's Title Insurance (optional) to Pioneer Title Company				$1,447.00		
07						
08						
I. TOTAL OTHER COSTS (Borrower-Paid)		**$3,961.02**				
Other Costs Subtotals (E + F + G + H)		$3,961.02				

		Borrower-Paid		Seller-Paid		Paid by Others
J. TOTAL CLOSING COSTS (Borrower-Paid)		**$10,296.77**				
Closing Costs Subtotals (D + I)		$10,296.77		$23,971.00		$12.00
Lender Credits						

CLOSING DISCLOSURE

Figure 6 - Buyer Closing Disclosure - Page 3 of 6

Calculating Cash to Close	Loan Estimate	Final	Did this change?
Use this table to see what has changed from your Loan Estimate.			
Total Closing Costs (J)	$10,718.00	$10,296.77	YES • See **Total Loan Costs (D)** and **Total Other Costs (I)**
Closing Costs Paid Before Closing	$0	$0	NO
Closing Costs Financed (Paid from your Loan Amount)	$0	$0	NO
Down Payment/Funds from Borrower	$100,000.00	$100,000.00	NO
Deposit	$0	-$3,500.00	YES • You increased this payment. See Deposit in **Section L.**
Funds for Borrower	$0	$0	NO
Seller Credits	$0	-$4,420.00	YES • See Seller-Paid column on page 2 and Seller Credits in **Section L.**
Adjustments and Other Credits	$0	-$1,733.19	YES • See details **Section L.**
Cash to Close	**$110,718.00**	**$100,643.58**	

Summaries of Transactions
Use this table to see a summary of your transaction.

BORROWER'S TRANSACTION

K. Due from Borrower at Closing	$373,296.77
01 Sale Price of Property	$363,000.00
02 Sale Price of Any Personal Property Included in Sale	
03 Closing Costs Paid at Closing (J)	$10,296.77
04	
Adjustments	
05	
06	
07	
Adjustments for Items Paid by Seller in Advance	
08 City/Town Taxes to	
09 County Taxes to	
10 Assessments to	
11	
12	
13	
14	
15	

L. Paid Already by or on Behalf of Borrower at Closing	$272,653.19
01 Deposit	$3,500.00
02 Loan Amount	$263,000.00
03 Existing Loan(s) Assumed or Taken Subject to	
04	
05 Seller Credit	$4,420.00
Other Credits	
06	
07	
Adjustments	
08	
09	
10 MIP Refund	
11	
Adjustments for Items Unpaid by Seller	
12 City/Town Taxes to	
13 County Taxes 07/01/19 to 03/06/20	$1,669.08
14 Assessments to	
15 HOA	$64.11
16	
17	

CALCULATION	
Total Due from Borrower at Closing (K)	$373,296.77
Total Paid Already by or on Behalf of Borrower at Closing (L)	– $272,653.19
Cash to Close ☒ From ☐ To Borrower	**$100,643.58**

SELLER'S TRANSACTION

M. Due to Seller at Closing	$363,000.00
01 Sale Price of Property	$363,000.00
02 Sale Price of Any Personal Property Included in Sale	
03	
04	
05	
06	
07	
08	
Adjustments for Items Paid by Seller in Advance	
09 City/Town Taxes to	
10 County Taxes to	
11 Assessments to	
12	
13	
14	
15	
16	

N. Due from Seller at Closing	$30,124.19
01 Excess Deposit	
02 Closing Costs Paid at Closing (J)	$23,971.00
03 Existing Loan(s) Assumed or Taken Subject to	
04 Payoff of First Mortgage Loan	
05 Payoff of Second Mortgage Loan	
06	
07	
08 Seller Credit	$4,420
09	
10	
11	
12	
13	
Adjustments for Items Unpaid by Seller	
14 City/Town Taxes to	
15 07/01/19 03/06/20	$1,669.08
16 Assessments to	
17 HOA	$64.11
18	
19	

CALCULATION	
Total Due to Seller at Closing (M)	$363,000.00
Total Due from Seller at Closing (N)	– $30,124.19
Cash ☐ From ☒ To Seller	**$332,875.81**

Figure 7 - Buyer Closing Disclosure - Page 4 of 6

Additional Information About This Loan

Loan Disclosures

Assumption
If you sell or transfer this property to another person, your lender
- ☐ will allow, under certain conditions, this person to assume this loan on the original terms.
- ☒ will not allow assumption of this loan on the original terms.

Demand Feature
Your loan
- ☐ has a demand feature, which permits your lender to require early repayment of the loan. You should review your note for details.
- ☒ does not have a demand feature.

Late Payment
If your payment is more than *15* days late, your lender will charge a late fee of *5% of the monthly principal and interest payment.*

Negative Amortization (Increase in Loan Amount)
Under your loan terms, you
- ☐ are scheduled to make monthly payments that do not pay all of the interest due that month. As a result, your loan amount will increase (negatively amortize), and your loan amount will likely become larger than your original loan amount. Increases in your loan amount lower the equity you have in this property.
- ☐ may have monthly payments that do not pay all of the interest due that month. If you do, your loan amount will increase (negatively amortize), and, as a result, your loan amount may become larger than your original loan amount. Increases in your loan amount lower the equity you have in this property.
- ☒ do not have a negative amortization feature.

Partial Payments
Your lender
- ☐ may accept payments that are less than the full amount due (partial payments) and apply them to your loan.
- ☐ may hold them in a separate account until you pay the rest of the payment, and then apply the full payment to your loan.
- ☒ does not accept any partial payments.

If this loan is sold, your new lender may have a different policy.

Security Interest
You are granting a security interest in
3456 Anywhere Boulevard, Meridian, ID 83646

You may lose this property if you do not make your payments or satisfy other obligations for this loan.

Escrow Account
For now, your loan
- ☒ will have an escrow account (also called an "impound" or "trust" account) to pay the property costs listed below. Without an escrow account, you would pay them directly, possibly in one or two large payments a year. Your lender may be liable for penalties and interest for failing to make a payment.

Escrow		
Escrowed Property Costs over Year 1	$4,285.32	Estimated total amount over year 1 for your escrowed property costs: *Homeowner's Insurance Property Taxes*
Non-Escrowed Property Costs over Year 1	$360.00	Estimated total amount over year 1 for your non-escrowed property costs: *Homeowner's Association Dues* You may have other property costs.
Initial Escrow Payment	$1,849.14	A cushion for the escrow account you pay at closing. See Section G on page 2.
Monthly Escrow Payment	$357.11	The amount included in your total monthly payment.

- ☐ will not have an escrow account because ☐ you declined it ☐ your lender does not offer one. You must directly pay your property costs, such as taxes and homeowner's insurance. Contact your lender to ask if your loan can have an escrow account.

No Escrow		
Estimated Property Costs over Year 1		Estimated total amount over year 1. You must pay these costs directly, possibly in one or two large payments a year.
Escrow Waiver Fee		

In the future,
Your property costs may change and, as a result, your escrow payment may change. You may be able to cancel your escrow account, but if you do, you must pay your property costs directly. If you fail to pay your property taxes, your state or local government may (1) impose fines and penalties or (2) place a tax lien on this property. If you fail to pay any of your property costs, your lender may (1) add the amounts to your loan balance, (2) add an escrow account to your loan, or (3) require you to pay for property insurance that the lender buys on your behalf, which likely would cost more and provide fewer benefits than what you could buy on your own.

Figure 8 - Buyer Closing Disclosure - Page 5 of 6

Loan Calculations

Total of Payments. Total you will have paid after you make all payments of principal, interest, mortgage insurance, and loan costs, as scheduled.	$486,921.29
Finance Charge. The dollar amount the loan will cost you.	$223,285.79
Amount Financed. The loan amount available after paying your upfront finance charge.	$256,444.87
Annual Percentage Rate (APR). Your costs over the loan term expressed as a rate. This is not your interest rate.	4.717%
Total Interest Percentage (TIP). The total amount of interest that you will pay over the loan term as a percentage of your loan amount.	82.732%

 Questions? If you have questions about the loan terms or costs on this form, use the contact information below. To get more information or make a complaint, contact the Consumer Financial Protection Bureau at **www.consumerfinance.gov/mortgage-closing**

Other Disclosures

Appraisal
If the property was appraised for your loan, your lender is required to give you a copy at no additional cost at least 3 days before closing. If you have not yet received it, please contact your lender at the information listed below.

Contract Details
See your note and security instrument for information about
• what happens if you fail to make your payments,
• what is a default on the loan,
• situations in which your lender can require early repayment of the loan, and
• the rules for making payments before they are due.

Liability after Foreclosure
If your lender forecloses on this property and the foreclosure does not cover the amount of unpaid balance on this loan,
[X] state law may protect you from liability for the unpaid balance. If you refinance or take on any additional debt on this property, you may lose this protection and have to pay any debt remaining even after foreclosure. You may want to consult a lawyer for more information.
[ ] state law does not protect you from liability for the unpaid balance.

Refinance
Refinancing this loan will depend on your future financial situation, the property value, and market conditions. You may not be able to refinance this loan.

Tax Deductions
If you borrow more than this property is worth, the interest on the loan amount above this property's fair market value is not deductible from your federal income taxes. You should consult a tax advisor for more information.

Contact Information

	Lender	Mortgage Broker	Real Estate Broker (B)	Real Estate Broker (S)	Settlement Agent
Name	Acme Bank		Super Great Realty Group	Super Great Realty Group	Pioneer Title Company
Address	4321 Random Blvd. Somecity, ST 12340		100 Realty Way Boise, ID 83706	987 Suburb Ct.	8151 W. Rifleman St Boise, ID 83704
NMLS ID	654321				
ST License ID			SGRG0001	SGRG1000	000001
Contact	Joe Smith		Bill Broker	Rudy Realtor	Sally Settlement
Contact NMLS ID	12345				
Contact ST License ID			P000001	P100000	987654321
Email	joesmith@acmebank.com		billbroker@email.com	rudyrealtor@email.com	ssettlement@pioneertitleco.com
Phone	123-456-7890		208-555-1000	321-555-7171	208-377-2700

Confirm Receipt

By signing, you are only confirming that you have received this form. You do not have to accept this loan because you have signed or received this form.

_____   _____
Jane Doe   Date

CLOSING DISCLOSURE   PAGE 5 OF 6 • LOAN ID # 123456789

Figure 9 - Buyer Closing Disclosure - Page 6 of 6

Addendum to Closing Disclosure

This form is a continued statement of final loan terms and closing costs.

Seller	Sue Smith and John Smith 2456 Anywhere Boulevard Meridian, ID 83646

CLOSING DISCLOSURE

PAGE 6 OF 6 • LOAN ID # 123456789

Can You Explain or Define:

Purpose Of a Walk Through

RESPA

HUD 1 Settlement Statement

3 Day Rule

Potential Errors To Look For

Responsible Broker

Agent Responsibilities

C.L.U.E Report

Questions – Chapter 16

1. RESPA requires lenders to provide borrowers with a closing disclosure at least ___ business days prior to closing a mortgage.

   A. No requirements

   B. 1 day

   C. 2 days

   D. 3 days

2. Why should a walk through prior to closing be scheduled 2-3 days before closing?

   A. To make sure the property is substantially the same condition as when the offer was accepted

   B. So the buyer can request changes they didn't see when they made their offer

   C. Get any information from the seller necessary to take possession

   D. Make arrangements to get keys to move in

3. What type of financing is not regulated by the Real Estate Settlement Practices Act?

   A. Loans with VA program

   B. Any federal related loan program

   C. Loans with FHA program

   D. Commercial loans

4. When should application for homeowner insurance be initiated?

   A. Prior to making an offer

   B. As soon after acceptance as possible

   C. Upon closing

   D. After closing and recording

5. The Claim Loss Underwriting Exchange tracks claims up to how many years?

   A. 1 year

   B. 4 years

   C. 6 years

   D. 7 years

6. HUD 1 closing statements are required for:

   A. All loans requiring financing

   B. Title insurance

   C. IRS record keeping for audits

   D. Federally related loans

7. How long must transaction files be held by a real estate broker?

   A. 1 year after closing

   B. 3 years after the year of closing

   C. 3 calendar years after the year of closing

   D. 5 calendar years following closing.

8. Who is responsible for the accuracy and delivery of a closing statement?

    A. The buyer and seller

    B. The buyer's real estate agent

    C. The escrow agent

    D. The responsible broker

Answer Key - Chapter Review Questions

Chapter 1

1. A
2. C
3. C
4. C
5. D
6. C
7. B
8. B
9. B
10. B
11. C
12. C
13. B
14. D
15. B
16. D
17. A
18. C
19. B
20. D
21. C
22. D
23. C

Chapter 2

1. C
2. A
3. D
4. C
5. C
6. B
7. D
8. A
9. A
10. B

Chapter 3

1. D
2. B
3. B
4. D
5. D
6. C
7. C
8. A
9. A
10. C
11. C
12. B
13. D

14. D
15. C
16. C
17. D
18. D
19. B
20. B
21. B
22. D
23. C
24. A
25. C
26. A
27. C
28. A
29. D
30. B
31 D
32. C

Chapter 4

1. B
2. A
3. C
4. D
5. B

6. D
7. A
8. D
9. A
10. C

Chapter 5

1. B
2. C
3. A
4. B
5. A
6. B
7. C
8. D
9. C
10. B
11. C
12. D
13. A
14. B
15. A
16. D
17. C
18. B
19. D

20. A
21. C
22. B
23. B
24. B

Chapter 6

1. D
2. A
3. C
4. B
5. C
6. C
7. A
8. B
9. D
10. B
11. D
12. C
13. D
14. D
15. B
16. A
17. C
18. D
19. D

20. C
21. D

Chapter 7

1. B
2. C
3. C
4. D
5. C
6. D
7. C
8. C
9. B
10. D
11. D
12. A
13. A
14. A
15. B

Chapter 8

1. A
2. D
3. C
4. D

5. B

6. C

7. C

8. A

9. B

10. B

11. C

12. A

13. A

14. C

15. D

16. D

Chapter 9

1. A

2. C

3. A

4. C

5. B

6. D

7. D

8. B

9. C

10. C

11. B

12. C

13. C

14. A

15. D

Chapter 10

1. A

2. A

3. C

4. D

5. D

6. C

7. B

8. B

9. A

10. B

11. C

12. B

13. A

14. D

15. C

16. B

17. C

18. C

19. D

20. D

21. A

22. B

23. D

24. B

25. C

Chapter 11

1. D

2. C

3. C

4. C

5. C

6. D

7. D

8. A

9. B

10. C

11. B

12. A

13. C

14. D

15. C

16. B

17. B

18. A

19. C

20. C

Chapter 12

1. D

2. D

3. A

4. D

Chapter 13

1. A

2. B

3. D

4. C

5. A

6. B

7. C

8. C

9. A

10. C

11. D

Chapter 14

1. C

2. D

3. B

4. D

5. B

6. D

7. C

8. A

9. D

Chapter 15

1. C

2. D

3. C

4. C

5. C

6. A

7. C

8. C

Chapter 16

1. D

2. A

3. D

4. B

5. D

6. D

7. C

8. D

Index

236

238

Made in the USA
Middletown, DE
27 September 2023

39526901R00137